100 Literacy Hours

YEAR 6

Published by Scholastic Ltd,
Villiers House,
Clarendon Avenue,
Leamington Spa,
Warwickshire CV32 5PR

AUTHOR
Chris Webster

EDITORS
Kate Element
Lorna Gilbert

ASSISTANT EDITORS
Christine Lee
Lesley Suldow

SERIES DESIGNER
Joy White

DESIGNERS
Anna Oliwa
Rachel Warner
Sarah Rock

COVER ARTWORK
Peter Stevenson

ILLUSTRATIONS
Maggie Downer

British Library Cataloguing-in-Publication Data
A catalogue record for this book is available from the British Library.

ISBN 0-590-53918-3

ACKNOWLEDGEMENTS

The publishers gratefully acknowledge permission to reproduce the following copyright material:

Jonathan Clowes Ltd, London on behalf of Andrea Plunket, Administrator of the Sir Arthur Conan Doyle Copyrights for the adaptation of the story and the right to use Sir Arthur Conan Doyle's characters Sherlock Holmes and Dr Watson as they appeared in 'The Red-Headed League' © 1996, The Sir Arthur Conan Doyle Copyright Holders.
Faber & Faber Ltd for the use of the opening two lines from 'Nessie' by Ted Hughes from *Moon-Bells and Other Poems* by Ted Hughes © 1978, Ted Hughes (1978, Chatto & Windus; 1986, The Bodley Head).
Jon Greefield for the use of the new Globe Yard Level Plan.
David Hingham Associates for the use of 'Old Mrs Thing-um-e-bob', 'I saw a jolly hunter' and 'As I went down the cat-walk' by Charles Causley from *Figgie Hobbins* by Charles Causley © 1970, Charles Causley (1970, Macmillan).
Wes Magee for the use of 'What is...the sun?' by Wes Magee from *The Witches Brew And Other Poems* by Wes Magee © 1989, Wes Magee (1989, Cambridge University Press).
Janet Perry for the following units: 'Origins of Proper Names', 'Investigating Humorous Verse' and 'Experimenting with Language'.
Marian Reiner, Literary Agent, New York on behalf of the authors for the use of 'New notebook' by Judith Thurman from *Flashlight and Other Poems* by Judith Thurman © 1976, Judith Thurman and 'Mean Song' by Eve Merriam from *There Is No Rhyme For Silver* by Eve Merriam © 1962, Eve Merrriam (1962, Atheneum Publishhers, Inc).
**RoSPA, Birmingham for the use of text from *The RoSPA Bicicyle Owners's Handbook* © RoSPA.
Scholastic Inc, New York for the use of adaptation of 'Light Makes the Winter Blues Glow Away' by Courtney Silk from *Scholastic News* 14.2.92 © 1992 Scholastic Inc; for use of 'Skimming, scanning and studying' from *Reading for Understanding Book D* © 1995, Scholastic Inc.
Anne Serraillier for the use of 'After Ever Happily' or 'The Princess and the Woodcutter' by Ian Serraillier from *Happily Ever After* by Ian Serrallier © 1963, Ian Serrallier (1963, OUP).
University of Texas Press for the use of 'Propp's Functions' adapted from *Morphology of the Folktale* by Vladimir Propp © 1973, University of Texas Press.
Usborne Publishing, 83–85 Saffron Hill, London EC14 8RT for the use of an extract from *Usborne Book of Better English* by Robyn Gee and Carol Watson © 1983, Robyn Gee and Carol Watson (1993, 1990, Usborne Publishing).

Every effort has been made to trace copyright holders for the works reproduced in this book, and the publishers apologize for any inadvertent omissions.

Contents

INTRODUCTION

ABOUT THE SERIES

100 Literacy Hours is a series of year-specific teachers' resource books that provide a core of material for the teaching of the English curriculum within the context of the National Literacy Strategy *Framework for Teaching* and within the structure of the Literacy Hour. Each book offers term-by-term lesson plans, complete with objectives and organization grids and accompanied, where relevant, with photocopiable texts and activity sheets. The materials are ready-to-use, and their adaptable format enables them to be used as flexibly as possible. The 100 hours provided offer a balance of both reading and writing, and of range: fiction and poetry and non-fiction. However, it is expected that you will wish to personalize the material – altering the order, interleaving lessons plans with complementary materials from your school's existing schemes, consolidating work by using the structure of a lesson plan as a model for a lesson with different content, and so on. The loose-leaf format of each book, with hole-punched, perforated, tear-out pages, makes the integration of other tried-and-tested and favourite material into the core very easy.

USING THIS BOOK

The materials

This book provides 100 literacy hours for Year 6, presented as 'units' of between 1 and 5 hours. There is a balance of reading and writing units, most of which are linked in order to demonstrate and reinforce the close relationship. The bulk of the 100 hours is fully supported with detailed lesson plans and integrated photocopiable resources. The remainder of the hours are plans for suitable follow-on or follow-up hours linked to some of the units. These can be found at the end of the unit to which they refer, and are presented as grids outlining objectives and organization. Together, these materials should be regarded as a core, as a starting point for developing your own personalized folder for the year.

Adapting and personalizing the materials

During the trialling of these resources, wide differences in ability were found in classes of the same year group in different schools. This means that the *precise* content of the plans and resources will almost certainly need modification to suit the children in a particular school. One way to do this is as follows:
■ Separate the pages of the book and place them in an A4 ring-binder.
■ Adjust the level of the photocopiable resource sheets to match the needs of the children in your year group.
■ 'Trade' materials with higher or lower year groups so that the average level matches that of the target year group.
■ Add your own favourite teaching materials in the appropriate places.
■ Substitute materials for others if necessary (for example, if you have a set of books which you wish to use instead of one of the ones recommended).
    You have now created a tailor-made folder of plans and resources for your year group!

Preparing a scheme of work

All schools are required to write detailed schemes of work, and these materials have been designed to facilitate this process. The termly Overview grids provided on pages 12–17 have been compiled by extracting the 'Objectives' grids from each teaching unit and putting them together to provide you with what are, essentially, medium-term plans. These grids are photocopiable so, should you wish to alter the order of units and/ or add your own, they can be copied, cut and pasted to make your own plans. On page 18 there is also a photocopiable set of blank objectives grids for you to use when inserting your own material.

ORGANIZATION OF TEACHING UNITS

Each term is divided into teaching units comprising between 1–5 hours. Each of the main units has either a reading or a writing focus (although there is, of course, overlap) and a fiction, poetry or non-fiction content. The units are organized as follows:

Objectives grid
Outlines the word-, sentence- and text-level objectives of the unit.

Organization grid
Outlines the key activities for each part of each hour.

UNIT LESSON PLANS
Each unit of lesson plans is written to the following headings:

Resources
Provides a list of what you need for teaching the whole unit.

Preparation
Outlines any advance preparation needed before the hour(s) begins.

Synopsis
Gives a synopsis of the story, where whole published fiction texts are used as the basis of units.
  Each hour is then set out as follows:

Introduction
Sets out what to do in the whole-class shared reading/writing session.

Whole-class skills work
Sets out what to do in the whole-class word- and sentence-level skills session. (See page 8 for further information about whole-class skills work.)

Differentiated group work
Sets out what each group does in the guided group and independent work session. (See page 8 for further information about differentiated group work.)

Conclusion
Sets out what to do in the whole-class plenary session.

Follow-up
Some units lend themselves particularly to follow-up hours. These are indicated in the lesson plans and are provided as grid plans at the end of the relevant unit.

Further ideas
Provides ideas for extending what is done within the hours of the unit.

Photocopiable sheets
Photocopiable resource and activity sheets that support each unit. These can be found at the end of each relevant unit and are marked with the photocopiable symbol .

Many of the sheets have more than one application and are therefore used in several units.

READING UNITS

These teaching units have three aims:
■ to develop basic reading skills across a wide range of texts – fiction, poetry and non-fiction
■ to develop skills of comprehension, inference, deduction and literary appreciation
■ to encourage enjoyment of reading.

Using the texts

All shorter texts are provided on the photocopiable resource sheets. The following longer texts will be needed (half-class sets are recommended for fiction and group sets for non-fiction):

■ *The Wizard of Oz* by L Frank Baum, Puffin Classics, ISBN 0-14-036693-8.
■ *Fantasy Stories* chosen by Diana Wynne Jones, Kingfishter, ISBN 1-85697-209-7.
■ *The Silver Sword* by Ian Serraillier, Puffin, ISBN 0-14-030146-1.

All the texts are intended for use as *shared texts*; that is to say, texts for whole-class and/or guided group reading. Use of appropriate teaching methods enables children to read and understand texts beyond their *independent* reading level. These methods include:

■ preparation, for example giving the background to a story, prior study of difficult words
■ an initial reading to the whole class with children following the text
■ re-reading in groups with less able groups supported by the teacher
■ differentiated follow-up activities which allow more able children to respond independently to the text while further support is given to less able readers
■ guided reading, in which the teacher takes children through the text helping them with phonic or contextual clues (less able readers), or higher-level reading skills (more able readers).

Additional suggestions are given, where relevant, in the detailed lesson plans, for example use of different versions of the same story.

It is assumed that children will be following a programme of guided reading alongside their reading of these shared texts.

Managing the reading of longer texts

In those units where the whole of longer texts is read, it is assumed that sometimes the chunks of reading allocated to the Introduction session (whole-class shared reading) may need to be undertaken outside of the session or lesson time. It could be included in guided group reading, or in other shared reading time or as homework. Recording and making copies of an audio tape of the text will enable those children who cannot read the text independently to have access to the story.

Responding to texts

Since the mid-1980s, a complete methodology for teaching children how to respond to texts has developed, and is becoming well established from KS1 to KS4. The materials in this book try to exemplify as many types of responses as possible, so that, as well as providing specific lessons, they also offer models which can be adapted for use with other texts. Some examples of responses to texts are:

■ cloze – fill in gaps in a text
■ sequencing – place a cut-up text in order
■ design a storyboard – such as plan a film version of the text
■ use drama techniques to explore a text – for example role-play, hot-seating
■ design a newspaper front page about an aspect of the text
■ comprehension questions answered orally or in writing.

Written comprehension

The majority of written tasks set in these materials encourage a creative response to reading. These often reveal children's comprehension of the text as clearly as any formal comprehension, and, like the oral and dramatic activities, they are just as effective in developing comprehension skills. However, children do need to practise formal written comprehension of different kinds, and activities for this have been provided in many of the units.

Note that the main purpose of the comprehension material is to develop understanding of the texts, not to provide detailed numerical assessments. Marking should therefore be kept simple. On most occasions the marking can be done orally in a concluding session. You might take each question in turn, asking for responses from the children and discussing them. The correct answer (or answers) can then be identified and the children can mark their own answers, simply placing a tick if they have got it right. Queries can be dealt with immediately. You can look at the comprehensions later to see at a glance which children are doing well at basic recall, which are doing well at inference and deduction, and most important of all, which children are struggling with basic understanding. These children should then be given further support during the next guided reading session.

WRITING UNITS

These units provide a series of structured writing experiences throughout the year leading to a more integrated, creative and open-ended approach in Term 3 which draws together and puts into practice previous skills taught and developed. The idea is to provide 'props' for learning and then to remove them gradually in the hope that children will be able to write with increasing independence and creativity. Examples of props are the many 'templates' to support writing. These include sentence and paragraph prompts for fiction, and page-layout templates for certain types of non-fiction (see 'Design a CD-ROM Page' unit, Term 2). Other kinds of props are the Story Planner (see 'Victorian Story Cards' unit, Term 2) and the Redrafting Checklist (see 'Golden Arrow Publications' unit, Term 2). Regular use of these will help children to internalize the prompts they contain, and so help them build independence as writers. Towards the end of Term 3 the Writing Simulation unit ('Summer Camp Experience') provides a context for children to write in a range of forms for a range of purposes and audiences, so bringing together in a creative way, the wide range of skills covered throughout the year.

Cross-curricular writing

The best opportunities for most non-narrative writing occur in other curriculum areas. Therefore, when the necessary skills have been introduced through one of the non-fiction units, they should be applied to another curriculum area soon afterwards. It would be well worth holding year-group meetings specifically to 'map' opportunities for non-narrative writing across the curriculum.

REFERENCE AND RESEARCH SKILLS UNITS

Within each term there are two 1-hour Reference and Research Skills units. The purpose of these units is to focus attention on important skills that may otherwise not get appropriate time within the context of other lesson plans. In this book for Year 6, the Reference and Research Skills units deal with the following skills:
Term 1:
Using an etymological dictionary.
Distinguishing between biography and autobiography.
Term 2:
Investigating root words, prefixes and suffixes.
Paraphrasing and summarising.
Term 3:
Setting purposes for reading.
Carrying out a language investigation.

WORD PLAY UNITS

At the end of each term there is a Word Play unit. The purpose of these units is to demonstrate that playing with words is not only 'OK' and fun, but also a powerful learning tool. The Word Play units for Year 6 are:
Term 1:
Origins of Proper Names.
Term 2:
Investigating Humorous Verse.
Term 3:
Experimenting with Language.

SPEAKING AND LISTENING

Speaking and listening is also an essential part of literacy, and development of skills in this important area has been integrated into the units for both reading and writing. Speaking and listening is *the* most important way of developing higher-order reading skills. Children must be able to explore texts through discussion, role-play and other forms of oral 'comprehension' before they can do justice to more formal written comprehension. 'Brainstorming' sharing ideas, helping each other to check work and so on, will all help children to write more effectively. The challenge for the teacher is to ensure that this discussion is clearly focused on the task and not merely idle chatter.

TIMING OF THE LITERACY HOUR

A brisk pace is an important feature of an effective Literacy Hour. The following suggestions, based on experience in trialling these materials, will help to keep things moving:
■ Train pupils in efficient classroom routines (see below under 'Differentiated group activities').
■ Don't talk too much! Keep explanations brief. Get children on task as soon as possible, and give further clarification and help in the context of the activity.
■ Don't let skills sessions overrun, unless there is a good reason which has been previously planned for. Skills will be revised and practised several times throughout the year within the context of other slots in the Literacy Hour and outside of it.
■ When starting group activities sessions, give a clear message about what you want children to have achieved in the time allocated, and encourage them to work efficiently such as not wasting time decorating a border before starting writing and so on.

Introductory session

Most often, these sessions involve the reading aloud of a shared text. Where possible, children should follow the reading in their own copy of the text. Using an overhead projector is the best way of doing this (see below). It allows a shared text to be used as a focal point for the whole class in the same way as a Big Book. Find ways to make them interactive by involving children in reading, asking questions and so on. Give appropriate background information and briefly discuss vocabulary and ideas. However, in all this, do not lose sight of the need to keep the pace of the lesson moving!

Whole-class skills work

It is during these sessions that the majority of grammar, punctuation, spelling and phonic skills are taught. The main principle is that the skills arise from the shared text and will also be used in the related writing unit. Over the year, key skills should be revisited many times so that children's mastery of them will grow incrementally. A word of warning: many grammatical concepts are difficult and abstract, so do not expect children to grasp them all at once. Expect it to be a slow process in which their understanding develops over several years. For example, many children may not achieve mastery of writing in paragraphs until they reach their teens – but they will not achieve it at all if a start is not made when they are much younger.

Although the materials in this book include spelling activities based on spelling rules and patterns arising from the texts, they cannot take the place of a programme of individualized spelling for children. Children could collect a list of words they need to learn in a spelling book. This could be supplemented at least once a week with words from a standard list to make a list of, say, ten (or more for more able/older children). Children then learn their lists using the LOOK/SAY/COVER/WRITE/CHECK method. Pairs of children can test each other on their own lists. Any words not learned can be carried over into the next list.

The same book, used backwards, can be used to collect new items of vocabulary. Again, these should be a mixture of words which children have come across themselves, and words introduced during teaching (for example, character adjectives, synonyms of 'said').

Differentiated group activities

For most group activities, three levels of differentiation are suggested, usually shown as four groups to reflect a normal distribution of ability:
Group 1:   above average pupils.
Groups 2 & 3:   average pupils.
Group 4:   below average pupils.

In the average KS2 class, group sizes would be between 7–8 (with some trade-off between groups according to the spread of ability in the class). This is fine for organizational purposes, and working with the teacher, but too large for most collaborative activities. These groups will therefore need to be subdivided into smaller groups of fours or pairs for many activities. There will also be occasions when mixed-ability groups are most appropriate for the activities (for example, the drama units).

Children need to know which main group they are in and be able to subdivide into fours or pairs quickly and efficiently. To help this process, teachers could name the groups, for example 'Home Group', 'Small Groups', 'Pairs', and train children to get into the appropriate group immediately the group is named.

When this routine is firmly established, children should then be given the experience of working with children from other groups, for example opposite sex pairs, fours made up of pairs from different 'Home Groups' and so on. It is also important to give them the experience of working in mixed-ability groups for appropriate activities.

The teacher should try to divide teaching time equally between all groups over the course of the week – the more able need help just as much as the less able if they are given suitably demanding tasks. **[NB An asterisk (*) after the group number is used on the grids and in the lesson plans to show which groups the teacher should be working with during the group activities session.]**

Finally, it is important to stress that even when a teacher is working intensively with one group, the first priority is always the overall work rate of the whole class. The following tips will help:
■ Train children to work independently. Tell them that you cannot help them while you are working with a group – their turn will come. In the meantime, they must find out for themselves, or ask a friend or a classroom assistant.
■ When working with a group, sit in a position so that the rest of the class can be seen.
■ Break off group work immediately to deal with lazy or disruptive children. They will soon learn that they are under supervision even when you are working with a group.

Concluding sessions

The key objective in most of these sessions is to review the teaching points of the lesson and ensure that the work of *selected* children, pairs or groups is shared with the class for discussion and evaluation. Enough should be heard to exemplify the variety of work produced, but not so much that it becomes boring, or takes too much time. Keep a record of who has presented what to ensure that all children have the opportunity to present their work in due course.

Finishing off

When the time arrives for the concluding session, children will be at different stages of their work. Some will have finished, but many will still have work to do. The following strategies are recommended for dealing with this situation:
■ Expect children to be *on task* during the time allocated for writing.
■ Encourage them to work at a reasonable pace.
■ Make expectations of each group clear: 'I expect you to write at least a side during the next 20 minutes' (Groups 2 & 3). 'I want one paragraph of four or five lines written very carefully and checked over by the end of this session' (Group 4).
■ Give frequent time warnings such as 'We will have to stop writing in ten minutes'.
■ For key pieces of writing plan either a) homework to finish them off, or b) another hour of careful redrafting and presenting.
■ Discourage time-wasting activities such as decorating margins. Pictures should only be encouraged when they have a specific part to play (as in many non-fiction writing activities).

PHOTOCOPYING

Please note:
■ Where there is instruction to copy material from copyright texts, *you need to ensure that this is done within the limits of the copying licence your school has.*
■ If pupils are using their own exercise books or paper for answers, then all photocopiable resources are reusable.

USE OF OVERHEAD PROJECTOR

Having the use of an overhead projector (OHP) is ideal for whole-class work. Photocopiable texts and skills activities can then be copied onto acetate to make overhead transparencies (OHTs) which can be projected onto a screen or a bare, white or light-coloured wall. For best effect, try to clear a whole section of wall from floor to ceiling and have it painted white. A partial black out would be an advantage. You will then be able to project a huge impressive text or picture. It can also be used to project backgrounds for drama improvisations. Where an OHP is not available, photocopiable sheets should be enlarged to at least A3 size.

INFORMATION AND COMPUTER TECHNOLOGY

Word processors have revolutionized the way we write, making redrafting less of a chore, and allowing documents to be well presented. However, the benefits of word processing only begin to be felt when the user has acquired a reasonable typing speed. It is therefore recommended that all children should use both hands on the keyboard and spend enough time practising so that they do not have to search for letters. To achieve this, word processing should be 'on the go' at all times. In most classrooms this will mean that a rota will have to be set up. When children have mastered the basics of word processing, they should be encouraged to make judgements about choice of fonts and page layout. The 'Design a CD-ROM Page' and Writing Simulation ('Summer Camp Experience') units provide good opportunities for this.

ASSESSMENT

Regular and ongoing assessment of children's achievements and progress is, of course, essential. These materials assume that you and your school have satisfactory methods and systems of assessing and recording already in place and therefore don't attempt to suggest an alternative. However, what these materials also assume is that your current procedures are based on clearly stated teaching objectives. Therefore the objectives grids at the beginning of each unit should be invaluable in providing you with a framework for ongoing assessment.

In addition, to facilitate individual children conferencing at the end of each half-term, a photocopiable record sheet has been provided on page 11. Specific targets for reading and writing can be set for each pupil at the end of the previous half-term and recorded on the sheet in the left-hand column. Interim progress towards these targets can be assessed when appropriate and noted in the middle column. Then, at the end of each half-term, during the conference, pupil and teacher together can record achievement and agree further targets for the next half-term.

HOMEWORK

The amount of homework should be increased throughout the Key Stage. In Year 6, it might take the form of:
■ Finishing off work that could not be finished in class. *Note:* be careful how you manage this. Less able pupils are often the slowest workers, and could end up with the most homework. If there seems to be a lot of finishing off needed in children's own time, consider revising lesson plans to allow more time in school.
■ Preparation – for example finding texts, such as cereal packets, newspapers and so on, to be used in the next day's lesson; making notes or plans for storywriting; research such as interviewing or surveying family members.

PUPIL ASSESSMENT GRID

Pupil's name:

Term	1	2	3	Class 1st half	Year group 2nd half
	TARGET(S)			INTERIM PROGRESS (inc dates)	ACHIEVEMENT AT END OF HALF TERM
Reading					
Writing					

OVERVIEW: YEAR 6
TERM 1

UNIT	SPELLING/ VOCABULARY	GRAMMAR/ PUNCTUATION	COMPREHENSION/ COMPOSITION
HOUR 1 — 5 (+3) READING FICTION Classic fiction: *The Wizard of Oz* by L Frank Baum.	Extend vocabulary through reading the text. Understand function of and use etymological dictionaries.	Revise all parts of speech. Study author's sentence construction.	Investigate features of fantasy. Study and respond to plot, setting, characters and ideas. Write a summary. Turn a story scene into a playscript. Write a literacy essay. (Follow-up: Compare novel and film.)
HOUR 2 — 4 WRITING FICTION Guided writing: 'Pleasant Afternoon'.	Identify misspelled words in own writing.	Revise layout and punctuation of dialogue. Revise earlier work on verbs. Explore two additional forms of the future tense.	Explore story structure. Write interesting dialogue. Understand use of irony. Plan effectively the plot, characters and structure of own narrative writing. Explore events from a different point of view. Revise types of story endings.
HOUR 3 — 4 READING NON-FICTION Recount genre: 'The Bermuda Triangle'.	Study vocabulary in the text. Make a glossary.	Understand the use of colons and semicolons. Investigate connecting words.	Revise the features of recount texts. Distinguish between fact and opinion. Comment critically on the success of recount texts.
HOUR 4 — 2 WRITING NON-FICTION Recount genre: 'The *Mary Celeste*'.	Explore technical vocabulary. Check own work for correct spelling.	Check own work for correct grammar and punctuation. Understand the terms 'active' and 'passive'.	Explore features of a recount text. Distinguish between fact and fiction. Write a well-structured narrative based on a factual event. Revise key skills for redrafting. Comment critically on the success of recount texts.
HOUR 5 — 1 REFERENCE AND RESEARCH SKILLS The origins of English.	Understand function of etymological dictionary and use it to study words of interest and significance.	Develop grammatical awareness about parts of speech.	Investigate Chaucer's language. Read and understand explanatory text about the origins of English.
HOUR 6 — 4 READING POETRY Classic poetry: 'The Pied Piper of Hamelin' by Robert Browning.	Explore key words in the poem. Understand how words have changed or fallen out of use over time. Compile a glossary of difficult/archaic words.	Secure knowledge of more sophisticated punctuation marks as used in poetic form.	Read classic poetry by a long-established poet. Revise how to study verse forms. Revise similes and metaphors. Write a literacy essay using the appropriate conventions. Express a personal response to a poem.

NB 5 (+3) = Number of hours in unit (plus number of follow-up hours)

OVERVIEW: YEAR 6
TERM 1 (CONTINUED)

UNIT	SPELLING/ VOCABULARY	GRAMMAR/ PUNCTUATION	COMPREHENSION/ COMPOSITION
WRITING POETRY Simile poems: 'New Notebook' by Judith Thurman.	Identify common, everyday expressions that are similes.	Recognize and use active verbs in writing.	Revise similes. Write own poems using effective similes. Write own poems experimenting with active verbs and personification.
READING PLAYS Extract from *A Midsummer Night's Dream* by William Shakespeare.	Understand how words and expressions have changed over time.	Explore sentence structure, recognizing sentences, clauses and phrases.	Study extract from Shakespeare play as example of classic drama. Read, prepare and present a playscript.
WRITING PLAYS 'Pyramus and Thisbe' from *A Midsummer's Night Dream* by William Shakespeare.	Understand how words and expressions have changed over time.	Demonstrate an understanding of the grammatical construction of archaic language.	Be familiar with the work of established authors. Practise improvisations. Prepare a story as a script using the correct conventions.
READING NON-FICTION Recount genre: 'The Marwell Manor Mystery'.	Study vocabulary in recount/report texts.	Understand the terms 'active' and 'passive' voice. Note how changes from active to passive affect word order.	Read a range of non-fiction recount texts. Revise the conventions of the report genre. Write a non-chronological report. Revise the conventions of diaries. Revise key skills of writing stories.
WRITING NON-FICTION Journalistic writing: 'Marwell Manor Special Report'.	Identify and use journalistic vocabulary and phrases.		Report on an imagined event using journalistic styles and conventions. Develop a journalistic style, investigating balanced reporting and presentation of information.
REFERENCE AND RESEARCH SKILLS Life stories.	Investigate the etymology of 'biography' and 'autobiography'.	Revise the difference between 1st and 3rd person narrative.	Investigate the etymology of 'biography' and 'autobiography'.
WORD PLAY Origins of proper names.	Investigate the origins of proper names.	Revise the conventions of Standard English.	Plan quickly and effectively the plot and characters of a piece of narrative writing.

OVERVIEW: YEAR 6
TERM 2

UNIT	SPELLING/ VOCABULARY	GRAMMAR/ PUNCTUATION	COMPREHENSION/ COMPOSITION
READING FICTION Classic fiction: Extract from *Nicholas Nickleby* by Charles Dickens.	Extend vocabulary from reading. Create glossary.	Revise paragraphing. Revise simple, compound and complex sentences.	Read extract from longer established novel. Increase familiarity with significant writer of the past.
WRITING FICTION Victorian Story Cards.	Extend vocabulary from reading. Use glossary.	Revise 1st and 3rd-person pronouns. Extend writing of dialogue.	Revise key writing skills and story structures. Write own story using story read as model.
REDRAFTING SIMULATION 'Golden Arrow Publications'.	Identify misspelled words in own writing.	Revise structure and paragraphing. Revise all parts of speech, verb tenses and 1st and 3rd - person viewpoints. Revise all forms of punctuation, including that for dialogue.	Review, edit and evaluate own writing. Redraft content and format.
READING NON-FICTION 'Shakespeare's Theatre'.	Develop new vocabulary from reading.	Understand use of past tense in text. Identify sequencing words. Understand features of formal language.	Read and understand information text. Revise features of non-fiction recount. Interpret illustrative and diagrammatic information. Write public information leaflet.
WRITING NON-FICTION Design a CD-ROM page.	Develop IT-related vocabulary. Develop and extend knowledge of acronyms.	Compare layout features of print and IT information texts.	Compare features of non-fiction texts in print and IT. Write text for a CD-ROM encyclopaedia page.
REFERENCE AND RESEARCH SKILLS Establishing roots.	Use personal reading, a range of dictionaries and previous knowledge to investigate words with common prefixes, suffixes and word roots.	Understand that words can be changed by adding prefixes and suffixes.	Know how to use alternative strategy when meaning is not clear from context.
READING POETRY Extract from 'Niassan Creation Myth'.	Use phonetic knowledge to pronounce unfamiliar and foreign words. Understand the meaning of 'creation', 'myth', 'literature'.	Consider the impact of the use of active verbs.	Read a myth in poetic form. Recognize how words in poetry are manipulated to create rhythms. Analyse how mood and feeling are reflected in poetry. Extend knowledge of the oral tradition.
WRITING POETRY Metaphor poems: 'The Beach' by William Hart-Smith and 'What is . . . the sun?' by Wes Magee.	Understand the terms 'imagery' and 'metaphor'.	Demonstrate awareness of parallel grammatical structures in writing own poems.	Recognize figurative language and use in own writing.

HOUR 3
HOUR 3
HOUR 3
HOUR 3
HOUR 2
HOUR 1
HOUR 1
HOUR 1

14

OVERVIEW: YEAR 6
TERM 2 (CONTINUED)

	UNIT	SPELLING/ VOCABULARY	GRAMMAR/ PUNCTUATION	COMPREHENSION/ COMPOSITION
HOUR 3	READING FICTION 'The Red-Headed League' by Sir Arthur Conan Doyle (a Sherlock Holmes story).	Use and understand vocabulary related to mystery genre.	Investigate the use of hyphens and dashes.	Read a mystery story by a well-established author. Identify characteristic features of mystery genre.
HOUR 2	WRITING FICTION 'Write a detective story'.	Identify misspelled words in own writing. Develop vocabulary related to mystery/ detective genre.	Demonstrate grammatical awareness and knowledge of punctuation in own writing.	Write a story in a genre similar to one read.
HOUR 3	READING NON-FICTION 'Lights', from The RoSPA Bicycle Owner's Handbook.	Study vocabulary in text. Revise bi- prefix and investigate words that include it.	Investigate conditional clauses. Understand features of formal official language.	Read a public information text and explore characteristic features of language and format.
HOUR 2	WRITING NON-FICTION 'The Hover-bike Owner's Handbook'.	Identify misspelled words in own writing. Use independent spelling strategies. Use vocabulary appropriate to content and style.	Revise use of conditionals. Use conventions of official language: imperatives and the auxiliary modal verb 'must'.	Use features of official language to produce a public information booklet.
HOUR 1	REFERENCE AND RESEARCH SKILLS Paraphrasing and summarizing.	Spell and understand meaning of words with prefix para-.	Revise work on contracting sentences by summarizing.	Develop key skills of paraphrasing and summarizing.
HOUR 1	WORD PLAY Investigating humorous verse: Three poems by Charles Causley.	Use known spellings as a basis for spelling other words.	Revise work on contracting sentences.	Investigate humorous verse. Explore three poems by a signficiant poet.

OVERVIEW: YEAR 6
TERM 3

UNIT	SPELLING/ VOCABULARY	GRAMMAR/ PUNCTUATION	COMPREHENSION/ COMPOSITION
READING POETRY Poems by William Blake.	Develop vocabulary to talk about poems. Understand that language changes over time.	Understand and demonstrate when reading aloud how punctuation signposts meaning. Identify and use contrastive connectives.	Read, describe, compare and evaluate poems by significant poet. Investigate meaning conveyed through figurative language. Write summaries.
WRITING POETRY The Poetry Machine.	Develop vocabulary to talk about poetry.	Revise parts of speech.	Write poems linked by form. Revise features of different poetic forms.
READING NON-FICTION Persuasive writing: 'Capital Punishment'.	Develop vocabulary through reading.	Revise language conventions and grammatical features of persuasive texts.	Read and review characteristics of argument texts. Distinguish fact from opinion. Express personal responses to text.
WRITING NON-FICTION Persuasive writing: 'Corporal Punishment'.	Identify misspelled words in own writing. Develop vocabulary of argument.	Extend knowledge and use of connectives.	Write a persuasive argument in paragraphs with appropriate links. Secure control of impersonal writing.
READING FICTION Fantasy genre: Fantasy Stories, chosen by Diana Wynne Jones.	Develop vocabulary through text. Extend literary vocabulary for talking about texts.	Identify the language features of fantasy genre. Identify and understand complex sentences. Revise conditional clauses.	Examine different authors' treatment of same themes and genre. Look at contrasts and connections in the work of different writers. Write a brief synopsis of a text. Understand the use of paragraphs.
WRITING FICTION Writing fantasy stories.	Check spelling in own writing. Use vocabulary appropriate to fantasy genre.	Demonstrate grammatical awareness and check grammar in own writing.	Write a story based on fantasy genre. Revise key plot structures. Revise redrafting skills.
REFERENCE AND RESEARCH SKILLS Setting a purpose for reading.	Understand and differentiate the terms 'scanning', 'skimming' and 'studying'.		Set purposes for reading so that research is fast and effective. Use reading style appropriate to purpose.

OVERVIEW: YEAR 6
TERM 3 (CONTINUED)

HOUR	UNIT	SPELLING/ VOCABULARY	GRAMMAR/ PUNCTUATION	COMPREHENSION/ COMPOSITION
5 (+2)	READING FICTION *The Silver Sword* by Ian Serraillier.	Revise and consolidate work during past year by learning and inventing spelling rules. Use independent strategies by applying knowledge of rules and exceptions. Practise and extend vocabulary through crosswords.	Revise the language conventions and grammatical features of narrative text. Consolidate work on complex sentences.	Read a work by a significant children's author and compare it (in next unit) with a poem by same author. Describe and evaluate the style of an individual writer. Write a summary, deciding on priorities relevant to purpose.
2	WRITING FICTION 'After Ever Happily' by Ian Serraillier.	Appreciate poet's use of language to create humour. Use independent spelling strategies when writing own poem and fairy tale.	Revise language conventions and grammatical features of different types of text.	Compare works by a single writer. Iinvestigate humorous verse. Revise and extend writing of free verse. Write own story using flashback structure.
5	WRITING SIMULATION 'Summer Camp Experience'.	Practise use of independent spelling strategies. Demonstrate use of extended vocabulary in own writing. Identify misspelled words in own writing.	Revise language conventions and grammatical features of a range of text types. Revise and use the impersonal voice and the passive voice.	Review a range of non-fiction text types and their characteristics. Use appropriate style and form to suit a specific purpose and audience. Secure control of impersonal writing.
1	REFERENCE AND RESEARCH SKILLS Talking slang: a language investigation.	Understand the term 'slang'. Collect and define slang words and phrases, using a variety of information sources.	Conduct a language investigation through interviews and research.	Write a dictionary of slang. Locate information efficiently.
1	WORD PLAY Experimenting with language.	Experiment with language, creating new words.	Secure control of complex sentences. Understand how clauses can be manipulated to achieve different affects. Secure understanding of parts of speech.	Comment critically on overall impact of poem.

NB.  5 (+2) = Number of hours in unit (plus number of follow-up hours)

OBJECTIVES GRIDS:
BLANK TEMPLATES

UNIT	SPELLING/ VOCABULARY	GRAMMAR/ PUNCTUATION	COMPREHENSION/ COMPOSITION

UNIT	SPELLING/ VOCABULARY	GRAMMAR/ PUNCTUATION	COMPREHENSION/ COMPOSITION

UNIT	SPELLING/ VOCABULARY	GRAMMAR/ PUNCTUATION	COMPREHENSION/ COMPOSITION

UNIT	SPELLING/ VOCABULARY	GRAMMAR/ PUNCTUATION	COMPREHENSION/ COMPOSITION

Term 1

THE WIZARD OF OZ

OBJECTIVES

UNIT	SPELLING/ VOCABULARY	GRAMMAR/ PUNCTUATION	COMPREHENSION/ COMPOSITION
READING FICTION Classic fiction: *The Wizard of Oz* by L Frank Baum.	Extend vocabulary through reading the text. Understand function of and use etymological dictionaries.	Revise all parts of speech. Study author's sentence construction.	Investigate features of fantasy. Study and respond to plot, setting, characters and ideas. Write a summary. Turn a story scene into a playscript. Write a literacy essay. (Follow-up: Compare novel and film.)

ORGANIZATION (5 HOURS)

	INTRODUCTION	WHOLE-CLASS SKILLS WORK	DIFFERENTIATED GROUP ACTIVITIES	CONCLUSION
HOUR 1	Shared reading of Chapters 1–3 of *The Wizard of Oz* (pages 1–25, approximately 16 minutes).	Distinguish between 'summary' and 'abridgement'. Model process of writing a summary.	1*: Guided reading and discussion. Preparation for writing essay. 2 & 3: Write a 150-word summary of Chapter 1. 4*: Guided reading and discussion. Preparation for writing essay.	Several summaries are read out and compared. The class discusses and evaluates which summaries contain all the essential points.
HOUR 2	Sum up events in Chapters 1–3. Shared reading of Chapters 4–6 (pages 26–49, approximately 16 minutes).	Revise all eight parts of speech.	1: Write a 150-word summary of Chapter 6. 2 & 3*: Guided reading and discussion. Essay preparation. 4: Write a summary of Chapter 1.	Key points from the day's reading are discussed. Pupils are encouraged to make notes towards their essays.
HOUR 3	Briefly sum up what happened in Chapters 4–6. Briefly summarize Chapters 7–9 (pages 50–73). Shared reading of Chapters 10 & 11 (pages 74–98, pproximately 20 minutes).	Investigate language and style of the text, including the vocabulary and sentence construction. Describe features of plot structure.	1*: Guided reading and discussion. Essay preparation. 2 & 3: Turn a scene from the story into a playscript. 4*: Guided reading and discussion. Essay preparation.	Key points from the day's reading are summed up.
HOUR 4	Briefly sum up what happened in Chapters 10 & 11. Shared reading of Chapters 12–14 (pages 99–129, approximately 20 minutes).	Investigate the etymology of words from the novel.	1: Turn a scene from the story into a playscript. 2 & 3*: Guided reading and discussion. Essay preparation. 4: Create a storyboard with production notes for a chapter.	Key points from the day's reading are discussed. Pupils are encouraged to make notes towards their essays.
HOUR 5	Briefly sum up what happened in Chapters 12–14. Shared reading of Chapters 15 & 16 (pages 130–147, approximately 14 minutes).	Explore the conventions of writing a literary essay.	1–4*: All pupils write an essay on *The Wizard of Oz* using their notes and the essay template on photocopiable page 26.	Read Chapter 17 (pages 148–153) and summarize the author's ending.

RESOURCES

The Wizard of Oz by L Frank Baum (Puffin Classics, ISBN 0-14-036693-8) – if possible, enough copies for half the class, photocopiable page 26 (Essay Template), dictionaries (at least one between two) which contain etymological references, board or flip chart, OHP and acetate (optional), writing materials.

Note: The recommended readings cover the main events, but omit Chapters 7, 8, 9 an[d] 18 to the end. The selected chapters cover all the events in the film *The Wizard of Oz* (Metro Goldwyn Mayer, 1939) so the remaining chapters can be omitted. However, if desired, these could be read at other times during the day or as homework. The former will work with a half class set, whereas the latter will require a copy for every child.

PREPARATION

Make copies of the Essay Template (photocopiable page 26) for each child in Groups 1–3. Prepare a separate version of the sheet for the children in Group 4, omitting sections 5–7. If possible, prepare an OHT of the sheet or make an A3 enlargement. Do the same with the author information on the first two pages of *The Wizard of Oz*.

SYNOPSIS

Dorothy and her dog Toto are whirled away in their house by a cyclone. They arrive in the land of Oz, killing the Wicked Witch of the East, who is crushed by the house. Dorothy takes the Witch's silver shoes which have magic powers. To get back home, she has to follow the yellow brick road to where the great Wizard lives – the only one who can help her. On her way, she meets the Tin Woodman, Scarecrow and Cowardly Lion, who accompany her to the City of Emeralds to ask the Wizard's help. The Wizard refuses any favours until they kill the Wicked Witch of the West. Dorothy accidentally manages to do this and they return to claim the Wizard's favours, but he turns out to be a total impostor. Despite this, he manages to help Dorothy's companions although he fails to grant her wish. Dorothy's final hope is to travel to the country of the Quadlings. There, Glinda, the Witch of the South, tells Dorothy to click the heels of her magic shoes three times, and almost instantly Dorothy and Toto find themselves back home in Kansas.

Introduction

Start by explaining to the children that they are going to study *The Wizard of Oz* and then write an essay about it. They will be given the outline for the essay at the start of the group activities session, and should refer to the headings to help them make appropriate notes throughout the five hours.

Before sharing the text, ask if any of the children know the story of *The Wizard of Oz*. Do they know who the author is? Have any of them seen a film version of the story? Read the information about the author at the start of the book, then read Chapters 1–3. Ask the children to identify the genre of the book (a classic fantasy novel with fairy-tale elements). How can the children tell this? Try to establish the characteristic features of fantasy. (The narrative is not possible in real life with its setting in an imaginary world, the magical events, the traditional fairy-tale characters which include witches and wizards, talking animals and so on, the triumph of good over evil.)

Whole-class skills work

Begin by asking the children to define the word 'summary'. Do they know what an abridgement of a text is? Discuss their ideas then provide these definitions:
Summary: A short account of the key facts, points or events in a piece of writing. A summary usually uses different wording to the original.
Abridgement: A shortened, condensed version made by omitting words, sentences and even whole sections from the original text.

Briefly discuss why summaries are useful – for example, to get information across quickly and to fit it in a limited amount of writing space such as in a book/film review, a cover blurb and so on. Move on to discuss abridged texts. Explain that lengthy classic novels are often shortened or 'abridged' to help readers – for example, young children who would find it difficult to read a long text, or readers who want to experience famous classic writing but are happy to have less detail than that provided in the full version.

Now demonstrate the process of shortening a text by making a 100-word summary of the information about the author on the first two pages of *The Wizard of Oz*. (Ideally, this text should be displayed on an OHP so that the children can follow the process.) Explain and go through each stage as follows:
■ Pick out the most important facts. As 100 words is about one-fifth of the original length, only the most essential details can be included. Ask the children what these might be, then underline them.

- Count the number of underlined words. If it is close to 100, more facts will have to be cut. If it is a very low number, more facts could be added.
- Encourage the children to provide suggestions.
- Put the facts into sentences. Work together to do this.
- Count the words again and add or cut information as necessary.
  Briefly list the stages and keep it to display in the group activities for Hours 1 and 2.

Differentiated group activities

Give a copy of the Essay Template on photocopiable page 26 to each child, providing the shortened version for children in Group 4 (see Preparation). Explain that they should use the spaces between the paragraph prompts to make notes.

1*: Guided reading and discussion of Chapters 1–3. Use the following questions as a starting point, encouraging children to refer to the text to support their responses:
- In your own words, describe the contrast between Kansas and Oz.
- What do we learn about Dorothy's character from these chapters?
- How do you think Dorothy feels about landing in Oz?
- Describe Scarecrow's character.
  Remind the children that they should be making notes throughout this session in preparation for their essay writing.

2 & 3: Write a 150-word summary of Chapter 1 following the process given in the whole-class skills session. Display the list of stages for the children to refer to.

4*: Guided reading and discussion followed by essay preparation, as for Group 1.

Conclusion

Select several children from Groups 2 and 3 to read out their summaries and ask the rest of the class to evaluate them. Which summaries contain all the essential points? If time allows, those in Groups 1 and 4 could report back briefly on their discussion of the day's readings, while children in Groups 1 and 3 make notes towards their essay.

Introduction

Briefly recap on Chapters 1–3 of the story:

> Dorothy and Toto land in Oz, killing the Wicked Witch of the East. Dorothy is given the witch's magic shoes by the Munchkins in gratitude. She sets off for the City of Emeralds to seek help from the Wizard of Oz in returning home. She meets the Scarecrow who goes with her to see if the Wizard can give him some brains.

Read Chapters 4–6. Discuss the introduction of the new characters (Tin Woodman and Cowardly Lion) and what they add to the story at this point – for example, further interest and variety in that they become Dorothy's companions; each has his own story and needs the Wizard's help; touches of humour (such as Dorothy slapping the Cowardly Lion); the building up of suspense as they travel to meet the Great Wizard, and so on.

Whole-class skills work

Hold a question-and-answer session to revise all eight parts of speech (some grammars list nine, including articles *a* and *the*). Write each one on the board and ask the children to find other examples in Chapters 4–6, following the suggestions below.

Noun: a naming word, for example *Dorothy, road, bricks*.

Pronoun: takes the place of a noun, for example *he, she, them, him*.

Adjective: describes a noun, for example *rough, difficult, yellow*.

Verb: a 'doing' word, for example *walk, stumbled, stepped*.

Adverb: describes a verb or adjective, for example *merrily, carefully, quite, very*.

Preposition: shows where things are in relation to each other, for example *with, under, on*.

Conjunction: joins statements, clauses and words in phrases, for example *and, but, because, when*.

Interjection: an exclamation, for example *'Oh!'*.

Differentiated group activities

1: Write a 150-word summary of Chapter 6. Display the list of stages of the summarizing process from Hour 1 for the children to refer to.

2 & 3*: Guided reading and discussion of Chapters 4–6. Use the following questions as

a starting point, encouraging children to refer to the text to support their responses:
- What else do we learn about Scarecrow in Chapter 4?
- In your own words, describe Tin Woodman and his history.
- Describe Lion's character.

Encourage the children to make notes in preparation for their essay.

4: Write a summary of Chapter 1. The children will be supported by the fact that they have heard similar summaries read aloud by Groups 2 and 3 in the previous hour.

Conclusion

Select children from Groups 2 and 3 to report back on their discussion of the day's reading and ask the other children to make notes towards their essays.

Introduction

Briefly recap on Chapters 4–6:

Dorothy listens to the Scarecrow's story. The next day, they meet Tin Woodman whom they rescue by oiling his rusted joints. Tin Woodman joins them on their journey, intending to ask the Wizard to give him a heart. They meet Cowardly Lion who goes with them on their journey in the hope that the Wizard will give him courage.

Chapters 7–9 describe various adventures on the road to Oz and are not essential to the understanding of the whole story. They can be summarized for the children as follows:

Dorothy, Toto, Scarecrow, Tin Woodman and Cowardly Lion come to a wide deep ditch. Cowardly Lion jumps over it (showing courage, even though he thinks he has none), then carries the others across one at a time on his back. They come to another gulf and Tin Woodman has the idea of felling a tree to make a bridge. They are pursued by beasts called Kalidahs, and Scarecrow has the idea (even though he thinks he has no brains) of chopping down the bridge so that they fall into the gulf. Next Dorothy and Toto are drugged to sleep by some poppies in a field. Lion is affected soon after, but Scarecrow and Tin Woodman are not affected because they are not mortal. They save Dorothy and Toto, but cannot lift the heavy Lion. Luckily, they are helped by the Queen of the Field Mice who summons all her subjects to drag Lion out of the field.

Next, read Chapters 10 and 11. Note that the length of the reading in this hour will reduce the time available for the whole-class skills and group sessions.

Whole-class skills work

Explain to the children that they are going to look in detail at various language and style aspects of *The Wizard of Oz*, including vocabulary, and briefly examine plot structure. Ask them to look in detail at Chapter 11, then discuss the following:
- At the opening of the chapter, Baum describes the land of Oz and begins to build up an image of the Great Wizard. What techniques does he use to do this? (He uses many adjectives to build up a picture of fairy-tale beauty and splendour – *dazzled, wonderful, sparkling, glittering, lovely, beautiful*, and so on. The constant repetition of the word *green* reinforces the notion of the Emerald City and its riches. The sense of the Great Wizard's awesome power is built up by the use of a traditional fairy-tale royal setting, for example *Palace* and *Throne Room*. The Wizard's mystery and power are further enhanced by the fact that no one inside or outside of the Emerald City has ever been allowed to see him.)
- How does the author create the feeling that this is a fantasy land? (By making everything green, by using phrases such as *The Guardian of the Gates, The Palace of Oz, The Great Wizard, The Wicked Witch of the West*, and so on, by including details of the Wizard appearing in different forms to each of the characters – for example, *he saw...a most lovely Lady...dressed in green silk gauze...Growing from her shoulders were wings, gorgeous in colour...* – so we feel that almost anything is possible in the land of Oz.)
- The Wizard sees Dorothy and her companions separately, and says much the same thing to each of them. Why is this plot structure similar to a traditional fairy tale? (Traditional fairy tales often use repetition in their plots. Point out that a similar structure is used in Chapters 3–6 when Dorothy meets her journeying companions – each tells his own story and each has a problem that requires the Wizard's help.)

Finally, ask the children to identify words they do not know or are not sure about. Ask them to look them up in dictionaries, then help them to understand their meaning in the context of the passage.

Differentiated group activities

1*: Guided reading and discussion of Chapters 10 and 11. The following questions can be used as a starting point:
- How does Baum describe the Wizard's Throne Room and the Wizard himself?
- What are Dorothy's impressions of the Wizard?
- How do her companions react to the Wizard?
- What does the Wizard ask them to do?

Encourage the children to make notes for their essay during the discussion.

2 & 3: Turn the scene in which Dorothy sees the Wizard (Chapter 11) into a short playscript. The children should be encouraged to use the correct layout and playscript conventions such as set description, stage directions and so on.

4*: Guided reading and discussion as for Group 1.

Conclusion

Sum up on the key points of the lesson, particularly the way that Baum uses language and plot structure to create the effect of a fairy story. Encourage the children in Groups 2 and 3 to make notes towards their essays.

Introduction

Briefly recap on Chapters 10 and 11:

Dorothy and her friends are near the Emerald City at last and rest overnight in a cottage. The next day, they set off and reach the Emerald City. The Guardian of the Gates gives them all green spectacles and allows them in. They stay at the Palace while they await the Wizard's audience. Each is finally granted a separate interview with Oz, but is refused help until they have killed the Wicked Witch of the West. They decide to try to meet the Wizard's request and plan to begin their journey the following day.

Next, read Chapters 12–14. Note that the length of the reading in this hour will reduce the time available for the whole-class skills and group work sessions.

Whole-class skills work

Introduce the term 'etymology'. Have any of the children heard it before? Does anyone know its meaning? Explain that etymology is the study of the origins of words. Tell the children that they are going to learn about etymological dictionaries. Explain that most dictionaries contain etymological information about the history of words, including the original language from which they were derived. This information is usually provided in the form of abbreviations. Provide the children with one etymological dictionary between two, and together explore these abbreviations. Some common ones include:

L Latin **Gk** Greek **F** French **G** German **It** Italian
ME Middle English (c. 1200–1500) **OE** Old English (c. 700–1200)

Write the above abbreviations on the board or flip chart, then ask the children to see if they can find the origins of the following words which can be found in Chapters 12–14:

basket	chariot	comrade	country	diamonds
guardian	next	obey	plague	polite
soldier	spectacle	telescope	terrible	umbrella

Discuss the results. Generally, it will be found that most words are of Old or Middle English origin. But many words have French origins. Why do the children think this is? Discuss the various languages that have contributed to the development of English.

Differentiated group activities

1: Choose one scene from Chapters 12–14 to turn into a playscript. Use the correct layout and write suitable production notes to go with the script.

2 & 3*: Guided reading and discussion of Chapters 12–14. The following questions can be used as a starting point:

■ How do Dorothy and her companions feel as they leave the Emerald City?
■ Why does the author use the Winged Monkeys as a means of returning the characters to the Emerald City? (To add variety and avoid repeating details of the journey back.)
■ What are the characters hoping for when they return to see the Wizard?
The children should make notes throughout the session to prepare for their essay.
4: Create a simple storyboard with production notes for one of the chapters.

Conclusion

Key points from the day's reading should be discussed and the children in Groups 1 and 4 encouraged to make notes towards their essays.

Introduction

Briefly recap on Chapters 12–14:

Dorothy and her companions travel West to meet the Wicked Witch. The Witch uses various means to attack them, and eventually, Scarecrow and Tin Woodman are almost destroyed by the Winged Monkeys, while Lion is captured. Dorothy is enslaved by the Witch who eventually manages to steal one of Dorothy's magic silver shoes. Dorothy pours a bucket of water over her in anger. This destroys the Witch and everyone in her land is set free. Dorothy's companions are rescued and the Winged Monkeys return them all to the City of Emeralds.

Next, read Chapters 15 and 16. Briefly discuss the characters' reactions to the Wizard of Oz when his tricks are discovered.

Whole-class skills work

Display the Essay Template (photocopiable page 26) on an OHP. Explain essay-writing conventions – the fact that each paragraph should make a series of points, and the most important points should be supported by evidence. This can be done in three ways:
■ An indirect reference to the text, for example *We can see that Lion already has courage because he offers to go with Dorothy to try to kill the witch.*
■ Using a short quotation, for example *We can see that Scarecrow already has brains because when the Kalidahs were pursuing them 'he was thinking what was best to be done'.*
■ Using a longer quotation which should be set out on indented lines, for example *Baum makes Oz seem a fairy-tale place by making everything green:*
  'Green candy and green pop corn were offered for sale, as well as green shoes, green hats, and green clothes of all sorts. At one place a man was selling green lemonade.'
In writing their essays as part of the group activities session below, children in Group 1 should be encouraged to use all three kinds of evidence in their essays. Children in Groups 2 and 3 would do best to avoid longer quotations. Children in Group 4 should use indirect reference only.

Differentiated group activities

1–4*: Children in all groups use their notes, the above guidance and the Essay Template (photocopiable page 26) to write an essay on *The Wizard of Oz*. Children in Group 4 use a shorter version of the template (see 'Preparation'). Provide support as appropriate.

Conclusion

Read Chapter 17, then summarize the author's ending for the children:

Dorothy does not get back to Kansas with the Wizard because she leaps from the balloon to save Toto. There follows a series of adventures until Glinda explains that Dorothy's shoes have the power to take her back if she clicks her heels together three times. She does this and reappears in Kansas outside Uncle Henry's new farm house.

Discuss: is this ending essential? Should the author have ended with Dorothy returning by balloon with the Wizard? Is he just spinning out the story to make it longer?

FOLLOW-UP (3 HOURS)

Page 27 provides a grid plan for a 3-hour follow-up unit comparing the book *The Wizard of Oz* and the film.

ESSAY TEMPLATE

Write your notes in the spaces provided. Turn over the page if you need more space.

Paragraph 1: Write an introduction to the book including a few sentences about the author and the genre of the book. Follow with a summary of the main events of the story in about 100 words.

Paragraph 2: Describe the main character, Dorothy.

Paragraph 3: Describe Dorothy's three companions: Scarecrow, Tin Man and Cowardly Lion.

Paragraph 4: Describe the Wizard of Oz as he appears in Chapter 11.

Paragraph 5: Write about the qualities shown by Dorothy's companions in Chapters 12–14.

Paragraph 6: Describe how Dorothy's companions' wishes come true. Explain how this can happen although the Wizard is a fraud.

Paragraph 7: Discuss the language and style used by the author (focus on Chapter 11).

Paragraph 8: Write about what you liked and disliked about the book. What did you learn about the qualities of intelligence, love and courage?

THE WIZARD OF OZ: FOLLOW-UP

OBJECTIVES

UNIT	SPELLING/VOCABULARY	GRAMMAR/ PUNCTUATION	COMPREHENSION/ COMPOSITION
READING FICTION Classic fiction: *The Wizard of Oz* – Follow-up.	Revise technical vocabulary of film.	Compare how the grammar and punctuation of written word differ from that of spoken word.	Compare and evaluate a novel in print and the film version.

ORGANIZATION (3 HOURS)

	INTRODUCTION	WHOLE-CLASS SKILLS WORK	DIFFERENTIATED GROUP ACTIVITIES	CONCLUSION
HOUR 1	Watch the opening scenes of the 1939 film *The Wizard of Oz* to the point where Dorothy arrives in the land of Munchkins.	Revise technical vocabulary of film, eg *long shot, close-up, pan, tilt, zoom* etc.	1*: Discuss similarities and differences between film and book. Make notes. 2 & 3: Make notes on each film scene referring to the type of shot used. 4*: Discuss similarities between film and book.	Discuss ideas arising from the group activities.
HOUR 2	Watch the scene in which Dorothy meets the Tin Man.	Compare descriptive techniques in book and film: **Book:** Use of descriptive language, particularly adjectives and adverbs; attention to detail. **Film:** Costume design, set design, camera, angle, use of colour.	1–4*: Write a description of Tin Man from film only. Compare this with description in book. If time allows, the same activity can be done with all the main characters. The scene showing the first audiences with the Wizard is particularly interesting, and varies in several ways from book.	Discuss similarities and differences between the film and the book.
HOUR 3	After watching more of the film in times outside literacy hours, show the last scene in which Dorothy returns to Kansas.	Examine the plot structures in film and book, with particular attention to the endings.	1: Write an essay examining similarities and differences between film and book. 2 & 3*: Write a film review saying how well film does justice to book. 4: Write a short review of the film.	Selected pupils share their essays and film reviews followed by discussion and evaluation.

PLEASANT AFTERNOON

OBJECTIVES

UNIT	SPELLING/VOCABULARY	GRAMMAR/ COMPREHENSION	COMPREHENSION/ COMPOSITION
WRITING FICTION Guided writing: 'Pleasant Afternoon'.	Identify misspelled words in own writing.	Revise layout and punctuation of dialogue. Revise earlier work on verbs. Explore two additional forms of the future tense.	Explore story structure. Write interesting dialogue. Understand use of irony. Plan effectively the plot, characters and structure of own narrative writing. Explore events from a different point of view. Revise types of story endings.

ORGANIZATION (4 HOURS)

	INTRODUCTION	WHOLE-CLASS SKILLS WORK	DIFFERENTIATED GROUP ACTIVITIES	CONCLUSION
HOUR 1	Read 'Pleasant Afternoon' on photocopiable page 33. Examine story structure.	Use photocopiable resource sheets to support writing character descriptions.	1*: Begin guided writing of 'Desert Disaster' story. 2 & 3: Reading Comprehension – parts A & C. 4*: As for Group 1, following template on photocopiable page.	Selected pupils from Groups 1 & 4 read out their story beginnings. The class briefly evaluates how effectively the different story elements are blended.
HOUR 2	Re-read 'Pleasant Afternoon'. Briefly discuss the events from the viewpoints of Jim and Maxwell.	Revise: layout and punctuation of dialogue; use of interesting/varied reporting clauses; adding descriptive phrases to reporting clauses.	1: Reading Comprehension: all parts. 2 & 3*: Begin guided writing of 'Desert Disaster' story using template as a guide. 4: Reading Comprehension – part A.	Go over answers to the Reading Comprehension exercise.
HOUR 3	Re-read a specified extract of 'Pleasant Afternoon', then discuss possible alternatives endings.	Explore irony. Identify where title is referred to literally or ironically in story.	1*: Continue writing 'Desert Disaster'. Develop main plot and subplots using 'Pleasant Afternoon' as model. 2 & 3: Write an alternative ending to 'Pleasant Afternoon'. 4*: Continue writing 'Desert Disaster' story.	Selected pupils from Groups 2 & 3 read out their alternative endings. The class evaluates how effectively they follow on from the original story.
HOUR 4	Re-read the ending of 'Pleasant Afternoon'. Explain how it brings main plot and subplots back together again.	Revise previous work on verbs. Explore two additional forms of the future tense.	1: Write an alternative ending to 'Pleasant Afternoon'. 2 & 3*: Continue writing 'Desert Disaster' story. 4: As for Group 1, according to ability.	Selected pupils from Groups 1 & 4 read out their alternative endings. The class evaluates how effectively they follow on from the original story.

RESOURCES

Photocopiable pages 33 and 34 (Pleasant Afternoon), 35 (Desert Disaster: Characters), 36 (Desert Disaster: Story Template) and 37 (Reading Comprehension), board or flip chart, OHP and acetate (optional), writing materials.

PREPARATION

Prepare a complete set of the above photocopiable sheets for each pair of children. If possible, make an OHT or A3 enlargement of 'Pleasant Afternoon' (pages 33 and 34) and the Desert Disaster: Story Template (page 36).

HOUR 1

Introduction

Explain to the children that they are going to read a story entitled 'Pleasant Afternoon' and then write a story entitled 'Desert Disaster'. Their story will use a different situation and characters, but will have the same structure as 'Pleasant Afternoon'.

Display the 'Pleasant Afternoon' as an OHT or A3 enlargement then read it aloud. Discuss the structure of the story and see if the children can identify a clear beginning, middle and end. Then summarize the structure on the board as follows:

Beginning: Sets the scene, with dialogue, action and description blended together.
Middle: Two parallel story lines (plot and sub-plot) created by the two groups of characters trying to survive in different ways.
Ending: Jim's idea for survival turns out to be best and the whole group is saved by the arrival of a plane.

Go through the story again, looking at how details of character and setting are built up gradually, bit by bit. Point out how dialogue, action and description are integrated rather than presented as separate blocks:

> ...it's not safe to leave the track; there are no landmarks out there – just sand, sand and more sand, and the wind-blown stuff is bad news, even for this tough old Land Rover.

Through Jim's dialogue, the reader learns that the setting is a desert. There is no separate descriptive paragraph to introduce the setting; instead, the author has used dialogue to convey this, adding small bits of description later in the story (*the sand reached to the horizon in smooth rippling dunes*). Similarly, character is built up gradually, through dialogue and interaction with other characters, as well as through occasional description.

Tell the children that when they come to write their stories, they should try to build up character and place description bit by bit in the same way. Explain that this is how most modern authors handle description of place and character.

Whole-class skills work

Say to the children that most good stories grow out of the characters involved. Explain that, in their work so far, the main focus in character description has been on appearance, but the following aspects are even more important:

Personality: what a person is like *inside*, for example determined, adventurous, moody and so on.
Abilities: what they are good at, for example they may be intelligent, good with their hands, artistic and so on.
Motivation: what makes them tick, for example a desire to impress people, desire for money and so on.

List these aspects on the board or flip chart, then give out one copy of photocopiable page 35 (Desert Disaster: Characters) between two. Ask the children to choose two characters from the sheet. One of these is to be the main character of their story. This person will need to be a strong leader, but also sensible and wise. The second character will also have a strong personality but could be impulsive, arrogant, bad tempered, and so on. Ask the children to spend a few minutes writing a brief life history for each one. Tell them to focus particularly on the three aspects above.

Use the last few minutes of this session to share a couple of examples.

Differentiated group activities

1*: Begin guided writing of their own 'Desert Disaster' story. Encourage the children in this group to use 'Pleasant Afternoon' as a model for structure and style. Emphasize the importance of integrating action, dialogue and description. The children can use the characters prepared in the skills session, but should remember to feed in the descriptive information a piece at a time. Emphasize that they should try to show what a character is like by what they say and do as well as how they are described.

2 & 3: Complete parts A and C of the Reading Comprehension exercise for 'Pleasant Afternoon' (photocopiable page 37).

4*: Begin guided writing of their own 'Desert Disaster' story following closely the story template on photocopiable page 36.

Conclusion

Select children from Groups 1 and 4 to read out their story beginnings, following with a brief class discussion. Are character and place description, action and dialogue blended together effectively? Do the main characters stand out clearly?

Introduction

Display 'Pleasant Afternoon' as an OHT or A3 enlargement and re-read the story. Briefly discuss the events from the different viewpoints of Jim and Maxwell. What would be the opinions of these characters on the events that unfold? For example, Jim sees things from a highly practical viewpoint and feels that Maxwell is acting foolishly. Maxwell thinks he knows better about travelling in the desert and views Jim's objections to going off the track as mere nonsense. Encourage the children to support their ideas with evidence from the text.

Finish by looking at how the story switches between the plot and subplot, as the narrative focuses in turn on Jim and Jeremy, then on Maxwell's group. Explain that the children should use a similar structure in their own 'Desert Disaster' stories.

Whole-class skills work

Display the photocopiable story template (page 36) as an OHT or A3 enlargement. Use the dialogue on the sheet to revise the following:

■ How dialogue is set out on separate indented lines for alternate speakers.

■ The punctuation of dialogue – correct placement of speech marks, commas and so on.

■ Writing interesting reporting clauses using synonyms of 'said' and adverbs.

■ Adding a phrase of description to the reporting clause.

In previous units, the emphasis has been on writing blocks of dialogue, but in their 'Desert Disaster' stories, the children should be encouraged to integrate dialogue and description freely throughout the story. However, give them this rule of thumb: the dialogue should not exceed more than half of the length of the story (otherwise it would be more suitable written as a play!).

Differentiated group activities

1: Complete all parts of the Reading Comprehension sheet.

2 & 3*: Write the 'Desert Disaster' story as described for Group 1 in Hour 1, but use the template as a guide. In other words, the children follow it closely, but are encouraged to expand on the sentences provided and add in extra description.

4: Complete part A of the Reading Comprehension sheet. Part C can be used for discussion if time allows.

Conclusion

Now that all the children have worked on the Reading Comprehension exercise, go over the answers with the whole class.

Introduction

Read from *They were crawling now...* to *...everything went black* in 'Pleasant Afternoon', then discuss possible alternative types of ending to the story, for example:

■ A twist in the tale

■ An anti-climax

■ A 'cliff-hanger'.

Whole-class skills work

Consider the meaning of the term 'irony' with reference to the title 'Pleasant Afternoon'.

Do the children know what irony is? Explain that irony is saying one thing and meaning the opposite – for example, looking out of the window on a rainy day and saying, 'What a *lovely* day!' Point out that a different tone of voice is used to say something with irony. Ask the children to make up some ironic comments, for example about the weather, or their likes and dislikes, and so on. Write these on the board or flip chart and ask volunteers to read them out using an appropriate tone of voice.

Next, display 'Pleasant Afternoon' on an OHP. Look at the title: it is used in both a literal and an ironic sense:
■ It really is a 'pleasant afternoon' for Jim and Jeremy in that they make the best of the situation and find a way to enjoy it.
■ For the rest of the group, it is a 'pleasant afternoon' only in a deeply ironic sense because they are exposed to real danger and great discomfort.
Ask the children to find specific places where the title appears in the story. Are these references literal or ironic? (They should find four examples – two ironic and two literal.) Now see if they can pick out two further instances of irony:

Jim's comment: *"You know best, of course."*
Mark's comment: *"A real comfort to know we're in such good hands."*

Discuss these comments in the context of the story to make sure the children understand in what way they are ironic.

Differentiated group activities

1*: Continue writing their 'Desert Disaster' stories with a particular focus on developing both the plot and subplot. The children should use the 'Pleasant Afternoon' story as a model.
2 & 3: Write a different ending to 'Pleasant Afternoon' based on ideas from the introductory discussion.
4*: Continue writing their 'Desert Disaster' stories. The children in this group may find it helpful to write the full story of what happens to each group, cut them into sections, and then paste the sections together in alternate order.

Conclusion

Select children from Groups 2 and 3 to read their alternative endings. The rest of the class should evaluate how effectively they follow on from the beginning and middle of the original story.

Introduction

Re-read the ending of 'Pleasant Afternoon' and explain how it brings both the main plot and the subplots back together again in that both of the separate groups are finally reunited. Remind the children that the endings of their own 'Desert Disaster' stories should reflect a similar structure.

Whole-class skills work

Revise previous work on verbs by going through the different tenses. Ask the children to give you some examples for each tense. Then write the tenses on the board or flip chart using 'to run' as an example:
■ Simple present tense, for example 'I run'.
■ Simple past tense, for example 'I ran'.
■ Future tense using the auxiliary verbs 'will' and 'shall', for example 'I will run'.
■ Present continuous tense using the present tense of the verb 'to be' + present participle, for example 'I am running'.
■ Past continuous tense using past tense of verb 'to be' + present participle, for example 'I was running'.
Now introduce two additional forms of the future tense:
■ Future continuous using the future tense of the verb 'to be' + present participle, for example 'I will be running' (indicates certainty).
■ Future using 'be going to' + infinitive, for example 'I am going to run' (indicates intention).
Finally, ask the children to:
■ choose a simple verb and write it in all the tenses given above, using 'run' as a model
■ find examples of the future continuous and 'going to' in the story.

Differentiated group activities

1: Write an alternative ending to 'Pleasant Afternoon', based on ideas from the introductory session in Hour 3.

2 & 3*: Continue writing their 'Desert Disaster' stories.

4: Write an alternative ending to 'Pleasant Afternoon' as for Group 1, but keep the text short and the ideas relatively simple.

Conclusion

Select children from Groups 1 and 4 to read their alternative endings. The rest of the class should evaluate how effectively the alternative endings follow on from the original story.

Discuss how you might 'publish' the children's own stories in a class anthology. What would be a suitable title for the anthology?

Ensure that the children are given time outside the Literacy Hour to finish their stories.

FURTHER IDEA

Ask the children to look at how producers switch between plot and subplots in television programmes. For example, a typical soap opera may have several plots running at once, with rapid scene changes between them. This is a good way of keeping the viewers' attention. A section of a soap opera could be studied in class and the children could learn how to use this technique more effectively in their own writing.

PLEASANT AFTERNOON

"Drive towards those dunes," ordered Maxwell, in his best commanding tone.

"We oughta stick to the track," replied Jim, shaking his head wisely.

"Look, I'm paying you to drive us on this trip, so just do it!" snapped Maxwell.

"Okay, then, if that's what you want," said Jim, a frown creasing his tanned, weather-beaten features, "but it's not safe to leave the track; there are no landmarks out there – just sand, sand and more sand, and the wind-blown stuff is bad news, even for this tough old Land Rover..."

"Don't preach me a sermon, just do as I say!" Maxwell cut in haughtily, smoothing back the sleeves of his brand new safari jacket.

"You know best, of course," Jim muttered under his breath. Reluctantly, he started to drive in the direction of the dunes, putting the vehicle in four-wheel drive so that it could grip the shifting sands. Within minutes the track was far behind them and out of sight.

"We'll go due East, then all we have to do is to drive back this afternoon with the sun behind us and we'll find the track again," said Maxwell, convinced of his own navigational expertise. "That should make a very pleasant afternoon drive," he added smugly.

"Sun sets in the West if I remember rightly," said Jim quietly. "That means we're going to be heading back towards the setting sun."

"Yes...yes...just as I said," said Maxwell, not in the least put out.

They continued to drive on for some time, with the midday sun hammering mercilessly down on to the Land Rover until it was like an oven inside. No cooling air entered through the open windows, only more searing heat.

"Pleasant afternoon drive this is sure turning out to be," sighed Mary, Maxwell's wife. "Maxwell, let's turn back now, I've had enough of this."

"You wanted to see the desert, didn't you?" retorted Maxwell irritably. "If you'd worn something more appropriate you wouldn't feel so uncomfortable." As he spoke, he scowled at the elegant designer suit that his wife was wearing.

"She's right," said Jeremy, from the back seat, "I'm being fried alive in here!" Mark and David nodded in agreement.

Maxwell rolled his eyes, then turned to Jim impatiently: "Well, I suppose you'd better take us back – as everyone's having *such* a pleasant afternoon..."

But Jim wasn't listening, he was concentrating on the Land Rover which was rapidly losing its grip in the loose sand. He eased the accelerator to stop the wheels spinning, then tried again. It was no good. They were well and truly stuck.

Maxwell did his best to appear unconcerned. He assumed his commanding tone again: "Everybody out! We're going to have to push!" Somehow, though, his confidence seemed less convincing.

They pushed as hard as they could, but it didn't work; the Land Rover just sank deeper and deeper into the sand.

"What now?" wailed Mary, with a feeling of sudden despair.

"We'll have to walk back," said Maxwell. "All we have to do is follow the wheel tracks back to the road."

"Wheel tracks will be blown clear by now," said Jim calmly.

"Nonsense, man," snapped Maxwell, "look, you can see them clearly." He pointed to the tracks behind the Land Rover.

"They'll be gone in half an hour," said Jim. "Tracks further back will be gone already."

"What do you suggest, then?" said Maxwell, his irritation growing.

"Stay here, try to keep cool. The company knows whereabouts we're headed. They'll send out a search when we don't turn up."

Maxwell flew into a temper. He told Jim he was an idiot and that they'd all die of thirst, and that anyone with any sense could see that the best thing was to walk back to the road then hitch a lift from a passing car. Everyone was convinced by the conviction with which he said it. Only Jeremy hesitated. "Seems to me that Jim knows this desert better than we do. Perhaps we ought to take his advice."

"Do what you like!" challenged Maxwell. "It's your funeral!"

With that, he led the others into the desert, taking the only water bottle with him.

"What are we going to do now?" asked Jeremy, when the others had disappeared over the horizon.

"Guess we make ourselves as comfortable as we can – and wait," said Jim, unruffled. "Give me a hand with this tarp, will ya?"

He pulled an old tarpaulin sheet from the back of the Land Rover and started to rig up an awning on the shady side of the vehicle. Then he took the tool kit and crawled under the front of the vehicle.

"What are you doing?" asked Jeremy.

"Trying to get us something to drink. I'm going to drain the radiator into this can. The water won't taste too good, but at least there's no anti-freeze in it!"

Hours later, Maxwell's party sank to the ground with exhaustion. Maxwell threw the empty water bottle to the ground and looked around for any signs of Land Rover tracks or the road. In every direction, the sand reached to the horizon in smooth rippling dunes. He was finally forced to admit it: they were lost. But they had to go on. If they stayed here, they would die.

"A real comfort to know we're in such good hands," scowled Mark.

"Oh, give it a rest," hissed Maxwell. "Come on!" he said, dragging Mary to her feet. "It's not far now. Keep going!"

The water didn't taste too bad once you got used to it. Jeremy took another sip and leaned back against the wheel listening to Jim as he told him some of his adventures in the desert. The tarpaulin kept out the sun and a slight breeze cooled the air underneath – Jeremy was beginning to feel a lot better.

They were crawling now. Their lips were dried and swollen and the breath rasped in their throats. Maxwell realized that if they didn't find help soon, they were finished. He dragged himself to his feet and surveyed the horizon. Nothing – but wait! He saw a tiny shape in the distance. What was it?

"Look!" he croaked, "There's something there! Come on! Don't give up now!"

They dragged themselves towards the shape. As they came nearer, Maxwell could see that it was a vehicle of some sort. "It must be the road!" he cried with delight. A few more steps and he could see that it was a Land Rover, a sandy-coloured, long-wheelbase Land Rover, like the one they had come out in. Someone had parked it beside the road and put up an awning to one side. But the heat, thirst and excitement were too much; he staggered, fell and everything went black.

He came round to a metallic taste in his mouth. Someone was giving him water. Then he realized it was Jim.

"Thought you'd be back," he smiled.

"But...but we walked in a straight line – away from here!"

"Sure you did, but perhaps I should have told you – the right leg is stronger than the left in a right-handed person, so it makes you walk in a great big circle."

"But...we could have missed you – and then..."

"Yeah, but you didn't. You're all safe now and perhaps next time you'll listen to an old hand. You might be a big boss in business, but out here you're helpless as a baby!"

"I'll bring two Land Rovers next time – no – Range Rovers – air-conditioned – with two-way radios..." mumbled Maxwell.

The drone of an aeroplane was heard in the distance. Soon, it was circling above them.

"What did I tell you?" said Jim to Jeremy, "They've found us. I'm looking forward to that ice cold beer!"

"Sure," said Jeremy, "the drinks are on me!"

"Not for them they're not – they're going to be in hospital for at least a week!"

Jeremy shook his head, then smiled as a thought struck him. "Maxwell should've listened to you like I did – after all, I had quite a pleasant afternoon!"

DESERT DISASTER: CHARACTERS

DESERT DISASTER: STORY TEMPLATE

The passengers cried out in horror as the ground came surging towards them. The plane was spiralling hopelessly downwards, with terrifying speed.

(Describe a plane crashing in the desert in 3–4 sentences.)

Moaning loudly, X slowly began to come to.

(Blend a description of how X feels with some character description, for example 'His face was deadly pale, but a deep cut in his forehead made his whole head throb with pain, as blood dripped onto his torn business suit.')

Slowly, painfully, he/she reached towards the window to look out. They had landed in a _____ , _____ desert. They were surrounded only by _____ and _____ . The heat penetrated the wrecked fuselage, a _____ , _____ heat, like _____ .

Suddenly, a voice shrieked in terror from the cockpit, 'He's dead! The captain's dead!'

There was a growing sense of deep panic and shock from the rest of the survivors.

Then Y, a _____ *(add brief description)*, said in a _____ tone, 'We have to get out of this plane – it could blow up at any moment!'

(Explain how passengers leave the plane. Describe what they look like. Write a conversation in which they discuss what to do. The conversation ends with Y telling everyone they must walk to safety.)

'Wait!' said X _____ . 'Surely we're supposed to stay with the plane!'

(Describe how more discussion follows and finally, how a group leaves with Y and another group stays with X.)

Now finish your story by writing alternate paragraphs describing what happens to each group. As X is the main character, his/her group should survive. The group led by Y could die of thirst and exhaustion, or could walk, unknowingly, in a circle back to the plane.

READING COMPREHENSION

PART A

1. What do we learn about Maxwell and Jim from the first four lines of the story?

2. Why does Jim think it is unwise to drive off the track?

3. What is the first sign that Maxwell, despite his dominant personality, may not know what he is talking about?

4. What does Mary, Maxwell's wife, think of their trip into the desert?

5. Why did the Land Rover get stuck?

6. What is Maxwell's plan to get back safely?

7. What does Jim say is wrong with the plan?

8. What does Jim say they should do?

9. Why does Jeremy decide to stay with Jim?

10. How does Jim make himself and Jeremy comfortable while they wait for help?

PART B

1. Maxwell shows at least one good quality while he is leading his party through the desert. What is it?

2. What explanation did Jim give for the fact that Maxwell's party had walked in a circle?

3. When Jim tells Maxwell off, what simile does he use to point out how helpless he is in the desert?

4. From Maxwell's reply, do you think he has learned his lesson, or not?

PART C

1. Give detailed descriptions of Maxwell and Jim, drawing on all the information in the story.

2. How do Maxwell and Jim's actions suit their individual characters?

3. How does the way they speak match their different personalities?

THE BERMUDA TRIANGLE

OBJECTIVES

UNIT	SPELLING/ VOCABULARY	GRAMMAR/ PUNCTUATION	COMPREHENSION/ COMPOSITION
READING NON-FICTION Recount genre: 'The Bermuda Triangle'.	Study vocabulary in the text. Make a glossary.	Understand the use of colons and semicolons. Investigate connecting words.	Revise the features of recount texts. Distinguish between fact and opinion. Comment critically on the success of recount texts.

ORGANIZATION (4 HOURS)

	INTRODUCTION	WHOLE-CLASS SKILLS WORK	DIFFERENTIATED GROUP ACTIVITIES	CONCLUSION
HOUR 1	Shared reading of 'The Bermuda Triangle' on photocopiable page 42. Revise features of recount texts.	Explore the differences between fact and opinion.	1*: Reading Comprehension – parts A & B. 2 & 3: Reading Comprehension – part C. 4*: Reading Comprehension – part A.	Pupils discuss their opinions of the Bermuda Triangle phenomenon.
HOUR 2	Shared re-reading of 'The Bermuda Triangle'.	Make a glossary for difficult vocabulary in 'The Bermuda Triangle'.	1: Reading Comprehension – part C. 2 & 3*: Reading Comprehension – parts A & B. 4: Reading Comprehension – part C, questions 1 & 3 only.	Go over part C of the Reading Comprehension sheet.
HOUR 3	Shared reading of 'Ten Facts About Flight 19' on photocopiable page 43.	Examine the use of colons and semicolons in 'Ten Facts About Flight 19'.	1–4*: All groups work on the following tasks: Carefully examine the facts in 'Ten Facts About Flight 19'. List differences between the two accounts. Say which is the most convincing. Identify facts that support the mystery aspect of the Bermuda Triangle.	Discuss the list of ten facts. Talk about which of the two accounts is the most convincing.
HOUR 4	Shared reading of 'The Mary Celeste' on photocopiable page 44.	Revise discursive connectives.	1–4*: All pupils work within their ability groups to discuss the Mary Celeste incident and write their own explanation.	Selected pupils share their different explanations of the Mary Celeste incident.

RESOURCES

Photocopiable pages 42 (The Bermuda Triangle), 43 (Ten Facts About Flight 19), 44 (The Mary Celeste) and 45 (Reading Comprehension), dictionaries, board or flip chart, OHP and acetate (optional), writing materials.

PREPARATION

Prepare enough copies of photocopiable page 45 (Reading Comprehension) for one per child. Prepare enough copies of pages 42, 43 and 44 for one between two children. You may wish to make an OHT or A3 enlargement of the 'Ten Facts About Flight 19' text on photocopiable page 43 for use in the skills session in Hour 3.

Introduction

Read 'The Bermuda Triangle'. Ask the children what type of text they think this is. Establish that it is a recount, and ask how we can recognize this. Use this opportunity to revise the features of recount texts:
- Introduction to orientate the reader
- Use of chronological sequence
- Formal tone of text
- Use of past tense
- Supporting illustrations
- Use of connectives, for example 'first...', 'next...', and so on.

Whole-class skills work

Explore the difference between fact and opinion. Ask the children to provide a definition of each word, then write these dictionary definitions on the board or flip chart:

Fact: something which is certainly known to have happened or to be true.
Opinion: what someone thinks, a belief without proof.

Ask the children to say which of the following sentences are presented as fact, and which are opinions:

- All dogs are vicious brutes.
- Cats are the most popular pet in the UK.
- The Battle of Hastings took place in 1066.
- The Normans were cruel, merciless soldiers.
- There are over 15 million television sets in the UK and they are turning us into illiterate imbeciles.

Emphasize that facts can sometimes be wrong, either because of a mistake, or because of a deliberate intention to mislead. Also, opinions can be presented as though they are facts.

Differentiated group activities

Each child will need a copy of the Reading Comprehension sheet on photocopiable page 45 for the activities here and in Hour 2.
1*: Complete parts A and B of the Reading Comprehension exercise on photocopiable page 45.
2 & 3: Complete part C of the Reading Comprehension exercise.
4*: Complete part A of the Reading Comprehension exercise.

Conclusion

Discuss the various opinions about the Bermuda Triangle. Is it a supernatural phenomenon, something that can be explained scientifically if further investigated, or simply a myth?

Introduction

Re-read 'The Bermuda Triangle'.

Whole-class skills work

Ask the children to pick out any words in 'The Bermuda Triangle' text that they find difficult or which they do not know the meaning of. These words are like include the following:

haywire, sailing tramp, bilges, authenticated, ditch, supernatural, surveillance, abduct, specimens, magnetic fields, phenomenon.

Encourage the children to try to work out the meaning of these words from the context, then check their ideas against the dictionary definitions. Together, work on compiling a glossary of these and any other difficult words in the text.

Differentiated group activities

1: Complete part C of the Reading Comprehension exercise. The children should write an explanation of the reasoning behind their choices.
2 & 3*: Complete parts A and B of the Reading Comprehension sheet.
4: Complete questions 1 and 3 in part C of the Reading Comprehension exercise.

Conclusion

Go over part C of the Reading Comprehension exercise. Some sentences are clearly opinion, for example the first sentence, while some are clearly fact, for example the reference to Charles Berlitz' book. However, much of the passage consists of statements that sound like facts, but which should be checked against other sources.

HOUR 3

Introduction

Read 'Ten Facts About Flight 19' on photocopiable page 43. Briefly discuss what new information this text provides compared to 'The Bermuda Triangle' text.

Whole-class skills work

Make sure that each pair of children has a copy of the 'Ten Facts About Flight 19' text in front of them or display it as an OHT or A3 enlargement. Draw a colon and a semicolon on the board or flip chart and establish with the children what they are – such as the punctuation marks called 'colon' and 'semicolon'. Ask the children to examine the use of colons and semicolons in the text and to try to explain exactly how they are used. After five minutes, discuss what they have found, and ensure that they have noted the following:
■ A colon is used to introduce the list of facts and means 'note what follows'.
■ The facts are treated as separate statements within one long sentence, therefore each item does not begin with a capital letter or end with a full stop.
■ A semicolon is used to separate each statement or item in the list.
■ A colon is used in the first 'fact' to introduce the second statement which explains or expands the first.
■ In the fifth 'fact' a semicolon is used to replace a full stop. It links two complete but related sentences which are of equal importance and turns them into one sentence.
(Point out also the fact that bullets are used to emphasize each statement.)
   Explain that this is an increasingly common way of setting out and punctuating a list of items, particularly in reports and other business documents.

Differentiated group activities

1–4*: All the children work in their ability groups to compare the two accounts of Flight 19 on photocopiable pages 42 (The Bermuda Triangle) and 43 (Ten Facts About Flight 19). Set them the following tasks:

■ Examine carefully 'The Ten Facts about Flight 19'. Are they all pure fact?
■ Make a list of all the differences between the two accounts and say which version they think is the most convincing and why.
■ Some of the facts seem to support the mystery aspect of the Bermuda Triangle rather than explaining it away. Which facts are these?

Conclusion

Discuss the list of facts in 'Ten Facts About Flight 19'.
■ Point out that the tenth fact in the list is not a fact. It is the author's interpretation – his opinion – of what happened. However, slipped in at the bottom of a list of facts it comes across as forcefully as a fact. This exercise should alert the children to maintain a critical awareness even when working with what are presented as facts.
■ Conclude that the second version is the most convincing account, partly because of the title, and partly because of the greater detail.

HOUR 4

Introduction

Read 'The *Mary Celeste*' on photocopiable page 44. Ask the children if they can spot any discrepancies between the two accounts. (The name of the ship is spelled differently and the date is different, though similar enough to suggest a copying error. Both versions present the information as fact. We can only tell which is correct by further research – and you may wish to give children the opportunity to do this.)

Whole-class skills work

Revise discursive connectives. Remind the children that these are connectives used to present an argument. List the following examples on the board or flip chart:

as a result	for	next	therefore
because	however	on the other hand	these
but	instead	so	this
finally	nevertheless	then	yet

Explain to the children that they should refer frequently to this list when expressing their point of view about the *Mary Celeste* mystery in the group activities.

Differentiated group activities

1–4*: All the children work within their ability groups to discuss what they think happened to the *Mary Celeste*. They then write their own explanation, remembering to include some of the connectives listed in the skills session. The first paragraph of their explanation should briefly set out the key facts about the event.

Conclusion

Select children to share their different explanations of the *Mary Celeste* incident.

FURTHER IDEA

Ask the children to conduct further research into the Bermuda Triangle mystery (there are many interesting Internet sites expressing various points of view on this subject). The texts in this unit are based on a detailed analysis of two incidents, with brief reference to a few others. The children could investigate two or three more incidents in detail. They should then discuss how this affects their opinion about the nature of the Bermuda Triangle mystery.

THE BERMUDA TRIANGLE

The Bermuda Triangle is one of earth's great unsolved mysteries. It covers a huge area of the Atlantic Ocean bordered by Bermuda, Puerto Rico and Miami, Florida. It did not receive its name until 1964, but reports of strange happenings in the area have been recorded for centuries.

The first to bear witness to the Bermuda Triangle's weirdness was Christopher Columbus. As the *Nina*, the *Pinta* and the *Santa Maria* sailed through the area in 1492, Columbus' compass went haywire and weird lights were seen in the sky, which he described as 'a great flame of fire that crashed into the ocean'.

In 1892, the sailing tramp *Marie Celeste* was found drifting on the Atlantic Ocean with no one on board. There was some water in the ship's bilges, but she was nowhere near sinking. The ship's only lifeboat was missing. Strangest of all, the crew of the *Marie Celeste* were never seen again, and their boat was never found.

The best authenticated mystery took place on 5 December, 1945, with the disappearance of Flight 19. Five Navy Avenger bombers vanished while on a routine training mission on a clear day, as did one of the rescue planes sent to search for them. The men were trained to ditch in the sea, and all the planes carried life rafts. Yet no survivors and wreckage from Flight 19 were found. Even the official Navy report stated that the Avengers had disappeared 'as if they had flown to Mars'.

About 200 other mysterious incidents have taken place in this area. Many of these are described in Charles Berlitz' book *The Bermuda Triangle* (1974).

Some people say that accidents will happen wherever people travel and the area of ocean in the Bermuda Triangle is no exception to this rule. This is true, but it is the strangeness of the accidents that has attracted attention. This had led investigators to suggest a range of explanations from the scientific to the supernatural. One of the strangest explanations is that the Bermuda Triangle is an area which is kept under surveillance by aliens and that from time to time they abduct specimens for analysis. This would explain the complete disappearance of the crew of the *Marie Celeste* and the 27 men of Flight 19. Another strange explanation is that the area is under the influence of the inhabitants of the lost continent of Atlantis which sank below the waves thousands of years ago. A more scientific explanation is that the area is subjected to abnormal magnetic fields. This could have affected the compasses of the Avengers on Flight 19, causing them to fly in the wrong direction until they ran out of fuel in the middle of the Atlantic.

Whether the explanation is scientific or supernatural remains to be seen, but all the facts point to a highly unusual and dangerous phenomenon which should be taken seriously and properly investigated.

TEN FACTS ABOUT FLIGHT 19

The fate of Flight 19 is said to be one of the strongest pieces of evidence that there is something strange about the Bermuda Triangle, yet the story is often told in a misleading way. Here are ten key facts about Flight 19:

■ 'Flight 19' was a training mission: Patrol leader Lt. Charles Taylor was the only experienced pilot;

■ soon after take-off, Taylor's compass malfunctioned, so he decided to fly by 'dead reckoning', an alternative method of navigation;

■ Taylor was not wearing a watch (which is necessary for navigation by 'dead reckoning');

■ one of the Avengers developed a faulty radio;

■ the weather gradually deteriorated into a major storm; visibility was poor;

■ at 19.01, the last message was received from Flight 19: a faint, repeated 'FT, FT' – the call letters of Flight 19;

■ the Mariner search plane was not lost, but exploded 23 minutes after take-off. Other planes carried on the search;

■ the official report did state that the planes had vanished 'as if they had flown to Mars' – but this is only a figure of speech not meant to be taken literally;

■ upon the termination of the search, the Navy issued the warning that travellers in the area should remain on the alert;

■ the most likely explanation is that Taylor, flying without a compass in a major storm, led his mission in the wrong direction. They flew East into the Atlantic instead of West to Florida and must have crash landed and sunk off the continental shelf where the sea is so deep that the wreckage would never be found.

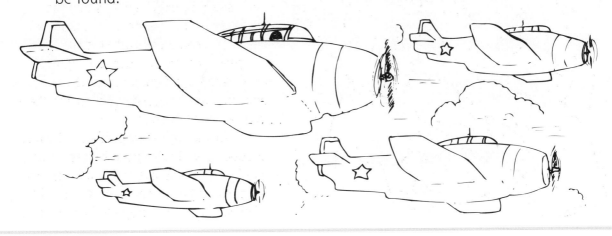

THE *MARY CELESTE*

The *Mary Celeste* was an ordinary sailing tramp of about 230 tons. Her skipper, Captain Benjamin Briggs, was a respectable and religious man. The *Mary Celeste* was sailing from New York to Genoa on 7 November, 1872. She had a cargo of oil and raw alcohol in barrels. Captain Briggs had his wife and two-year-old daughter with him. The crew consisted of a mate, second mate, cook and four seamen.

Twenty-eight days later, on 5 December, the ship was found drifting in the Atlantic Ocean with no one on board. She was found by the brig *Dei Gratia* which had previously been in New York with her. Captain Morehouse sent his mate on board. He found nothing wrong. The sails were set, though a little torn. There was water in the ship's bilges, but not enough to put the ship in danger. The ship's lifeboat was missing. Some hatch covers were off, but the cargo seemed undamaged. The cabin skylight was open and everything inside was wet.

The ship's log was in the cabin and showed no unusual entries, but the ship's other papers and navigation instruments were missing. There was plenty of food and water on board and no sign of fire or any other calamity that might have caused the crew to abandon ship.

There was a deep cut in the ship's rail and two long scratches marked the ship's bow planking. There was a darkened bloodstain on the deck and a blood-stained sword in the captain's cabin which someone had tried to clean. The clock in the cabin had been turned upside down.

The captain and the crew were never seen again.

READING COMPREHENSION

PART A

1. Who was the first person reported to have experienced something strange in the area now known as the Bermuda Triangle?

2. What did he experience that was strange?

3. What was strange about the *Marie Celeste* incident?

4. What happened to Flight 19?

PART B

1. Why is Flight 19 described as the 'best authenticated' incident?

2. How many other strange incidents are said to have taken place in this area? How could the reader find out more about them?

3. What explanations does the author offer for the Bermuda Triangle mystery?

PART C

1. Underline all the statements in 'The Bermuda Triangle' text that you think are definite facts.

2. Underline in another colour all the statements that might be facts, but that you would like to check.

3. In a third colour, underline all the statements that you think are opinions.

FACT AND FICTION

OBJECTIVES

UNIT	SPELLING/VOCABULARY	GRAMMAR/ PUNCTUATION	COMPREHENSION/ COMPOSITION
WRITING NON-FICTION Recount genre: 'The *Mary Celeste*'.	Explore technical vocabulary. Check own work for correct spelling.	Check own work for correct grammar and punctuation. Understand the terms 'active' and 'passive'.	Explore features of a recount text. Distinguish between fact and fiction. Write a well-structured narrative based on a factual event. Revise key skills for redrafting. Comment critically on the success of recount texts.

ORGANIZATION (2 HOURS)

	INTRODUCTION	WHOLE-CLASS SKILLS WORK	DIFFERENTIATED GROUP ACTIVITIES	CONCLUSION
HOUR 1	Shared reading of 'The *Mary Celeste*' on photocopiable page 44 from 'The Bermuda Triangle' unit. Explore the maritime vocabulary.	Explore features of *Mary Celeste* text which identify it as a recount. Explore the use of the 'passive' and 'active' voice in the text.	1–4*: All pupils work within ability groups to discuss unusual events from their own experience and write a brief recount of the event.	Selected pupils read out their recounts. The class evaluate how effectively the recount genre has been used.
HOUR 2	Discuss ways in which a narrative version of 'The *Mary Celeste*' would be different to the recount text.	Distinguish between fact and fiction.	1–4*: All pupils work on turning 'The *Mary Celeste*' text into a narrative.	Selected pupils read out the first drafts of their narratives. The class evaluates how effectively the factual material has been incorporated.

RESOURCES
Photocopiable page 44 (The *Mary Celeste*) from 'The Bermuda Triangle' unit, a mixture of fiction and non-fiction from the class library, board or flip chart, OHP and acetate (optional), writing materials.

PREPARATION

If you have not already photocopied page 44 for the previous unit, you will need to make enough copies for one between two children. If possible, also prepare an OHT or A3 enlargement of this photocopiable page.

Introduction
Read (or re-read if the previous unit has been done) 'The *Mary Celeste*' and explain that the class is going to use the text as the basis for a story. Spend a few minutes exploring the maritime words and phrases, for example *sailing tramp, mate, second mate, brig, the sails were set, bilges, hatch covers, ship's log, ship's rail, ship's bow planking*. (The children may have covered some of these words in the previous unit.)

Whole-class skills work

Display 'The Mary Celeste' as an OHT or A3 enlargement. Begin by asking the children to identify what genre the text is written in. Once they have established that it is a recount, see if they can remember the main features of recount texts as covered in the previous unit on page 39 (Introduction to Hour 1). Move on to examine 'The Mary Celeste' text, asking the children to pick out any of these features. They should identify the introduction to orientate the reader, the use of chronological sequence for presenting the facts, the formal tone, the use of the past tense, and supporting illustration.

Next, look at the style of the text in more detail. Remind the children of the terms 'active' and 'passive' voice. Explain that a passive sentence is one where the subject is the person or thing acted on by the verb, rather than the one who performs the action. Give this example from the text: *She was found by the brig* Dei Gratia. Then ask the children to transform this to an active sentence: 'The brig *Dei Gratia* found the ship *Mary Celeste*'. Spend a few minutes picking out examples of active and passive sentences in the text.

Finish by explaining that the passive voice is often used in scientific reports (for example 'Water was poured into the tube...') but it is also sometimes used by writers when they do not know (or do not wish to reveal) the identity of the person responsible for the actions, as is the case in this particular text.

Differentiated group activities

1–4*: The children work in their ability groups to discuss any unusual events of which they have personal experience. They then write a brief recount of the event. Children in Group 4 could be asked to write the events in list form initially, and then combine each item into a one- or two-statement sentence.

It may be helpful to display a list of the typical features of recount texts on the board or flip chart for the children to refer to (see page 39).

Conclusion

Select children to read out the written version of their unusual event. Ask the rest of the class to evaluate how effectively the writer has used recount genre. Is the text written in the past tense? Does it state the facts plainly and in chronological order?

Introduction

Discuss with the children how a narrative (story) version of the *Mary Celeste* mystery would be different. For example, there would be more imaginative description, characters and dialogue, and a structure to the story that would leave us feeling satisfied rather than mystified.

Whole-class skills work

Discuss with the children the differences between fact and fiction. Provide some concrete examples by reading out some short sentences or passages from both fiction and non-fiction books from the class library. Talk about how the children distinguish between fact and fiction, then write these dictionary definitions on the board or flip chart:
Fact: something which is certainly known to have happened or to be true.
Fiction: invented statement or narrative.
Tell the children that, in the group activities session, they are going to turn 'The Mary Celeste' recount into a narrative. Explain that this is often done by professional authors. For example, the factual sinking of the *Titanic* has been turned into many different stories which include fictional characters and events against a background of the known facts.

Differentiated group activities

1–4*: All the children work in their ability groups to rewrite 'The Mary Celeste' text as a narrative. Emphasize that their versions should include the standard story elements of imaginative description of character and setting, plus interesting dialogue as well as a more satisfying ending based on their own interpretation of the incident. However, they must also be careful to incorporate the known facts into their stories. Children in Group 4 could focus on rewriting the first two paragraphs only, concentrating mainly on blending in the main facts with their own imaginative description.

Conclusion

Select children to read out the first drafts of their stories, while the rest of the class

evaluates how effectively they have incorporated the factual material into the narrative.
Briefly revise the key skills needed to redraft a narrative successfully:
■ Structuring a story with a beginning, middle and end.
■ Writing in paragraphs.
■ Writing detailed descriptions of characters and places.
■ Punctuating and setting out dialogue correctly.
■ Writing realistic dialogue with varied and descriptive reporting clauses.
■ Checking spelling, punctuation and grammatical correctness.
Ensure that the children are given additional time to redraft their stories.

FURTHER IDEA

Ask the children to experiment with further work on fact, fiction, recount and narrative in the following way:
■ Make up a mystery, for example a flying saucer seen over the school. This, of course, is pure fiction.
■ Write about the mystery in recount form, as though it had actually happened. The children should note that this often happens in writing. *Robinson Crusoe*, for example, is written in this way, though there is no intention to deceive readers. However, many ghost, UFO and mystery stories are written in this way with an intention to mislead.

THE ORIGINS OF ENGLISH

OBJECTIVES

UNIT	SPELLING/VOCABULARY	GRAMMAR/ PUNCTUATION	COMPREHENSION/ COMPOSITION
REFERENCE AND RESEARCH SKILLS The origins of English.	Understand function of etymological dictionary and use it to study words of interest and significance.	Develop grammatical awareness about parts of speech.	Investigate Chaucer's language. Read and understand explanatory text about the origins of English.

ORGANIZATION (1 HOUR)

	INTRODUCTION	WHOLE-CLASS SKILLS WORK	DIFFERENTIATED GROUP ACTIVITIES	CONCLUSION
HOUR 1	Investigate a few lines of 'The Prologue' to *The Canterbury Tales* by Geoffrey Chaucer. Read and discuss the explanatory text, 'The Origins of English' on photocopiable page 51.	Establish definition of 'etymology'. Explore the origins of some English words.	1*: Use etymological dictionary to study origins of words. 2 & 3: Guess the origins of a list of words, then look them up. 4*: As for 2 & 3 with teacher support.	Share results of etymological studies. Discuss the eclectic nature of the English language.

RESOURCES

Photocopiable page 51 (The Origins of English), dictionaries that give derivations and origins (including etymological dictionaries if possible), OHP and acetate (optional), board or flip chart, writing materials.
Note: If it is not possible to obtain some etymological dictionaries, an alternative would be to use a publication such as *Chambers Word Origins* (Fun with English series) by George Beal. This is a 32-page paperback that provides some useful word histories.

PREPARATION

Make enough copies of photocopiable page 51 (The Origins of English) for one between two children. If possible, prepare it also as an OHT – or enlarge to at least A3 size. Write the following lines from The Prologue to Chaucer's *Canterbury Tales* on the board or flip chart:

> Whan that Aprill with his shoures soote
> That droghte of March hath perced to the roote,
> And bathed every veyne in swich licour
> Of which vertu engendred is the flour;
> Whan Zephirus eek with his sweete breeth
> Inspired hath in every holt and heeth
> The tendre croppes, and the yonge sonne
> Hath in the Ram his halve cour yronne,
> And smale foweles maken melodye...

Prepare some lists of words for children in Groups 2–4 to study in their group activities.

Introduction

Introduce the hour by showing children the lines from Chaucer written on the board or flip chart. Ask the children what they think it is. They may well recognize it as a poem. Then ask them what language they think it is. Establish that it is, in fact, English, but a form of Middle English which was in use in the 14th century. You may wish to explain that it is the opening of a poetic work called the *Canterbury Tales* by Geoffrey Chaucer (have any of the children heard of it?), but use the lines essentially to demonstrate that a) many of the words in the poem are still used today, but that b) the English language has changed considerably over the centuries.

Now distribute copies of photocopiable page 51 (The Origins of English) and read this through with the class. Establish that it is an example of explanatory text and that it answers the question: What are the origins of the English language?

Whole-class skills work

Re-read the paragraph in the text that explains what etymology is. Ensure that the children understand that etymology is the study of the origin and history of words – and that they can pronounce the word! Distribute the dictionaries you have so that all children can at least see one. Now, write the following words beginning with 'a' on the board: *adder, alcohol, alligator, atlas*. Ask the children to look them up in their dictionaries to find out what the origin is and whether they can find any interesting stories about the words and their origins:

adder

This comes from the Old English word *naedre* which means 'snake'. It became 'adder' when the later version 'nadder' was mistaken referred to as 'an adder' rather than 'a nadder'!

alcohol

This comes from the Arabic words *al* (the) and *kohl* (fine black powder).

alligator

This is originally a Latin word (*lacertus*) but comes to English from the Spanish word *lagarto* (lizard). The Spanish word for 'the' is *el*. So *el lagarto* became the English 'alligator'.

atlas

This is a word of Greek origin. Atlas was the name of a god in Greek mythology who is said to have supported the heavens above the earth. The figure of Atlas with the world on his back was often used on the title page of map collections in the 16th century. The name has since been used to mean a book of maps.

Emphasize the various origins and the fact that the English language is made up of words from all over the world.

Differentiated group activities

All children should work within their groups, individually, in pairs or in small groups, depending on how many dictionaries are available.

1*: This group should work with the etymological dictionaries, if available. They should search for interesting origins and stories behind words that interest them – or words that are related to a topic they are studying in another area of the curriculum.

2 & 3: This group should use dictionaries to look up the etymology of a list of words supplied by the teacher. These can be words related to a current topic of study or interest, or a random selection such as the following:

butler (French), denim (French), grapefruit (USA), hamburger (German), hooligan (Irish), ketchup (Chinese), magazine (Arabic), money (Latin), monster (Latin), oboe (French), piano (Italian), robot (Czech), thesaurus (Greek), treacle (French), umbrella (Italian).

4*: As for 2 & 3, but with teacher support.

Conclusion

Share the results of the groups' etymological studies. Have they found any really interesting stories about words? How many different countries and languages were represented by the words they studied? What does this tell us about the English language? Do they think this is true for other modern languages?

THE ORIGINS OF ENGLISH

The English language that we use today has developed through a long history that reflects many influences.

Where do the words come from?

Long ago the British Isles were invaded by many different races, and each of these races contributed words to the language we now speak and write.

The Ancient Britons spoke a language called Celtic. Then Britain was invaded by the Romans who brought with them the Roman alphabet which we use today.

When Roman power declined, Britain was invaded by the Jutes, the Saxons and Angles. Eventually their languages mingled to form Anglo-Saxon (Old English).

Next came the Viking invasions which introduced Scandinavian words; and finally there was the Norman Conquest which was very important as it introduced French into the language.

Over the centuries words from many other countries were gradually introduced into English as merchants travelled across the world, and scholars were influenced by the Renaissance. Latin and Greek were used by educated people, and for more than a century Latin was the only language recognized in English schools.

The British ruled in India for two hundred years and many Indian words have been absorbed into English from there, for example: *thug, verandah* and *bungalow*.

More recently, our language has been influenced by the two World Wars and by American films and culture.

It is fun to discover where words came from. The study of word derivations is called 'etymology'. Most good dictionaries provide a certain amount of information on etymology, but if you want a lot of detail you will need a special 'etymological dictionary'.

Stories about words

In Roman times each Roman soldier was given an allowance to pay for the salt he needed. The Latin word for salt is *sal*. Nowadays there is an English word meaning 'wages paid by the month or by the year'. Do you know what it is?[1]

During the Middle Ages in England, the pilgrims going to Canterbury used to ride at a gentle gallop known as the 'Canterbury gallop'. There is now a six-letter word to describe this gallop. Can you think what that is?[2]

Words from names

Some of the words we use now are connected with the names of people or places.

Sardines are so called because they are caught off the shores of Sardinia.

Wellington boots are named after the 1st Duke of Wellington who wore very high boots covering his knees.

The 4th Earl of Sandwich was an English nobleman who loved hunting. One day he hunted for twenty-four hours without stopping, and the only food he ate was meat placed between slices of bread. Food eaten like this has been called after him ever since.

[1] salary
[2] canter

THE PIED PIPER OF HAMELIN

OBJECTIVES

UNIT	SPELLING/VOCABULARY	GRAMMAR/ PUNCTUATION	COMPREHENSION/ COMPOSITION
READING POETRY Classic poetry: 'The Pied Piper of Hamelin' by Robert Browning.	Explore key words in the poem. Understand how words have changed or fallen out of use over time. Compile a glossary of difficult/archaic words.	Secure knowledge of more sophisticated punctuation marks as used in poetic form.	Read classic poetry by a long-established poet. Revise how to study verse forms. Revise similes and metaphors. Write a literary essay using the appropriate conventions. Express a personal response to a poem.

ORGANIZATION (4 HOURS)

	INTRODUCTION	WHOLE-CLASS SKILLS WORK	DIFFERENTIATED GROUP ACTIVITIES	CONCLUSION
HOUR 1	Briefly discuss the life of Robert Browning. Shared reading of parts I–IV of 'The Pied Piper of Hamelin' (photocopiable pages 57–59).	Revise how to study verse forms, focusing on rhyme pattern and metre.	1*: Guided reading and discussion of parts I–IV of the poem. 2 & 3: Write a character description of the Mayor. 4*: Guided reading and discussion.	Pupils in Groups 1 & 4 report back on discussion of the poem.
HOUR 2	Shared reading of parts V–VIII of the poem.	Revise the term 'simile' and 'metaphor'. Look for and explain examples in the poem.	1: Write a description of the Pied Piper. 2 & 3*: Guided reading and discussion of V–VIII of the poem. 4: Write a description of the Pied Piper.	Selected pupils in Groups 2 & 3 report back on their discussion of the poem. Selected pupils in Groups 1 & 4 share their descriptions of the Pied Piper.
HOUR 3	Shared reading of parts IX–XI of the poem. Discuss how pupils think the poem might end.	Pick out key words in the poem to explain in context. Discuss how some words have changed or fallen out of use. Make a glossary of difficult, archaic or unusual words used in poem.	All pupils write a continuation of the poem as below. 1*: Write in rhyming verse, in the style of Browning. 2 & 3: Write in unrhymed or free verse. 4*: Write in a simple prose version suitable for young children.	The continuations of the poem are shared.
HOUR 4	Shared reading of parts I–XI, plus one of the endings from Group 1.	Revise the conventions of writing a literary essay.	1: Write a review of the poem using the Poetry Review: Writing Template on photocopiable page 60 as a guide only. 2 & 3*: As Group 1, but avoid using longer quotations for evidence. 4: Write a review of the poem directly on to the template.	All pupils are invited to share and discuss their responses to the last two sections of the template.

RESOURCES

Photocopiable pages 57–59 ('The Pied Piper of Hamelin'), 60 (Poetry Review: Writing Template), dictionaries, board or flip chart, OHP and acetate (optional), writing materials.

PREPARATION

Make enough copies of the poem on photocopiable pages 57–59 for one between two children. If possible, also prepare the poem as OHTs or make an enlarged version. Make enough copies of photocopiable page 60 (Poetry Review Writing Template) for one per child. If more space for writing is needed by some children, you could enlarge this sheet to A3 size.

Introduction

Tell the children that they are going to study the poem 'The Pied Piper of Hamelin'. Do they know who wrote the poem? Establish that it was Robert Browning and provide these brief biographical details:

> Robert Browning was born in 1812, the son of a bank clerk, and struggled most of his life to gain recognition as a successful poet. He was still dependent on his family well into adulthood. In 1846, Browning married the poet Elizabeth Barrett, then considered one of the outstanding poets of the day. They moved to Italy because of her ill health and she died there in 1861. Sadly, it was only after her death that Robert Browning came into his own as a poet. Although his wife's reputation as a poet was greater than his own during his lifetime, Robert Browning is today believed to be one of the great poets of the Victorian era. He died in 1889.
> 'The Pied Piper of Hamelin', written in 1845, is one of Browning's best-known poems. It is a retelling in verse of a German folk tale. The story is still re-enacted every year in the Westfalian town of Hamelin.

Find out what the children already know about the story of the Pied Piper. Have any of them seen a television or pantomime version of the story? Write their ideas on the board or flip chart.

Now read parts I–IV of 'The Pied Piper of Hamelin' on photocopiable page 57. Discuss what the poem is about, ensuring children can identify the main characters and the story line.

Whole-class skills work

Find out how much the children remember about studying verse forms in terms of metre and rhyme patterns. Do they know the symbol used to mark stressed syllables? Can they explain the system used to identify rhyme patterns? Revise the following points:

- Use the / symbol to mark stressed syllables.
- Use a different letter of the alphabet to mark each different rhyme (begin with a again with each new stanza).

Next, analyse the first four lines of the opening verse, inviting the children's help. Write the following marked-up section of verse on the board or flip chart as a model:

```
     /        /        /
Hamelin Town's in Brunswick,              a
     /        /        /
By famous Hanover city;                   b
     /        /        /        /
The river Weser, deep and wide,           c
   /        /              /        /
Washes its wall on the southern side;     c
```

Now allocate sections of between eight and twelve lines (of parts I–IV) to each pair of children and ask them to analyse them in the same way. When everyone has finished, sum up what has been discovered about the verse form of the poem:

- The rhyme scheme is different in each verse.
- The metrical pattern is mainly four stresses per line.

■ The poem is written in stanzas (verses) of varying length.

Differentiated group activities

1*: Guided reading and discussion. The following questions can be used as a starting point:
■ What do the rats do? What is the funniest thing that they do?
■ What action do the people take about the problem?
■ What complaints do they make against the Mayor and the Corporation?
■ What kind of person is the Mayor?
The group should prepare to report back to the rest of the class.
2 & 3: Write a character description of the Mayor. Make it as detailed as possible by referring closely to the poem.
4*: Guided reading and discussion as for Group 1 above.

Conclusion

Ask selected children from Groups 1 and 4 to report back on their discussion of parts I–IV of the poem. Select children from Groups 2 and 3 to share their descriptions of the Mayor.

Introduction

Read parts V–VIII of the poem on photocopiable pages 57–59. Ask the children to explain what happens in these four verses and discuss any words or lines that they find difficult to understand.

Whole-class skills work

Start by asking the children what they remember about the terms 'simile' and 'metaphor'. Establish the meaning of each term using the following explanations and examples:

A **simile** is a figure of speech that makes a comparison using the words 'like' or 'as', or 'than' as in this example from the poem:
'Nor brighter was his eye, nor moister
Than a too-long-opened oyster.'
A **metaphor** is also a figure of speech that makes a comparison, but it makes a direct comparison which says one thing *is* another. An example from the poem is:
'The world is grown to one vast drysaltery*!'
(*drysaltery: a word from the 18th century which means a store selling oils, sauces and pickles)

Discuss the meaning of the above examples and encourage the children to find more of each in the poem. They will find that while the poem is rich in similes that are easy to spot, the metaphors are far fewer and more elusive!

Differentiated group activities

1: Write a description of the Pied Piper, describing both his appearance and his character in as much detail as possible.
2 & 3*: Guided reading and discussion. The following questions can be used as a starting point:
■ What is unusual about the Pied Piper's appearance?
■ What striking simile does one member of the Corporation use to describe the effect of his entrance?
■ What similar jobs has the Pied Piper done recently?
■ What fee does he ask, and how do the Mayor and Corporation reply?
■ One rat survives to describe why the Piper's music is so alluring. How does he describe it?
4: Write a short description of the Pied Piper, focusing particularly on his unusual appearance.

Conclusion

Select children from Groups 2 and 3 to report back on their discussion of parts V–VIII of the poem. Select children from Groups 1 and 4 to share their descriptions of the Pied Piper.

Introduction

Read parts IX–XI of the poem. Discuss with the children how they think the poem might end. Most of them will know the story, but tease out the details, as these will be needed in the activities session:

The Pied Piper plays another tune which lures the children to follow him. He leads them to a mountain which opens up, lets them in and then shuts behind them. Only one lame boy is left outside. He describes the wonderful things he heard in the music. The poem ends with a moral: keep your promises.

Whole-class skills work

Display the poem as an OHT or A3 enlargement. Such a text offers a rich opportunity to explore difficult, unusual and archaic vocabulary. The children are likely to find many words or phrases which need further explanation. Start by picking out some key words such as these taken from parts I–III of the poem:

spied	*ermine*	*ditty*	*dolt*
vermin	*determine*	*keg*	*obese*

Encourage the children to work out their meaning from the context of the poem. How many of these words do we still use today? Which words have now disappeared from our language? Invite the children to help you compile two lists on the board or flip chart using the headings 'Words we still use' and 'Words we no longer use'. For those words still in use, for example *spied*, look at whether its meaning in the poem is still the same today. What words would we now use instead? (For example, for *spied* in the context of the poem, we would say 'saw'.)

Finish the exercise by making a short glossary of some of the most difficult words. The children should contribute by first looking up the words in a dictionary and then agreeing on a final definition according to the context in the poem.

Differentiated group activities

All children should write a continuation of the poem as described below. Explain that they do not have to continue it in the same way as the traditional version; they can invent a completely different ending if they wish.

1*: Write a continuation of the poem in rhyming verse, trying to imitate Browning's style as closely as possible.

2 & 3: Write a continuation of the poem in unrhymed verse, or free verse.

4*: Write a continuation of the poem in a simple prose version suitable for young children.

Conclusion

Share some examples of the children's continuations of the poem.

Introduction

Re-read parts I–XI of the poem, plus a continuation from Group 1 which has the traditional ending, if available. Alternatively, read the whole poem if a complete version is to hand and discuss how the ending differs from those read out at the end of the previous hour.

Whole-class skills work

Revise the conventions of writing a literary essay. Emphasize that each paragraph should make a series of points. One or two of the most important points should be supported by evidence. This can be done in three ways:

■ An indirect reference to the text, for example *The people were dissatisfied with the Mayor because he was old and lazy.*

■ A direct reference to the text using a short quotation, for example *The people were so dissatisfied with the Mayor that they said 'Our Mayor's a noddy.'*

■ A direct reference to the text using a longer quotation which should be set out on indented lines, for example: The effect of the Pied Piper's entrance is so surprising that one of the Corporation uses this simile to describe it:

'It's as my great-grandsire,
Starting up the Trump of Doom's tone,

Had walked this way from his painted tombstone!'

Give each child a copy of the Poetry Review: Writing Template on photocopiable page 60, and briefly talk through it. Remind the children of their work in previous sessions and say that they should use this to help them complete each section.

Differentiated group activities

1: Write a review of the poem using the template as a guide only. The children should be encouraged to write suitable introductions to each paragraph so that the final result reads like a self-contained essay, not a response to a series of prompts. They should also be encouraged to use all three kinds of evidence as explained in the skills session.

2 & 3*: Write a review of the poem using the template as a guide. However, the children in this group should avoid using longer quotations for evidence.

4: Write about the poem directly onto the template.

Conclusion

Invite all the children to share and discuss their responses to the last two sections of the template.

FURTHER IDEA

All the children could be asked to retell the whole story of the Pied Piper in prose form (Group 4 will have only completed the end section as prose for Hour 3). They could then compare their versions with some of the many others available.

THE PIED PIPER OF HAMELIN

A child's story
(Written for, and inscribed to, W M the younger)

I

Hamelin Town's in Brunswick,
By famous Hanover city;
The river Weser, deep and wide,
Washes its wall on the southern side;
A pleasanter spot you never spied;
But, when begins my ditty,
Almost five hundred years ago,
To see the townsfolk suffer so
From vermin, was a pity.

II

Rats!
They fought the dogs, and killed the cats,
And bit the babies in the cradles,
And ate the cheeses out of the vats,
And licked the soup from the cook's own ladles,
Split open the kegs of salted sprats,
Made nests inside men's Sunday hats,
And even spoiled the women's chats,
By drowning their speaking
With shrieking and squeaking
In fifty different sharps and flats.

III

At last the people in a body
To the Town Hall came flocking:
''Tis clear,' cried they, 'our Mayor's a noddy;
'And as for our Corporation – shocking
'To think we buy new gowns lined with ermine
'For dolts that can't or won't determine
'What's best to rid us of our vermin!
'You hope, because you're old and obese,
'To find in the furry civic robe ease?
'Rouse up, Sirs! Give your brains a racking
'To find the remedy we're lacking,
'Or sure as fate, we'll send you packing!'
At this the Mayor and Corporation
Quaked with mighty consternation.

IV

An hour they sate in council,
At length the Mayor broke silence:
'For a guilder I'd my ermine gown sell;
'I wish I were a mile hence!
'It's easy to bid one rack one's brain –
'I'm sure my poor head aches again
'I've scratched it so, and all in vain.
'Oh for a trap, a trap, a trap!'
Just as he said this, what should hap
At the chamber door but a gentle tap?

'Bless us,' cried the Mayor, 'what's that?'
(With the Corporation as he sat,
Looking little though wondrous fat;
Nor brighter was his eye, nor moister
Than a too-long-opened oyster,
Save when at noon his paunch grew mutinous
For a plate of turtle green and glutinous)
'Only a scraping of shoes on the mat?
'Anything like the sound of a rat
'Makes my heart go pit-a-pat!'

V

'Come in!' – the Mayor cried, looking bigger:
And in did come the strangest figure!
His queer long coat from heel to head
Was half of yellow and half of red;
And he himself was tall and thin,
With sharp blue eyes, each like a pin,
And light loose hair, yet swarthy skin,
No tuft on cheek nor beard on chin,
But lips where smiles went out and in –
There was no guessing his kith and kin!
And nobody could enough admire
The tall man and his quaint attire:
Quoth one: 'It's as my great-grandsire,
'Starting up the Trump of Doom's tone,
'Had walked this way from his painted
      tombstone!'

VI

He advanced to the council-table:
And, 'Please your honours,' said he, 'I'm able,
'By means of a secret charm, to draw
'All creatures living beneath the sun,
'That creep, or swim, or fly, or run,
'After me so as you never saw!
'And I chiefly use my charm
'On creatures that do people harm,
'The mole, and toad, and newt, and viper;
'And people call me the Pied Piper.'
(And here they noticed round his neck
A scarf of red and yellow stripe,
To match with his coat of the selfsame cheque;
And at the scarf's end hung a pipe;
And his fingers, they noticed, were ever straying
As if impatient to be playing
Upon this pipe, as low it dangled
Over his vesture so old-fangled.)
'Yet,' said he, 'poor piper as I am,
'In Tartary I freed the Cham,
'Last June, from his huge swarms of gnats;
'I eased in Asia the Nizam
'Of a monstrous brood of vampyre-bats:
'And, as for what your brain bewilders,
'If I can rid your town of rats
'Will you give me a thousand guilders?'
'One? Fifty thousand!' – was the exclamation
Of the astonished Mayor and Corporation.

VII

Into the street the Piper stept,
Smiling first a little smile,
As if he knew what magic slept
In his quiet pipe the while;
Then, like a musical adept,
To blow the pipe his lips he wrinkled,
And green and blue his sharp eyes twinkled
Like a candle flame where salt is sprinkled;
And ere three shrill notes the pipe uttered,
You heard as if an army muttered;
And the muttering grew to a grumbling;
And the grumbling grew to a mighty rumbling:
And out of the houses the rats came tumbling.
Great rats, small rats, lean rats, brawny rats,
Brown rats, black rats, gray rats, tawny rats,
Grave old plodders, gay young friskers,
Fathers, mothers, uncles, cousins,
Cocking tales and pricking whiskers,
Families by tens and dozens,
Brothers, sisters, husbands, wives –
Followed the Piper for their lives.
From street to street he piped advancing,
And step for step they followed dancing,
Until they came to the river Weser
Wherein all plunged and perished
– Save one who, stout as Julius Caesar,
Swam across and lived to carry
(As he the manuscript he cherished)
To Rat-land home his commentary,
Which was, 'At the first shrill notes of the pipe,
'I heard the sound as of scraping tripe,
'And putting apples, wondrous ripe,
'Into a cider-press's gripe:
'And a moving away of pickle-tub-boards,
And a leaving ajar of conserve-cupboards,
'And a drawing the corks of train-oil-flasks,
'And a breaking the hoops of butter-casks;
'And it seemed as if a voice
'(Sweeter far than by harp or by psaltery
'Is breathed) called out, Oh rats, rejoice!
'The world is grown to one vast drysaltery!
'So munch on, crunch on, take your nuncheon,
'Breakfast, supper, dinner, luncheon!
'And just as a bulky sugar-puncheon,
'All ready staved, like a great sun shone
'Glorious scarce an inch before me,
'Just as methought it said, Come, bore me!
'– I found the Weser rolling o'er me.'

VIII

You should have heard the Hamelin people
Ringing the bells till they rocked the steeple;
'Go,' cried the Mayor, 'and get long poles!
'Poke out the nests and block up the holes!
'Consult with carpenters and builders,
'And leave in our town not even a trace
'Of the rats!' – when suddenly up the face
Of the Piper perked in the market-place,
With a, 'First, if you please, my thousand guilders!'

IX

A thousand guilders! The Mayor looked blue;
So did the Corporation too.
For council dinners made rare havock
With Claret, Moselle, Vin-de-Grave, Hock;
And half the money would replenish
Their cellar's biggest butt with Rhenish
To pay this sum to a wandering fellow
With gipsy coat of red and yellow!
'Beside,' quoth the Mayor with a knowing wink,
'Our business was done at the river's brink;
'We saw with our eyes the vermin sink,
'And what's dead can't come to life, I think,
'So, friend, we're not the folk's to shrink
'From the duty of giving you something for drink,
'And a matter of money to put in your poke;
'But, as for the guilders, what we spoke
'Of them, as you very well know, was in joke.
'Beside, our losses have made us thrifty;
'A thousand guilders! Come, take fifty!'

X

The piper's face fell, and he cried,
'No trifling! I can't wait, beside!
'I've promised to visit by dinner time
'Bagdat, and accept the prime
'Of the Head Cook's pottage, all he's rich in,
'For having left, in the Caliph's kitchen,
'Of a nest of scorpions no survivor –
'With him I proved no bargain-driver,
'With you, don't think I'll bate a stiver!
'And folks who put me in a passion
'May find me pipe to another fashion.'

XI

'How?' cried the Mayor, 'd'ye think I'll brook
'Being worse treated than a Cook?
'Insulted by a lazy ribald
'With idle pipe and vesture piebald?
'You threaten us, fellow! Do your worst,
'Blow your pipe there till you burst!'

Robert Browning

POETRY REVIEW: WRITING TEMPLATE

■ **What is the poem about?**
Tell the story of the poem, briefly, in your own words.

■ **Write about the verse form of the poem.**
Is it in free verse, blank verse or rhymed verse? If it is in rhymed verse, what is the rhyme scheme? Why do you think the poet chose this verse form?

■ **Choose three or four interesting descriptive words in the poem.**
Say what they mean and explain why you found them interesting.

■ **Quote a comparison (for example simile, metaphor, personification) from the poem.**
Explain why you liked it.

■ **What did the poem make you think of, or feel?**

■ **Did you like the poem? Explain your answer.**

SIMILE POEMS

OBJECTIVES

UNIT	SPELLING/VOCABULARY	GRAMMAR/ PUNCTUATION	COMPREHENSION/ COMPOSITION
WRITING POETRY Simile poems: 'New Notebook' by Judith Thurman.	Identify common, everyday expressions that are similes.	Recognize and use active verbs in writing.	Revise similes. Write own poems using effective similes. Write own poems experimenting with active verbs and personification.

ORGANIZATION (1 HOUR)

	INTRODUCTION	WHOLE-CLASS SKILLS WORK	DIFFERENTIATED GROUP ACTIVITIES	CONCLUSION
HOUR 1	Read the poem 'New Notebook' by Judith Thurman and identify similes. Read simile poem writing frames on photocopiable pages 63 and 64. Fill in the gaps in the poem.	Revise the term 'simile'. Look at what makes an effective simile, including the use of active verbs and personification.	1*: Complete 'Beach' and 'The storm' simile poems. Underline similes with personification and active verbs. Write own simile poem based on 'The storm'. 2 & 3: As for Group 1, but complete 'Double bass' and 'Beach'. Use 'Beach' as a model for own shorter poems. 4*: Complete 'Monster' poem. Write own poem using 'Monster' as a model.	Selected pupils share their simile poems. The class comment on how effective the similes are and on the use of personification and active verbs.

RESOURCES

Photocopiable pages 63 and 64 (Simile Poems: 1 and 2), board or flip chart. OHP and acetate (optional), writing materials.

PREPARATION

If possible, copy the following short poem onto the board or flip chart:

New Notebook
Lines
in a new notebook
run, even and fine,
like telephone wires
across a snowy landscape.

With wet, black strokes
the alphabet settles between them,
comfortable as a flock of crows.

Judith Thurman

Make enough copies of the poems 'Beach' and 'The storm' on photocopiable page 64 for each child in Group 1. Make enough copies of 'Double bass' and 'Beach' poems on photocopiable pages 63 and 64 for each child in Groups 2 and 3. (Mask off poems as appropriate to fit both on one sheet.) Make enough copies of 'Monster' poem on photocopiable page 65 for each child in Group 4. Prepare OHTs of all the poems or make A3 enlargements.

Introduction

Read out (and display if possible) the poem 'New notebook'. Talk about the 'picture' the poem 'paints' and how it does this. What comparisons does it make? (The blank lines in the notebook are compared to telephone wires against a snowy landscape; the writing is compared to crows sitting on the telephone wires.) Ask the children whether they think these are good images. Remind them that comparisons like these are called 'similes'.

Display the photocopiable poem frames as OHTs or A3 enlargements. Explain that these are simile poems, then read the examples together. Invite the children to suggest suitable similes to fill in the gaps. ('Monster' is the simplest; 'The storm' is the most challenging as it involves personification and active verbs – see skills section below.)

Whole-class skills work

Revise the term 'simile'. The children should refer to the poems to help them explain the term. Then provide this definition: a simile is a comparison using the words 'like' or 'as'.

Explain that many similes are used in everyday speech, for example 'she's as blind as a bat', 'he was like a bull in a china shop', and so on. Encourage the children to think of some other examples. However, a simile is most effective when it is fresh and striking, like in 'New notebook', not overused and worn out like the everyday examples above. This simile from the poem 'Nessie' by Ted Hughes describes the Loch Ness monster in a humorous and original way and is another good example of an effective simile:

No, it is not an elephant or any such grasshopper.
It's shaped like a pop bottle with two huge eyes in the stopper.

Explain that similes do not always need to use 'is'; they can use a different verb, as in this example: 'The wind bites like a hungry wolf'. Explain that this is an example of a simile with an active verb ('bites') and using this type of simile can produce a powerful effect. Ask the children to think of some similar examples and write them on the board or flip chart under the heading 'similes with active verbs'.

Introduce the term 'personification'. Explain that it involves using language normally linked with human action or emotion to refer to objects or abstract ideas, for example 'Winter has packed her bags and gone away' and 'Fear gripped him in a vice'. Although personification is technically a subtype of metaphor, it can be incorporated effectively into simile. Provide some examples of similes that use personification (for example 'The sea is like an angry tyrant'). Include examples with active verbs, such as 'The tree branch held her like a strong old friend' and 'The wind sang softly like a gentle child'. Can the children think of some other examples? Write their ideas on the board or flip chart.

Differentiated group activities

All the children should work in their ability groups to complete their own versions of the photocopiable simile poems as described below. They can then experiment with writing their own simile poems in a similar form.

1*: Complete the poems 'Beach' and 'The storm'. Underline any examples of personification and similes with active verbs and respond to these as imaginatively as possible. Write a simile poem using 'The storm' as a model and including similes with active verbs and personification.

2 & 3: Complete the poems 'Double bass' and 'Beach'. Underline examples of similes and personification with active verbs. Compose a poem using 'Beach' as a model, but with only two verses of four lines. Include similes with active verbs in their own poems.

4*: Complete the poem 'Monster'. Write a simile poem using 'Monster' as a model. If appropriate, the children can try to include examples of active verbs in their similes.

Conclusion

Select children to share their poems. The rest of the class evaluates the effectiveness of the similes, and discusses which ones are particularly fresh and striking. Have any of the children in Group 1 used similes with personification? Have those in Groups 2 and 3 used similes with active verbs? Evaluate the effectiveness of these examples.

FURTHER IDEA

Children could spend some time collecting examples of similes from poetry anthologies. They could share the most interesting examples and say what they like about them.

SIMILE POEMS: 1

Monster

There's a monster in my bedroom, mum,

I'll tell you what it's like,

Its head is like _____

Its body is like _____

Its claws are like _____

Its teeth are like _____

I know you don't believe me, mum,

But hurry up, it's getting closer,

It's...aaarrrggghhh!

Double bass

A double bass is a funny old instrument

It looks like _____

Its curves are like _____

It has a big fat belly like _____

When you bow it, it sounds like _____

But when you pluck it, it's more like _____

Yes, the double bass is a funny old instrument.

SIMILE POEMS: 2

The storm

The wild storm rages like an angry giant,

_____ lightning bolts through the sky like fiery weapons

As its thunderous voice _____ and echoes furiously.

The wind shrieks _____ like a _____

Its icy _____ grip the house as tightly as _____

The rain beats furiously against the windows like _____ .

Inside, the fire greets us like _____

And we feel as warm and snug as _____ .

Beach

Stretched out sleepily in the shade

On a day when the sun's as fierce as a _____

I'm feeling really hot and sticky

And my face is as red as a _____

The sea looks like _____

As I head towards it for a swim

But the sand _____ my feet like _____

Making me run as fast as _____

I'm so glad to reach the water

I splash about like a _____

The tiny waves welcome me like _____

And feel as _____ as _____

A MIDSUMMER NIGHT'S DREAM

OBJECTIVES

UNIT	SPELLING/VOCABULARY	GRAMMAR/ PUNCTUATION	COMPREHENSION/ COMPOSITION
READING PLAYS Extract from *A Midsummer Night's Dream* by William Shakespeare.	Understand how words and expressions have changed over time.	Explore sentence structure, recognizing sentences, clauses and phrases.	Study extract from Shakespeare play as example of classic drama. Read, prepare and present a playscript.

ORGANIZATION (2 HOURS)

	INTRODUCTION	WHOLE-CLASS SKILLS WORK	DIFFERENTIATED GROUP ACTIVITIES	CONCLUSION
HOUR 1	Introduce details about William Shakespeare. Shared reading of Act III, scene 1 of *A Midsummer Night's Dream* (photocopiable pages 68–70).	Use the play extract to investigate words and expressions that have changed over time.	1*: Guided reading and discussion. 2 & 3: Plan and rehearse a presentation of Act III, scene 1 of the play. 4*: Guided reading and discussion.	Pupils in Group 2 present their version of Act III, scene 1. The rest of the class evaluate its success.
HOUR 2	Pupils in Group 3 present their version of Act III, scene 1 of the same play.	Explore sentence structure, focusing on whole sentences, clauses and phrases. Study examples from the play extract.	1: Plan and rehearse a presentation of Act III, scene 1 of the play. 2 & 3*: Guided reading and discussion. 4: As for Group 1 above.	Pupils in Groups 1 & 4 present their versions of Act III, scene 1.

RESOURCES

Photocopiable pages 68–70 (from *A Midsummer Night's Dream*, Act III, scene 1), board or flip chart, OHP and acetate (optional), writing materials, an audio or video tape version of the play with cassette player or video recorder (optional).

PREPARATION

Prepare the play extract on photocopiable pages 68–70 as OHTs or A3 enlargements. Make enough copies of the extract to allow one per child. Practise reading the extract using a variety of different voices for the characters. Alternatively, if you are able to use an audio or video tape version of the play, set this to begin at Act III, scene 1.

Introduction

Display the photocopiable extract as OHTs or A3 enlargements. Explain to the children that this is Act III, scene 1 of a play called *A Midsummer Night's Dream* by William Shakespeare. Find out what the children already know about Shakespeare – and establish a few basic facts:

William Shakespeare (1564–1616), English poet and playwright, is said to be the greatest of all dramatists. His plays include *Hamlet*, *Macbeth*, *Romeo and Juliet* and *The Merchant of Venice*. *A Midsummer Night's Dream* (written around 1595) is a comic fantasy about how two pairs of noble lovers, who have been thwarted in their love, are brought together by a fairy realm. In Act III, scene 1, the comic townspeople, led by the blundering Bottom, rehearse a play (the tragedy of Pyramus and Thisbe) that they plan to perform for the Duke's wedding feast. Their bumbling efforts provide one of Shakespeare's greatest comic scenes.

Now *either* read through the play extract with appropriate expression and intonation, and providing plenty of support by explaining vocabulary and paraphrasing difficult speeches; *or* play the audio or video tape version of the scene. Ask the children to summarize briefly what is happening in this scene to check their level of understanding.

Whole-class skills work

Use the photocopiable play extract to investigate words and expressions that have changed over time. Point out to the children that there are three types of change in language to look out for in the text:
■ Changes in vocabulary, for example *tiring-house* (dressing room), *afeard* (afraid).
■ Changes in verb endings, for example *What sayest thou?* (The second-person singular -*est* ending has been dropped; 'thou' and its related words 'thy' and 'thine' have fallen into disuse except for the traditional version of the Lord's prayer still said in many churches. Ask: can anyone recite it?).
■ Changes in word order, for example *How answer you that?* (How do you answer that?).
   List these as headings on the board or flip chart, then go through the text with the children to find more examples of each type of change. Encourage them to try to work out meanings by using the context of the play. Note these down alongside the words or phrases. (You may wish to keep a permanent record of the list for the children to refer to later when preparing their performances.)

Differentiated group activities

1*: Guided reading and discussion of the photocopiable play extract. The following questions can be used as a basis for discussion:
■ Bottom tells Quince that he is worried about a scene in the play. What is he worried about?
■ What solution does Bottom suggest?
■ What is Snout worried about?
■ What solution does Bottom suggest to this problem?
■ Quince is worried about two things. What are they?
■ How do they decide to solve these two problems?
■ What do you think their presentation of the final play will be like?
2 & 3: Plan and rehearse a presentation of the text up to Bottom's speech: *If I were fair, Thisby, I were only thine.* The teacher will need to help allocate the parts appropriately. Encourage the children to focus on clarity and expression in their readings. They should project their voice as far as possible, and try to speak the lines with realistic intonation. Remind them to annotate their copy of the text to help support their readings.
4*: Guided reading and discussion, as for Group 1 above.

Conclusion

Ask the children in Group 2 to present their version of the scene. The rest of the class should be the audience and evaluate how effectively and clearly the text has been presented.

Introduction

Ask the children in Group 3 to present their version of the scene, as prepared in the previous hour. The rest of the class should follow the script to enhance their understanding of the text.

Whole-class skills work

Revise the terms 'sentence', 'clause' and 'phrase' with the children, writing the following explanations on the board or flip chart, for example:
Sentence: A word or group of words that makes complete sense on its own, for example 'We bought some sweets.'
Clause: A group of words containing a subject and a verb. There are two kinds: *main* clause which makes complete sense on its own; *subordinate* clause which is dependent on

the main clause to make sense, for example 'I woke up [main] when the alarm went off [subordinate].'

Phrase: a small group of words that does not make complete sense on its own and does not contain a verb, for example '...with four wheels'.

Explain that long sentences are often made up of a number of smaller sentences known as clauses. They may also contain phrases, e.g. 'She went home after completing the test without a single mistake'. Breaking long sentences down into these smaller parts can often make them easier to understand. Take this example from the play text:

> This green plot shall be our stage, this hawthorn-brake our tiring house; and we will do it in action as we will do it before the duke.

Point out that both the punctuation and conjunctions like 'and' and 'as' are useful guides as to how we can break up the sentence:

> This green plot shall be our stage,
> + this hawthorn-brake our tiring house;
> + and we will do it in action as we will do it before the duke.

Ask the children to explain the meaning of each part of the sentence (such as each clause), then discuss the overall meaning of the whole sentence. Pick out some more long sentences from the text and break them down in the same way. Ask the children to identify the separate clauses and any phrases that occur.

Differentiated group activities

1: Plan and rehearse a presentation of the text in the photocopiable play extract (see details for Groups 2 and 3, Hour 1).
2 & 3*: Guided reading and discussion (see details for Group 1, Hour 1).
4: Plan and rehearse a presentation of the text (as above).

Conclusion

Ask the children in Groups 1 and 4 to present their versions of Act III, scene 1. The rest of the class should evaluate the effectiveness and clarity of the presentations.

FURTHER IDEA

Show the class a film version of the play, and/or read a retelling of the story in one of the many versions available, for example Charles and Mary Lamb's *Tales from Shakespeare*.

A MIDSUMMER NIGHT'S DREAM

Act III, scene 1

[The wood. TITANIA lying asleep.]

Enter the clowns [QUINCE, SNUG, BOTTOM, FLUTE, SNOUT, and STARVELING].

BOTTOM: Are we all met?

QUINCE: Pat, pat; and here's a marvellous convenient place for our rehearsal. This green plot shall be our stage, this hawthorn-brake our tiring house; and we will do it in action as we will do it before the duke.

BOTTOM: Peter Quince!

QUINCE: What say'st thou, bully Bottom?

BOTTOM: There are things in this comedy of Pyramus and Thisby that will never please. First, Pyramus must draw a sword to kill himself, which the ladies cannot abide. How answer you that?

SNOUT: By'r lakin, a parlous fear.

STARVELING: I believe we must leave the killing out, when all is done.

BOTTOM: Not a whit! I have a device to make all well. Write me a prologue; and let the prologue seem to say, we will do no harm with our swords, and that Pyramus is not kill'd indeed; and, for the more better assurance, tell them that I Pyramus am not Pyramus, but Bottom the weaver. This will put them out of fear.

QUINCE: Well, we will have such a prologue; and it shall be written in eight and six.

BOTTOM: No, make it two more; let it be written in eight and eight.

SNOUT: Will not the ladies be afeard of the lion?

STARVELING: I fear it, I promise you.

BOTTOM: Masters, you ought to consider with yourselves. To bring in – God shield us! – a lion among ladies, is a most dreadful thing; for there is not a more fearful wild-fowl than your lion living; and we ought to look to't.

SNOUT: Therefore another prologue must tell he is not a lion.

BOTTOM: Nay, you must name his name, and half his face must be seen through the lion's neck; and he himself must speak through, saying thus, or to the same defect, – 'Ladies,' – or 'Fair-ladies, – I would wish you,' – or 'I would request you,' – or 'I would entreat you, – not to fear, not to tremble: my life for yours. If you think I come hither as a lion, it were pity of my life. No, I am no such thing; I am a man as other men are;' and there indeed let him name his name, and tell them plainly he is Snug the joiner.

QUINCE:	Well, it shall be so. But there is two hard things; that is, to bring the moonlight into a chamber; for, you know, Pyramus and Thisby meet by moonlight.
SNOUT:	Doth the moon shine that night we play our play?
BOTTOM:	A calendar, a calendar! Look in the almanac! Find out moonshine, find out moonshine.
QUINCE:	Yes, it doth shine that night.
BOTTOM:	Why, then may you leave a casement of the great chamber window, where we play, open, and the moon may shine in at the casement.
QUINCE:	Ay; or else one must come in with a bush of thorns and a lanthorn, and say he comes to disfigure, or to present, the person of Moonshine. Then, there is another thing: we must have a wall in the great chamber; for Pyramus and Thisby, says the story, did talk through the chink of a wall.
SNOUT:	You can never bring in a wall. What say you, Bottom?
BOTTOM:	Some man or other must present Wall; and let him have some plaster, or some loam, or some rough-cast about him, to signify wall; and let him hold his fingers thus, and through that cranny shall Pyramus and Thisby whisper.
QUINCE:	If that may be, then all is well. Come, sit down, every mother's son, and rehearse your parts. Pyramus, you begin. When you have spoken your speech, enter into that brake. And so every one according to his cue.
	[Enter PUCK behind.]
PUCK:	What hempen home-spuns have we swaggering here? So near the cradle of the fairy queen? What, a play toward! I'll be an auditor; An actor too, perhaps, if I see cause.
QUINCE:	Speak, Pyramus. Thisby, stand forth.
BOTTOM:	"Thisby, the flowers of odious savours sweet," –
QUINCE:	Odorous, odorous.
BOTTOM:	– "odours savours sweet; So hath thy breath, my dearest Thisby dear. But hark, a voice! stay thou but here awhile, And by and by I will to thee appear." *[Exit.]*
PUCK:	A stranger Pyramus than e'er played here. *[Exit.]*
FLUTE:	Must I speak now?
QUINCE:	Ay, marry, must you; for you must understand he goes but to see a noise that he heard, and is to come again.

FLUTE:	"Most radiant Pyramus, most lily-white of hue, Of colour like the red rose on triumphant brier, Most brisky juvenal and eke most lovely Jew, As true as truest horse that yet would never tire, I'll meet thee, Pyramus, at Ninny's tomb."
QUINCE:	"Ninus' tomb," man. Why, you must not speak that yet; that you answer to Pyramus. You speak all your part at once, cues and all. Pyramus enter. Your cue is past; it is, "never tire."
FLUTE:	O, – "As true as truest horse, that yet would never tire."

[Re-enter PUCK, and BOTTOM with an ass's head.]

BOTTOM:	"If I were fair, Thisby, I were only thine."
QUINCE:	O monstrous! O strange! we are haunted. Pray, masters, fly, masters! Help!

Exeunt QUINCE, SNUG, FLUTE, SNOUT, and STARVELING.

PUCK:	I'll follow you, I'll lead you about, a round, Through bog, through bush, through brake, through brier. Sometime a horse I'll be, sometime a hound, A hog, a headless bear, sometime a fire; And neigh, and bark, and grunt, and roar, and burn, Like horse, hound, hog, bear, fire, at every turn.

[Exit.]

BOTTOM:	Why do they run away? This is a knavery of them to make me afeard.

[Re-enter SNOUT.]

SNOUT:	O Bottom, thou art chang'd! What do I see on thee?
BOTTOM:	What do you see? You see an asshead of your own, do you?

[Exit SNOUT. Re-enter QUINCE.]

QUINCE:	Bless thee, Bottom! bless thee! thou art translated.

[Exit.]

PYRAMUS AND THISBE

OBJECTIVES

UNIT	SPELLING/VOCABULARY	GRAMMAR/ PUNCTUATION	COMPREHENSION/ COMPOSITION
WRITING PLAYS 'Pyramus and Thisbe' from *A Midsummer's Night Dream* by William Shakespeare.	Understand how words and expressions have changed over time.	Demonstrate an understanding of the grammatical construction of archaic language.	Be familiar with the work of established authors. Practise improvisations. Prepare a story as a script using the correct conventions.

ORGANIZATION (2 HOURS)

	INTRODUCTION	WHOLE-CLASS SKILLS WORK	DIFFERENTIATED GROUP ACTIVITIES	CONCLUSION
HOUR 1	Shared re-reading of *A Midsummer's Night Dream* Act III, scene 1 (photocopiable pages 68–70) from previous unit. Provide a brief outline of the play 'Pyramus and Thisbe'.	Explore/practise improvisation using 'Pyramus and Thisbe' as a focus.	1–4*: Each group plans its version of 'Pyramus and Thisbe' using the improvisation skills covered in the whole-class session. Pupils in Groups 1 should try to emulate the language of Shakespeare's play as far as possible.	Selected groups present their improvised versions of 'Pyramus and Thisbe'.
HOUR 2	Presentation of improvised version of 'Pyramus and Thisbe' by one group who did not perform in previous hour. Demonstrate how to turn this improvisation into a script.	Revise the conventions for setting out a playscript.	1–4*: All pupils transcribe their group's improvised version of the play into a playscript.	Selected pupils perform their plays from scripts. The rest of the class discuss the difference between the improvised and scripted versions.

RESOURCES

Photocopiable pages 68–70 (*A Midsummer Night's Dream*, Act III, scene 1) from previous unit, board or flip chart, OHP and acetate (optional), writing materials, an old sheet cut up to make four cloaks (optional, for improvisation).

PREPARATION

You will need to make one copy per child of the play extract on photocopiable pages 68–70, if you have not already done this for the previous unit. For the introduction in Hour 1, prepare an OHT or A3 enlargement of the cast and outline of the play 'Pyramus and Thisbe' (see 'Introduction' on next page). For the introduction in Hour 2, prepare the board or flip chart with the correct layout for a play script, including a margin for character names and these headings: title, cast, scene description.

Introduction

Read (or re-read) *A Midsummer Night's Dream*, Act III, scene 1 on photocopiable pages 68–70. Recap on the action in this scene, such as a comic group of locals rehearsing a tragic play called 'Pyramus and Thisbe'. Explain that other scenes in *A Midsummer Night's Dream* provide more information on what happens in 'Pyramus and Thisbe'. Provide the cast list and main outline of the play as an OHT or A3 enlargement (see 'Preparation') as follows:

> PYRAMUS AND THISBE
> CAST: Pyramus, Thisbe, Pyramus' father, Thisbe's father, Thisbe's mother, a lion.
>
> Pyramus falls in love with Thisbe, but their parents disapprove of their love. For this reason they have to be secretive and whisper to each other through a chink in a wall. They plan a meeting by moonlight at Ninus' tomb. Thisbe arrives first and is attacked by a lion. She manages to get away, but leaves her cloak, which the lion chews, leaving bloody marks. When Pyramus arrives, he sees the blood-stained cloak and thinks that Thisbe has been killed. He is so filled with grief that he takes his own life with his sword. When Thisbe returns, she finds her lover dead and stabs herself.

Ask the children if this story sounds familiar in any way. They may recognize how similar the plot is to another of Shakespeare's plays, *Romeo and Juliet*. Have any of them seen a film version of this play? Briefly identify the main similarities between the two plays: such as a young couple fall in love; their parents disapprove; they have to meet in secret; they plan a meeting at night; the male character mistakenly thinks the female character is dead and kills himself through grief. She then, seeing her lover dead, kills herself.

Whole-class skills work

Tell the children that they are going to produce their own improvised versions of the play 'Pyramus and Thisbe' using the story outline provided in the introduction. First, they will need to explore the different characters involved and their reactions to the events. Explain that this will help to bring the dialogue in their improvisations to life. They will also need to think about the sequence of the scenes.

Begin by focusing on the two main characters, Pyramus and Thisbe. As a starting point, read the description Thisbe gives of Pyramus *'Most radiant Pyramus...'* (these lines are spoken by Flute in the photocopiable play extract). What does this speech show about Thisbe's feelings for Pyramus? What might the couple think about having to meet secretly? Would it be frightening, or exciting, or perhaps both?

Choose a couple of volunteers to be Pyramus and Thisbe, and improvise the scene where Thisbe is attacked by the lion. Make the scene as realistic as possible, showing Thisbe's terror followed by her relief when she escapes, conveyed through a brief monologue. Then have Pyramus enter and find Thisbe's blood-stained cloak. His speech should reflect his deep horror, desperation and anguish, leading to his decision to kill himself. Finally, have Thisbe enter and find the dead Pyramus, then explore her reactions in a similar way.

Ask three other volunteers to play the parents of Pyramus and Thisbe. Hold a discussion between Thisbe and her mother and father when they discover her love for Pyramus. What might they all say to each other? Why might they disapprove of Pyramus? (Both families are old enemies.) Hold a similar discussion between Pyramus and his father. Finally, explore through dialogue the parents' reactions to the news of the deaths of Pyramus and Thisbe.

Finish by discussing how these separate scenes could be put together to represent the action of the whole play. What would be the best and most logical sequence? Which characters would be on stage in each scene? Emphasize that the children will need to consider these aspects carefully in their improvisations.

Differentiated group activities

1–4*: Each group prepares its own improvised version of 'Pyramus and Thisbe', using the ideas from the skills session as a starting point. The children will need to make notes to remind them of the sequence of events and the main points in their speeches. The children in Group 1 should try to emulate the language of Shakespeare's play as far as possible. The teacher provides support as appropriate, including the allocation of parts as necessary.

Conclusion

Ask selected groups to present their improvised version of the play.

Introduction

Choose one group (which did not perform at the end of the previous hour) to present its version of the play 'Pyramus and Thisbe'. Use the first half-dozen lines of the group's improvisation to demonstrate how this can be turned into a script. Remind the children of the correct layout of a playscript by showing them the outline prepared on the board or flip chart (see 'Preparation'). Emphasize that the process of writing the script is an opportunity to improve on the improvised version.

Whole-class skills work

Using the photocopiable play extract from *A Midsummer Night's Dream*, revise in detail the conventions for setting out playscripts. Explain that these vary slightly in different printed scripts, but for school use the following conventions are recommended.
■ Rule a wide margin (3cms) for the characters' names.
■ Begin with a title and cast list.
■ Underneath the subheading 'Scene 1', write a description of the set and which characters are on stage. Note that this is usually written in the present tense and is a guide to the producer of the play; it is not meant to be imaginative description.
■ Place other brief stage directions in brackets before the speech of the character they apply to.
■ Do *not* use quotation marks at the beginning and end of speeches.
   It may be helpful to list these conventions on the board or flip chart for the children to refer to, and to prompt discussion about the differences between them and the conventions used in the photocopiable play extract.

Differentiated group activities

1–4*: The children work in their ability groups to transcribe their improvised plays into scripted versions using the conventions outlined in the skills section. Children in Group 4 could concentrate on writing just the first two scenes in this way rather than the whole play, allowing them to focus mainly on using the correct conventions.

Conclusion

Ask selected groups to perform their plays or single scenes from their scripts. The class should discuss the difference between the improvised and scripted versions. Are the scripted versions better? In what ways are they an improvement on the improvisations?

FURTHER IDEAS

Read Act V, scene 1 of *A Midsummer Night's Dream*, to get an idea of what the original Pyramus and Thisbe play was like and to find out what a mess the locals made in presenting their version of it!

THE MARWELL MANOR MYSTERY

OBJECTIVES

UNIT	SPELLING/VOCABULARY	GRAMMAR/ PUNCTUATION	COMPREHENSION/ COMPOSITION
READING NON-FICTION Recount genre: 'The Marwell Manor Mystery'.	Study vocabulary in recount/report texts.	Understand the terms 'active' and 'passive' voice. Note how changes from active to passive affect word order.	Read a range of non-fiction recount texts. Revise the conventions of the report genre. Write a non-chronological report. Revise the conventions of diaries. Revise key skills of writing stories.

ORGANIZATION (4 HOURS)

	INTRODUCTION	WHOLE-CLASS SKILLS WORK	DIFFERENTIATED GROUP ACTIVITIES	CONCLUSION
HOUR 1	Introduce the 'Marwell Manor Mystery' unit and discuss the range of texts to be covered. Shared reading of all the texts on photocopiable pages 78 and 79. Discuss difficult vocabulary.	Revise the conventions of the report genre: present tense; data; non-chronological sequence. Explore which features Marwell Manor report contains.	1–4*: All pupils work in their ability groups to write a detailed report on the Marwell Manor mystery, using information from the photocopiable texts on pages 78 and 79.	Selected pupils read out their reports. The rest of the class evaluate and identify if any information is missing.
HOUR 2	Re-read Lady Anne's diary entries.	Revise the conventions of diary writing: mainly past tense; first person; informal style. Explore Lady Anne's diary entries.	1–4*: All groups discuss reasons for the haunting of Marwell Hall and how to stop it, drawing on evidence from the photocopiable texts. Pupils write own versions of their group's answers.	Pupils share their answers to the questions and any supporting evidence.
HOUR 3	Shared re-reading of all the Marwell Hall texts. Pupils listen for any evidence relating to the murder.	Explain the terms 'active' and 'passive' voice. Transform sentences from passive to active and vice versa.	1–4*: All groups discuss questions relating to the murder. Pupils write own versions of their group's answers.	Pupils share their answers to the questions and any supporting evidence.
HOUR 4	Discuss the differences if Marwell Mystery text were written as a story.	Revise skills covered in 'Pleasant Afternoon' unit, page 28, eg: structuring a story; developing character description; developing dialogue.	1–4*: Pupils choose to complete one of four writing tasks.	An example from each writing task is chosen for reading aloud to the class.

RESOURCES

Photocopiable pages 78 (Marwell Manor: 1), 79 (Marwell Manor: 2), board or flip chart, OHP and acetate (optional), writing materials.

PREPARATION

Prepare enough copies of photocopiable pages 78 and 79 for one between two. If possible, prepare an OHT or A3 enlargement of the Marwell Manor Report on photocopiable page 78.

Introduction

Tell the children that they are going to explore a range of non-fiction texts, including a report, some diary entries, newspaper reports, a will, and a small advertisement. Explain that from these texts, they will have to try to solve a mystery using skills of inference and deduction. The teacher should note that there is no absolute answer to the mystery – the evidence is sometimes conflicting and several interpretations are possible. The key skills are for the children to read the text carefully, and to find evidence to support their solutions.

Finally, it should be noted that all the photocopiable text provided in this unit is fictional, although based on a similar story associated with Burton Agnes Hall in North Yorkshire.

Read all the photocopiable texts to give the children an overview of the Marwell Manor mystery. Then go over some of the difficult vocabulary, for example:

paranormal	phenomenon	reception rooms
personal effects	neglected	ancestral
orchid	disrepair	small advertisement
occurrence	exorcism	orangery

Whole-class skills work

Revise the conventions of the report genre. Find out how much the children remember about these, then provide a brief summary. Remind them that reports are usually written in the present tense, though they may include sections of recount (in the past tense). They often contain data such as facts and figures. They are often written in sections which can be in any order. The sections are therefore arranged non-chronologically, though the content of some may be chronological. List these features on the board or flip chart.

Now display the Marwell Manor report on photocopiable page 78. Ask the children to examine how far the above criteria apply to this report. (Because the mystery began a few years ago, there is extensive use of the past tense. However, note that the conclusion is in the present tense.)

Differentiated group activities

The children will need one set of photocopiable pages 78 and 79 between two.
1–4*: The children work in their ability groups to write their own detailed report on the Marwell Manor Mystery. They should refer to the list of conventions compiled in the skills session. Explain that they will be adding further sections to this during Hours 2 and 3, and ask them to begin here with the subheading: '1. Background information'. They should write this first section using information from all the photocopiable texts, including names of those involved, dates, money amounts and so on. Emphasize that as this is a report, the details should be written as clearly and concisely as possible. For Group 1, a maximum word limit could be set, for example 100 words.

Conclusion

Ask selected children to read out their reports while the rest of the class evaluate them by indicating if any information has been missed out. By the end of this session, all the children should have a clear and detailed understanding of the background to the Marwell Manor mystery.

Introduction

Re-read Lady Anne's diary entries on photocopiable page 79.

Whole-class skills work

Revise the conventions of diary writing (recount genre). Find out how much the children remember about these, then provide a brief summary. Remind them that diaries are usually written in the past tense, though some parts may be in the present or future tense. They are written in the first person in an informal style.

Now display Lady Anne's diary entries and ask the children to examine how far the above criteria apply to these. They should look particularly for the mixture of tenses, but note the preponderance of the past tense.

Differentiated group activities

1–4*: The children discuss the following question in their groups: What is the reason for the haunting of Marwell Hall and how might it be stopped? They should give evidence from the texts for their views. (The reason for the haunting is that the conditions of Lady Anne's will have not been met – she has been buried at the church rather than in the grounds of Marwell Hall. Also, Dabbles the cat has gone missing and so cannot be cared for by Ruth Eckersley the housekeeper. The hauntings could possibly be stopped by fulfilling the conditions of the will.)

Following their discussions, the children each write their own version of the group's answers as part of their report begun in Hour 1. They should use the subheading: 2. How to stop the haunting.

Conclusion

The children share their answers to the question and provide any supporting evidence for their answers. Note that any answer is acceptable provided that the evidence is appropriate. (A possible alternative is to say that the haunting is in the Earl's mind. The evidence for this is that he is described as 'unstable'. However, this would still not explain why the servant and passers-by witnessed or heard the same phenomenon.)

Introduction

Explain to the children that in this lesson they are going to concentrate on the murder rather than the haunting. Ask them to listen carefully for all evidence relating to the murder as you re-read the photocopiable texts. Briefly discuss the evidence that they have identified.

Whole-class skills work

Introduce the terms 'active voice' and 'passive voice'. Illustrate the difference by using the following sentences:
Active voice: The cat chased the mouse.
Passive voice: The mouse was chased by the cat.
Ask the children to say what the difference in emphasis is. Sum up by explaining that in a passive sentence, the subject is the person or thing acted upon by the verb, rather than the one who performs the action. So, in the above passive sentence, the mouse is the subject acted upon by the verb 'chased'. In the active sentence, the cat is the subject and is the thing that 'acts' upon the mouse.

Use the following diagram to show how the active voice can be converted to the passive voice:

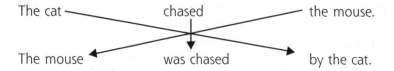

By repositioning the words as shown by the arrows, the sentence becomes passive. To change a sentence in the passive voice to the active voice, simply reverse the direction of the arrows and change the word order and verb form accordingly.

Now ask the children to experiment by changing these sentences into the passive voice:

- The boy kissed the girl.
- Timothy caught the shark.
- The car overtook the lorry.
- An architect designed this house.

Finally, find examples of passive voice sentences in the article 'Brutal Murder at Marwell Manor'. (Clue: look for the verb 'was'. Note that the passive voice is used here to avoid stating who found her as this is not important to the article.)

Differentiated group activities

1–4*: The children discuss the following question in their groups: Who do you think committed the murder? Following the discussion, they each write their own version of the group's answer under the subheading: 3. The murderer revealed. This will form the final section of their report begun in Hour 1.

Conclusion

The children share their answers to the question and give evidence to support their answers. Note that the texts have been designed to allow a number of interpretations for the murder, for example the thief, the Earl, Ruth – it is even possible to make a case for suicide. The main thing is that any interpretation must be supported by evidence from the texts.

Introduction

Explain to the children that the texts about Marwell Hall are fictional, even though they are written in forms normally used for factual writing, such as non-fiction. Discuss what differences there would be if the report text was written in a fictional form, such as a story. In what other ways could the story be told? (It could be written wholly in the past tense, including imaginative description and sections of dialogue. The events would unfold in chronological sequence.)

Whole-class skills work

Revise the key skills covered in the 'Pleasant Afternoon' unit (page 28). For example:
- Structuring a story – including a clear beginning, middle and end.
- Developing character description – exploring personality, ability and motivation of characters.
- Developing dialogue – making it as interesting and realistic as possible.
- Integrating character and place description and dialogue.

Differentiated group activities

1–4*: The children choose one of the following subjects to write about. Note that these writing tasks are in decreasing order of difficulty and would be suitable for the children in each of the four respective groups. However, it is desirable to allow some flexibility of choice.
- Re-write the Marwell Manor mystery in story form.
- Write a short version of the mystery which would be suitable for inclusion in a tourists' guide to Marwell Manor.
- Write a detailed report on your findings of the mystery using the same headings as those in Samuel Sheridan's report on photocopiable page 78.
- Write about what you think happened to the cat, Dabbles.

Conclusion

Choose an example from each task to be read out to the class. Discuss any weak points in the texts and how these could be improved.

FURTHER IDEA

The children could try to write their own story using a variety of text types. These might include:
- A collection of letters which tell a story.
- A series of diary entries which tell a story.
- A collection of different texts (like those for the Marwell Manor mystery) which tell a story.

MARWELL MANOR: 1

On these pages you will find a range of texts and pictures which throw some light on the Marwell Manor mystery. The most recent full investigation was by Professor Samuel Sheridan, the well-known paranormal investigator, but even he failed to get to the bottom of it. Can you do better?

A REPORT ON THE MARWELL MANOR MYSTERY

Date: 9th September, 1990
Author: Professor Samuel Sheridan, Paranormal Investigator

INTRODUCTION
This is a report on my investigation into the Marwell Manor mystery. The report is published by permission of the Earl of Marwell who asked me to investigate a strange phenomenon which has been troubling him recently.

BACKGROUND
Marwell Manor was built in 1750, but fell into disrepair in the early years of this century. However, in the 1980s, Lady Anne of Marwell, the Earl's wife, spent a great deal of money restoring and redecorating the house. Sadly, soon after her plans were completed, she was murdered in the course of a break-in. The Earl, who had for many years been an unstable personality, suffered a nervous breakdown and gave up his public duties.

THE PHENOMENON
The first occurrence of the phenomenon took place a few months ago – the Earl cannot remember the exact date. Recently, the phenomenon has been observed more and more frequently. The only eye-witnesses are the Earl and one of his servants. They state that, on the night of a full moon, a ghostly skull is seen floating down the corridors. The skull is said to make an ear-piercing scream as it floats along, and though no one else has seen the ghostly skull, many people, even passers-by, claim to have heard its scream. The Earl tried everything to end the haunting. He even asked Rev Hamilton, rector of the parish church, if he would conduct a service of exorcism, but the rector said the church no longer conducted such ceremonies. He gave the house a blessing instead, but the hauntings continued.

All the servants left except one: a deaf servant girl, Ruth Eckersley. The girl stayed on partly out of loyalty to the Earl, but also because she needed the wages he paid her. She was afraid that no one else would employ her because of her handicap.

CONCLUSION
When I reported to the Earl that I was unable to explain the phenomenon, or offer a solution, he decided that he had no option but to leave Marwell Manor before he finally went mad. The servant girl went with him. He is now living at 14 High Street, and is offering a large reward to anyone who can rid his ancestral mansion of its terrible curse.

I am convinced that there is something strange taking place at Marwell Manor, though it may not necessarily be supernatural. However, as I am unable to solve the mystery, I am making this report available, along with all the other papers I collected during my enquiry, to anyone who can perhaps do better.

MARWELL MANOR: 2

11th July, 1989
Dear Diary,
I have done so much work on the house. I've had the reception rooms re-decorated and furnished to my own designs – they look wonderful. It is a truly lovely house. I'd like to spend the rest of my life here – and to be buried here, if possible! My husband thinks I am silly to say such a thing. And I think he is silly to spend so much money on those stupid orchids!

12th July, 1989
Dear Diary,
I want to build an extension to Marwell Manor. This will cost £100,000 at least, and I'm afraid my husband is not very happy about it. He says it is a waste. I reminded him that the money is my own personal fortune and I can use it as I wish. He says, if he could get his hands on the money, he would use it for something sensible. When he mentioned orchids again, I went mad. I'm afraid we had a very bitter row and it has made me quite miserable.

The Marwell Chronicle

13th July, 1989

BRUTAL MURDER AT MARWELL MANOR

Lady Anne of Marwell Manor was today found brutally murdered in the Orangery in the grounds of Marwell Manor. She was found in a pool of blood with a deep stab wound in her neck, and an orchid lying beside her body. The police think she must have disturbed a thief in the act of stealing one of the Earl's rare orchids, some of which are worth over £1000. Strangely, they cannot find evidence of a break-in anywhere in the Orangery.

The Marwell Chronicle

16th July, 1989

FUNERAL OF LADY ANNE

The funeral of Lady Anne of Marwell Manor took place today at Marwell Church. There was much mourning at the funeral because of the tragic way in which she died - murdered for an orchid. She was buried in the family vault at the church. Lady Anne was a well-loved person in the village of Marwell and will be sadly missed by all.

THE LAST WILL AND TESTAMENT OF LADY ANNE OF MARWELL MANOR

I leave my personal fortune of £8,900,000, my jewellery, valued at £650,000, and all my personal effects to my beloved husband, and in the event of his death to my nearest relatives.

I leave the housekeeper, Ruth Eckersley, £1000 for being a good servant. I also leave her Dabbles, my cat, with £5000 for her upkeep.

Finally, I request that I be buried in the house that I have loved so much - Marwell Manor.

Signed: Anne Marwell
Witnessed: J. Ashton
Date: 12th July, 1989

The Marwell Chronicle

10th August, 1989

SMALL ADVERTISEMENTS

MISSING CAT. The Earl of Marwell's cat, Dabbles, went missing recently. She is black with a white patch behind her left ear, and will answer to the names 'Dabs' or 'Puss'. A £100 reward is offered to anyone who can give information leading to her recovery.

IN THE NEWS

OBJECTIVES

UNIT	SPELLING/VOCABULARY	GRAMMAR/ PUNCTUATION	COMPREHENSION/ COMPOSITION
WRITING NON-FICTION Journalistic writing: 'Marwell Manor Special Report'.	Identify and use journalistic vocabulary and phrases.		Report on an imagined event using journalistic styles and conventions. Develop a journalistic style, investigating balanced reporting and presentation of information.

ORGANIZATION (3 HOURS)

	INTRODUCTION	WHOLE-CLASS SKILLS WORK	DIFFERENTIATED GROUP ACTIVITIES	CONCLUSION
HOUR 1	Shared reading of the same news report as covered in a broadsheet and tabloid newspaper. Discuss the different styles.	Consider 'balanced and ethical reporting' in relation to the Marwell Manor mystery.	1–4*: Each ability group splits into two smaller groups for an 'investigative reporting' exercise, leading to a written news report draft in Hour 2.	Selected groups report on what they have found out from their partner group. The partner group comments on accuracy.
HOUR 2	Shared re-reading of the news report used in Hour 1 introduction.	Make a list of journalistic language collected from different newspapers. Display 'The Marwell Manor Mystery Special Report' template on photocopiable page 84 and discuss different styles of reporting.	1*: Write a draft of the 'Marwell Manor Mystery Special Report' on photocopiable page 84. 2 & 3: Write a draft of The 'Marwell Manor Mystery Special Report' following the template closely. 4*: Write a draft of the 'Marwell Manor Myster Special Report' on the template.	Selected pupils from each group read their draft articles.
HOUR 3	Display the news reports from Hours 1 & 2. Discuss the layout features used.	Revise newspaper layout features, including columns, headings, captions, fonts and bullet points. Pupils investigate layout features in different newspapers.	1–4*: All groups redraft and represent their news articles in as authentic a format as possible.	Pupils display and read from their finished newspaper articles.

RESOURCES
Photocopiable pages 84 ('The Marwell Manor Mystery Special Report' template), 78 and 79 (Marwell Manor: 1 and 2) from previous unit, a selection of tabloid and broadsheet newspapers (start collecting them a few weeks before they are needed, with the children's help), enough for one of each between two children (you may prefer to select several suitable pages from tabloid newspapers rather than using the whole thing), a recent news item as covered in a tabloid and a broadsheet newspaper, board or flip chart, OHP and acetate (optional), writing materials.

PREPARATION
'The Marwell Manor Mystery' unit must have been studied first. If more than a day or two has passed since the study of this unit, it would be worth spending an additional 15

minutes reading through the Marwell Manor texts on photocopiable pages 78 and 79 and discussing the various possible solutions to the mystery. Keep copies of these texts to hand for the children to refer to in the group activities below.

Prepare OHTs or A3 enlargements of one recent news item as covered in both a tabloid and a broadsheet newspaper (for comparison). Make copies of photocopiable page 84 ('The Marwell Manor Mystery Special Report' template) for one per child.

Introduction

Display the chosen news item taken from both a tabloid and broadsheet newspaper (see 'Preparation'). Read out the different versions from each newspaper. Discuss the different styles of reporting in the different types of newspaper. (Broadly speaking, tabloid newspapers will aim for popular appeal and will emphasize the exciting aspects of the story, perhaps including trivial, private details about those concerned to enhance its appeal. Broadsheet newspapers will aim for a more serious, balanced treatment and will go into more detail. At their worst, tabloid newspapers can sensationalize and exaggerate the story, intrude on people's private lives and so on.)

Now check to make sure that the children remember the Marwell Manor mystery texts (see 'Preparation') and if necessary, re-read them to recap on the basic facts.

Whole-class skills work

Discuss the meaning of the phrase 'balanced and ethical reporting' with the children. Ask them to consider how this might apply to news coverage of the Marwell Manor mystery. Start by discussing what could not be considered as balanced or ethical reporting, for example:
■ How a newspaper might sensationalize and exaggerate the story.
■ How reporters might intrude into the personal lives of those concerned.
■ How information might be distorted or exaggerated for effect, for example to suggest that the Earl and the servant had an affair, even though there is no evidence for it.

The next step is to discuss what a balanced and ethical report would be like:
■ It would keep to the established facts.
■ It would respect the feelings of the people concerned.
■ It would not probe unnecessarily into people's private lives, and would cover only those personal details which were considered essential to the case in question (such as in public interest).

Differentiated group activities

This activity simulates investigative reporting, and requires a form of 'jigsaw' grouping, as follows:
1–4*: Ability groups are split into two smaller groups, making eight groups in total. Each person in the group is given a role:
■ The Earl of Marwell
■ The servant girl (she can take part in the discussion because she has a hearing aid)
■ Samuel Sheridan
■ John Ashton (witness of Lady Anne's last will and testament – if an extra role is required).

All groups now follow these steps:
1. Review the mystery of Marwell Manor and make a collective decision about what happened – encourage a wide variety of interpretations.
2. Sub-group 1 play the role of reporters and interview sub-group 2 who play the above roles. The reporters have to ask questions to find out what happened (such as which version of events is sub-group 2 using?). They should make notes, particularly of quotations which may be useful in an article.
3. Groups reverse their roles.
4. Each group then discusses the information it has discovered in preparation for writing articles. The group should decide whether it will report in a tabloid or broadsheet format (guide pupils in making their decision – generally, the tabloid format will be easier to write and therefore more suitable for lower-ability groups).

Conclusion

Invite selected groups to report on what they have found out from their partner group. The partner group confirms the accuracy (or otherwise) of the reporting.

Introduction
Display the OHTs of the news item from the broadsheet and tabloid newspapers and re-read them. Explain to the children that they are going to explore journalistic language and style, so they should pay careful attention to this aspect during the reading.

Whole-class skills work
Begin by exploring the headlines in each version of the news article. What do the children notice about the style and language? What effect does this have? (The style is clipped and extremely concise, with words such as 'the' and 'a' often missed out. The number of words used is kept to a minimum to give headlines instant impact or 'punch'. There may be humour in the form of puns, word play and so on.) Move on to look at the opening sentences of each article. What do the children notice about these? (They are usually longer and contain a great deal of information to convey the main points of the story. The aim is to capture the reader's interest immediately so that they will read on.) Point out that the overall style of newspaper articles is concise and to the point, with the maximum amount of information presented in as few words as possible. Encourage the children to compare the way in which both the tabloid and broadsheet newspapers cover these particular features.

Next, give each pair of children one copy of a tabloid and a broadsheet newspaper (see 'Preparation') and ask them to collect examples of useful words and phrases often used in journalism, for example 'it is believed that...', 'is currently...', '...is thought to have', 'is alleged to have...' and so on. Make a list of these on the board or flip chart.

Finally, display 'The Marwell Manor Mystery Special Report' template on photocopiable page 84. Read the introduction, and invite suggestions for the following:
- How would a tabloid newspaper develop each section?
- How would a broadsheet newspaper develop each section?
- What would be the differences in language use/style?

Differentiated group activities
Each child will need a copy of 'The Marwell Manor Mystery Special Report' template on photocopiable page 84.
1*: Write 'The Marwell Manor Mystery Special Report' in draft form using the headings on the template as a guide if required. Try to achieve a balance between information from the Marwell Manor texts and information from the simulated interviews. Use quotations from the interviews.
2 & 3: Write a draft of the 'Special Report' following the template closely. Try to achieve the balance described above.
4*: Write a draft of the 'Special Report' directly onto the template, continuing over the page or using an additional sheet if more space is needed.

Conclusion
Ask selected children from each group to share their draft articles.

Introduction
Display the OHTs of the two newspaper articles used in the introductions for Hours 1 and 2 and ask the children to pick out as many specific layout features as they can.

Whole-class skills work
Use this opportunity to revise the following newspaper layout features:
- Columns
- Paragraphs
- Headlines and subheadings
- Captions
- Use of typefaces, bold, italic
- Bullet points.

Briefly discuss the purpose of these features – for example, to make the article easier to read, to enable readers to locate information quickly, to highlight important words or paragraphs, to add interest to and enhance the design. Then ask the children to investigate layout more closely on their own examples of tabloid and broadsheet newspapers. For example, they could:
- Find examples of each of the above features.
- Measure all margins and gutters (space between columns).

- Make notes on typeface style and measure typeface sizes (in millimetres).
- Gauge the aesthetic effect of the relative positioning of pictures and text.

Differentiated group activities

1–4*: Children in all groups redraft and represent their 'Special Report' articles, trying to achieve as authentic an effect as possible through layout. This can be achieved by:
- working on A3 paper
- using desktop publishing if possible
- writing their article in small, printed handwriting if computer access is not possible; perhaps just the headlines and subheadings could be printed out on a computer and pasted in place
- planning the page carefully and ruling all the columns and boxes using measurements from the actual newspapers
- allowing space for pictures or illustrations which can be drawn (or pasted in from other sources) later.

Conclusion

Ask selected children to display and read from their finished newspaper articles.

FURTHER IDEAS

- The children could read selected newspaper articles and try to identify those sentences which are fact and those which are opinion. (This could tie in with previous work on fact and opinion in 'The Bermuda Triangle' unit on pages 38).
- The children could carry out some research into the work of newspaper design and production, finding out all the different stages in the process of putting together a real newspaper.

The Marwell Manor Mystery

A Marwell Chronicle special supplement

The Marwell Chronicle presents this exclusive report on the Marwell Manor mystery with the special permission of the Earl of Marwell. It includes a full history of the Manor, details of the mysterious hauntings, and in-depth interviews with Samuel Sheridan, paranormal investigator, the Earl and his staff.

THE HISTORY OF MARWELL MANOR

THE HAUNTINGS

LADY ANNE'S SECRET PAPERS

IN-DEPTH INTERVIEWS

WHAT ACTUALLY HAPPENED

LIFE STORIES

OBJECTIVES

UNIT	SPELLING/VOCABULARY	GRAMMAR/ PUNCTUATION	COMPREHENSION/ COMPOSITION
REFERENCE AND RESEARCH SKILLS Life stories.	Distinguish between 'biography' and 'autobiography'.	Revise the difference between 1st and 3rd person narrative.	Investigate the etymology of 'biography' and 'autobiography'.

ORGANIZATION (1 HOUR)

INTRODUCTION	WHOLE-CLASS SKILLS WORK	DIFFERENTIATED GROUP ACTIVITIES	CONCLUSION
Read sample extracts from photocopiable page 87 of biography and autobiography. Establish as non-fiction genres. Discuss why we read and write about people's lives.	Identify the characteristic features of biography and autobiography.	1–4*: Work in pairs, first writing autobiographical text, then swapping and writing partner's piece as biographical text.	Share selected pieces of writing and identify in them characteristic features of the genres.

RESOURCES

Photocopiable page 87 (Life Stories), examples of biography and autobiography of people whose names the children are likely to recognize (these can be short – for example, biographical details about a famous person in an encyclopaedia or brief details given about an author or poet inside their book, or book-length – for example, the autobiography of a film, pop or sports personality), board or flip chart, OHP and acetate (optional), writing materials.

PREPARATION

Collect examples of biography and autobiography as outlined above. Make enough copies of photocopiable page 87 for one between two children. If possible, prepare the page as an OHT (or photocopied enlargement).

Introduction

Read aloud the short extracts of biography and autobiography from photocopiable page 87. (Do not, at this point, give out copies to the children.) Ask the children whether what you read was fiction or non-fiction. Having established the genres as non-fiction, ask the children what sort of non-fiction they are. Can they distinguish between the biography and autobiography? Now distribute copies of the sheet and, if possible, display it to focus class discussion. Read the page through again with the children. Then read some short representative extracts from the examples of biography and autobiography you have collected, and ask children whether they are biography (first-person or third-person) or autobiography.

Discuss the following questions:
■ What makes the lives of certain people interesting to you?
■ Why do you think someone would want to write about their own life for other people to read?
■ What can you learn about a person by reading about his or her life?

■ What do you think you might learn about yourself by exploring someone else's life?
■ Who would you choose to write a biography about? Why?
■ If you wrote an autobiography, who do you think might like to read it? Why?

Whole-class skills work

Write the words 'biography' and 'autobiography' on the board or flip chart and discuss the etymology of the two words (from the Greek *auto*: self; *bio*: life; *graph*: write).

Draw two webs on the board or flip chart around your 'biography' and 'autobiography' headings. Work with the children to complete the webs along the following lines:

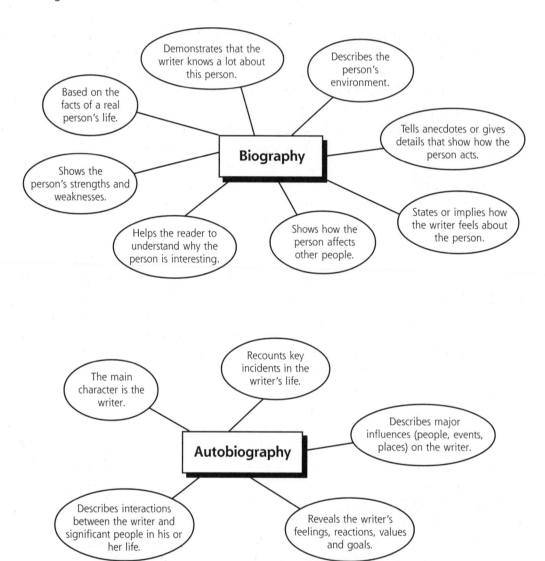

Differentiated group work

1–4*: Ask all the children to work in pairs within their groups. For the first half of the session, each child should write autobiographically about his or her life – or about a specific incident in his or her life. For the second half of the session, the partners should swap pieces of writing and each write their partner's autobiographical piece as a biographical piece. Encourage them to discuss the pieces if they need further information. For example, one child may have referred to 'my brother' in her autobiographical writing; her partner may wish to know the brother's name for her biographical piece.

Conclusion

Ask selected pairs to read their pieces. Refer back to the characteristic features webs that you created in the whole-class skills session and identify the characteristic features in the children's writing.

LIFE STORIES

Third-person biography

A third-person biography tells about a person that the writer may have met (for instance, to interview), but does not know personally. What the writer knows about that person has been gained from research.

Frances Hodgson Burnett was born in Manchester in 1849. When she was 16 her family emigrated to America, and Frances' hobby of writing stories earned her money when the stories were published in popular American magazines. She became famous when her first children's story, *Little Lord Fauntleroy*, was published in 1886. She came back to England for a while and lived in a large house called Maytham Hall, which had a walled garden. These surroundings inspired *The Secret Garden* which was the last and probably most popular of all her books. She died in 1924.

First-person biography

A first-person biography tells about a person that the writer knows personally and usually shows how that person has influenced or affected the writer's own life.

I knew, even from the first time I met Joshua Kentu, that he would be a famous footballer. I also knew that we would be lifelong friends, despite the fact that there is a world of differences in our backgrounds. The occasion of our meeting was an under-14's football match and we were playing on opposing teams. We ran into each other – quite literally! It was my fault entirely, and Josh would have been perfectly justified in beating me to a pulp. And he could have, because even then he was a physical powerhouse, but I know now the idea would never have entered his head. His first thought was for me – 'Hey man, you all right? That was some knock you gave us!'

Autobiography

Autobiography is always a first-person account because the writer is the subject of the narrative.

When anyone asks me where I'm from, or where I grew up, I have to answer: 'Most places.' Because it's true. From the time I was born in 1947 (a post-war baby) to the time I had my own second baby in 1976, I never lived in the same city, let alone the same house, for more than three years! But I remember each of the houses I have lived in (even the one I was born in), and attached to each one is at least one special memory. For example, outside the house where we lived when I was just beginning to discover the joys of reading, there was the most marvellous tree. Not only was it an excellent 'climber' (I broke my arm twice falling out of it!), but it also provided me with a special reading place. At the base of the huge trunk was a little hollow, just the right size for my bottom and back. I would snuggle up into it, hidden away by the tree's enormous foliage, and spend hours lost in other people's worlds.

ORIGINS OF PROPER NAMES

OBJECTIVES

UNIT	SPELLING/VOCABULARY	GRAMMAR/ PUNCTUATION	COMPREHENSION/ COMPOSITION
WORD PLAY Origins of proper names.	Investigate the origins of proper names.	Revise the conventions of Standard English.	Plan quickly and effectively the plot and characters of a piece of narrative writing.

ORGANIZATION (1 HOUR)

INTRODUCTION	WHOLE-CLASS SKILLS WORK	DIFFERENTIATED GROUP ACTIVITIES	CONCLUSION
Discuss names from the class list.	Examine place names and the names of products. Complete the 'Alphabetical Shopkeepers' framework using alliterative names.	1: Research origins of names on class list. 2*: Research origins of names used in partner's completed framework. 3: Design a poster for the chosen product. 4*: Use maps and dictionaries to complete framework.	Selected members of each group share their work, followed by a class discussion of how to present the work as a wall display.

RESOURCES

Photocopiable page 90 (Alphabetical Shopkeepers), map of the UK, local map, atlases, dictionaries of place names, surnames and first names, class list of children's names, board or flip chart, OHP and acetate (optional), writing materials.

PREPARATION

Prepare enough copies of the class list for Group 1 and enough copies of photocopiable page 90 (Alphabetical Shopkeepers) for Groups 2 and 4. If possible, make OHTs or A3 enlargements of both the photocopiable sheet and class list. Also, if possible, make OHTs of sample pages from the surnames, first names and place name dictionaries, preferably choosing pages that have relevance to various children's names in your class.

Introduction

Display the class list and ask each child to read out their own name. Ask the rest of the class to listen carefully, particularly to everyone's last name. Explain that, in most cases, our last names (or surnames) were given to us many years ago – some were given to us because of our ancestors' jobs (for example John Smith or Clare Baker) or because our ancestors lived near a particular place (for example Julie Hill, Joseph Wood). Are there any surnames from the class list whose origins are easy to explain in these terms?

Names from other countries may have similar origins and meanings. Do the children know any of these?

Do any of the children know the origin and meaning of their first name (for example Andrew – manly; Jane – gift of God)?

If possible, display the OHTs of the sample pages from the surnames and first names dictionaries and model how to use them.

Whole-class skills work

Display the maps of the UK and local area, pointing out that place names, too, have particular meanings – for example those containing '-borough', -'chester', '-ham', '-leigh', '-thorpe'. Use the place names dictionary to find out what these suffixes indicate. Refer to some local names and explain their meanings.

Now ask for volunteers to look for similar names on the maps. Write these on the board or flip chart and explain how to use the place names dictionary to find meanings. Choose one or two examples and then select children to find the meanings and write them on the board or flip chart.

Ask the children if they can think of any other kinds of proper names that are not of people or places – for example, names of products they might see in shops or advertised on television. Discuss how the product is often given a name that is associated with its best selling points – for example 'Jaguar' (fast and sleek). Make a list of these products.

Show the children the framework for 'Alphabetical Shopkeepers' on photocopiable page 90. Ask for volunteers to choose a letter and provide words for all the categories – for example:

My name is **Barbara**.
My husband's name is **Boris**.
We live in **Banbury**.
We sell **bicycles**
And we've lost our **budgie.**

Encourage them to have fun with words and add alliterative adjectives as well:

My name is **Zesty Zoe**.
My husband's name is **Zealous Zachariah**.
We live in a **Zambian zone**.
We sell **zigzag zebras.**
And we've lost our **zany zoo**!

Differentiated group activities

1: Work in pairs with the class list and dictionaries to research origins of the children's names.
2*: Work in pairs. Each partner fills in one or two sections of the 'Alphabetical Shopkeeper' photocopiable page. Partners then exchange verses and research the origins of the names their partner has used in their verse.
3: Choose a product and design a poster and advertising slogan which reflects the qualities of its name.
4*: Work in pairs to write sections of the 'Alphabetical Shopkeeper' sheet, using maps, atlases and dictionaries.

Conclusion

Selected members of each group present the outcomes of their group activities. Discuss with the class how the work might be presented as a wall display and arrange for time to do this outside of the hour.

ALPHABETICAL SHOPKEEPERS

My name is _____

My husband's name is _____

We live in _____

We sell _____

And we've lost our _____

My name is _____

My wife's name is _____

We live in _____

We sell _____

And we've lost our _____

My name is _____

My husband's name is _____

We live in _____

We sell _____

And we've lost our _____

My name is _____

My wife's name is _____

We live in _____

We sell _____

And we've lost our _____

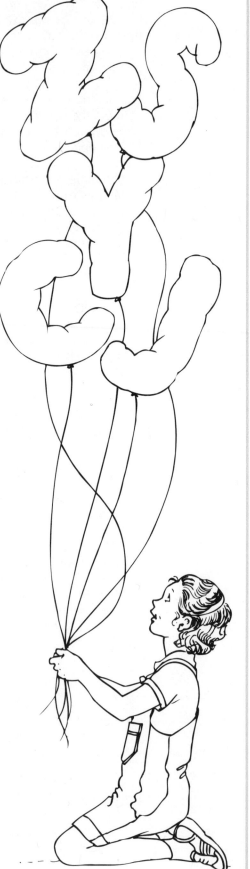

Term 2

THE FIRST CLASS IN ENGLISH

OBJECTIVES

UNIT	SPELLING/ VOCABULARY	GRAMMAR/ PUNCTUATION	COMPREHENSION/ COMPOSITION
READING FICTION Classic fiction: Extract from *Nicholas Nickleby* by Charles Dickens.	Extend vocabulary from reading. Create glossary.	Revise paragraphing. Revise simple, compound and complex sentences.	Read extract from longer established novel. Increase familiarity with significant writer of the past.

ORGANIZATION (3 HOURS)

	INTRODUCTION	WHOLE-CLASS SKILLS WORK	DIFFERENTIATED GROUP ACTIVITIES	CONCLUSION
HOUR 1	Introduce author. Shared reading of 'The First Class in English'.	Revise key writing skills: paragraphing, describing character and place, dialogue.	1*: Guided reading and discussion. 2 & 3: Write another scene in same style and language. 4*: Guided reading and discussion.	Selected pupils from Groups 2 & 3 share their next scenes.
HOUR 2	Re-read extract – preferably from original text.	Examine simple, compound and complex sentences.	1: Write another scene in same style and language. 2 & 3*: Guided reading and discussion. 4: Write another scene in same style and language.	Repeat some of the general discussion points with whole class.
HOUR 3	Discussion on simplifying text.	Compile glossary of difficult words in extract.	1*: Write simplified version of the next scene in chapter. 2 & 3: Simplify extract text for younger pupils. 4*: Simplify extract text for younger pupils.	Pupils read out different versions of texts. Class evaluation.

RESOURCES

Photocopiable pages 95 and 96 ('The First Class In English'), two or three copies of the original text of *Nicholas Nickleby* by Charles Dickens, OHP and acetate (optional), board or flip chart, writing materials.

PREPARATION

Photocopy enough copies of the story extract for one between two children. If possible, prepare text as OHT or enlarge to at least A3.

HOUR 1

Introduction

Briefly introduce the author, as follows:

Charles Dickens (1812–1870) is one of the most popular writers in the history of literature. Many of his books are well known, even to those who have never read them, through films and TV productions. For example, *A Christmas Carol* has been filmed several times, as well as turned into a musical and even a cartoon! Other well-known works are *Oliver Twist*, *Great Expectations* and *David Copperfield*. *Nicholas Nickleby*, from which the adapted extract used is taken, has been turned into a musical called *Smike*.

Read 'The First Class In English'.

Whole-class skills work

One of the aims of this unit is to provide a model for writing in the following writing unit (Victorian Story Cards). For this reason, the following key writing skills should be revised.

■ Paragraphing:

A paragraph is a section of writing that comprises sentences about a single idea, topic or scene. Each new paragraph represents a change of focus – in idea, time, place, character or speaker (in the case of dialogue). Although the formatting of paragraphs can be different in different pieces of writing, it is always consistent within one piece. Usually the first line of a paragraph is indented and there are no blank lines between paragraphs. Often the first paragraph of a story or chapter is *not* indented.

Analyse each paragraph and ask the children to give a reason why Dickens started a new paragraph at each point.

■ Describing character and place:

Remind the children that description is enhanced by the use of adjectives, adverbs, similes and metaphors, and by focusing on details that add to the reader's overall understanding of the text.

Ask children to find examples in the extract.

■ Dialogue:

Revise the punctuation and setting out of dialogue, and how to write interesting reporting clauses by using synonyms of 'said', adverbs, and phrases of description as appropriate.

Examine Dickens' use of dialogue in the extract.

Differentiated group activities

1*: Guided reading and discussion. Children could work from the original text. The following questions may be used as a starting point:
■ (If working from original text) which words and phrases are little used today? Which of the longer words are difficult?
■ In your own words, describe Dotheboy's Hall. How does it compare with your school?
■ Pick out the key words and phrases used to describe the children.
■ What kind of teacher was Mr Squeers?
■ What seems to be the main purpose of his 'system' of education?
■ What does Nicholas think to Squeers' 'system'?
■ How do you think the story might continue?
2 & 3: Write another short scene set in Dotheboy's Hall. Try to capture the style and language of the extract on the photocopiable pages.
4*: Guided reading and discussion (see above).

Conclusion

Ask selected children from Groups 2 and 3 to share some of their scenes set in Dotheboy's Hall. Comment on how the children's use of language and style have made them convincing 'follow-ons' to Dickens' writing.

Introduction

Re-read 'The First Class In English'. If the original book is available, the scene could be read out from it. As children have already worked with the slightly simplified version, they should be able to follow this. Follow this up by discussing style and language.

Whole-class skills work

Examine simple, compound and complex sentences.

A *simple sentence* contains one statement, for example:
What a Hell was breeding here!

A *compound sentence* contains two or more statements of equal importance joined by conjunctions (for example *and*, *but*) or a semi-colon, for example:
Smike shuffled out with the basin, and Mrs Squeers sent another little boy after him to bring wooden bowls.

A *complex sentence* contains a main clause or statement and a subordinate clause (or clauses), linked by subordinating conjunctions, for example:
After about half an hour, Mr Squeers came in...
Common subordinating conjunctions include: after, although, because, before, if, since, unless, until, when, while.

Ask the children to find other examples in the text. Simple sentences are easy to spot. Compound sentences can be identified by their use of *and* and *but*, and complex sentences by their use of subordinating conjunctions (see list above).

Differentiated group activities

1: Write another scene set in Dotheboy's Hall. Try to capture the style and language of Dickens' original text.
2 & 3*: Guided reading and discussion (see Hour 1).
4: Write another short scene set in Dotheboy's Hall.

Conclusion

Go over some of the discussion questions with the whole class, particularly the more general ones, for example, how do you think the story might continue?

Introduction

Explain to children that the text on the photocopiable pages has been slightly simplified from the original as follows: a few long and archaic words have been replaced with easier ones, and some of Dickens' very long complex and compound sentences have been shortened. Ask the children for what purposes they think texts might need to be adapted. What would they need to do to simplify the text for younger children, say children in Years 3 or 4?

In discussion with the children, work through the first paragraph as an example. The final result might be something like this:

Dotheboy's Hall was not a hall at all. It was a dirty room with broken windows. There were a few old desks for children and desks for Squeers and another teacher. The ceiling was like a barn's and the walls were dirty.

Whole-class skills work

Make a glossary of all the difficult words in the story and next to them write a simple word or phrase that can be used instead. This glossary will be used in the activities session.

Differentiated group activities

1*: Use the original text. Choose another scene, for example, the one immediately following in the chapter entitled 'The First Class Called Up' and write a slightly simplified version.
2 & 3: Simplify the extracted text on the photocopiable pages for use with younger children.
4*: As for Groups 2 and 3, but with teacher support.

Conclusion

Different versions of the text are read out and evaluated. The ideal way to do this is to try the texts out on Year 4 children if this can be arranged.

THE FIRST CLASS IN ENGLISH

Nicholas Nickleby is a new teacher at Dotheboy's Hall, a school for poor children, which is run by the cruel Wackford Squeers and his wife. This scene describes Nicholas' first impression of the school.

Dotheboy's Hall was not a hall at all, but a bare and dirty room with a couple of windows in which most of the glass was broken. There were a few old rickety desks, cut and notched, and inked and damaged, in every possible way; a detached desk for Squeers; and another for his assistant. The ceiling was supported, like that of a barn, by cross beams and rafters; and the walls were so stained that it was impossible to tell whether they had ever been painted or whitewashed.

But the pupils! How his last hopes faded as he looked around! Pale and haggard faces, lank and bony figures, children with the faces of old men, boys of stunted growth, and others whose long thin legs would hardly carry their stooping bodies, all crowded together; there were the bleary eye, the hare-lip, the crooked foot and every problem arising from cruelty and neglect. There were little faces which should have been handsome, darkened with the scowl of suffering; there were vicious-faced boys, brooding like prisoners in jail; and there were children who were weeping with loneliness. What a Hell was breeding here!

Mrs Squeers stood at one of the desks in front of a huge basin of brimstone and treacle, which she gave to every boy on a large wooden spoon. The boys had to stretch their mouths wide to take in the whole of the spoonful at one gasp, which they had to do, or face punishment.

'Now,' said Squeers, giving the desk a great rap with his cane, which made half the little boys nearly jump out of their skin, 'have they all taken their medicine?'

'Just finished,' said Mrs Squeers, choking the last boy in her hurry. 'Here, you Smike; take away the basin now. Look sharp!'

Smike shuffled out with the basin, and Mrs Squeers sent another little boy after him to bring wooden bowls.

Into these bowls, Mrs Squeers, helped by the hungry servant, poured out a brown mixture which looked like diluted pincushions, and she called porridge. A small wedge of brown bread was placed in each bowl, which they used to eat the porridge. When they had finished Mr Squeers said in a solemn voice, 'For what we have received, may the Lord make us truly thankful!' – and went away to his own breakfast.

Nicholas ate the porridge without appetite and sat down to wait for school time. He noticed how silent and sad the boys all seemed to be. There was none of the noise of a classroom; none of its boisterous play or hearty laughter. The children sat shivering together, and seemed to lack the spirit to move about. The only pupil who showed any sign of playfulness was Master Squeers who amused himself by treading on other boys' toes with his new boots.

After about half an hour, Mr Squeers came in, and the boys took their places and got out their books, which they had to share one between eight. After a few minutes, during which Mr Squeers looked very serious, as though he knew everything that was in the books by heart, he called up the first class.

Obediently a group of half-a-dozen scarecrows, their clothes torn at knees and elbows, sat themselves before Squeers' desk, and one of them placed a torn and filthy book in front of him.

'This is the first class in English spelling and philosophy, Nickleby,' said Squeers. 'We'll start a Latin class and hand that over to you. Now, then, where's the first boy?'

'Please, sir, he's cleaning the back parlour window,' said a small voice.

'So he is, to be sure,' replied Squeers. 'We go upon the practical mode of teaching, Nickleby; the regular education system. C-l-e-a-n, clean, verb active, to make bright, to scour. W-i-n, win, d-e-r, der, winder, a casement. When the boy knows this out of a book, he goes and does it. Where's the second boy?'

'Please, sir, he's weeding the garden,' came the reply.

'To be sure,' said Squeers, 'so he is. B-o-t, bot, t-i-n, tin, bottin, n-e-y, bottinney, noun, a knowledge of plants. When he has learned that bottinney means a knowledge of plants he goes and knows 'em. That's our system, Nickleby; what do you think of it?'

'It's a very useful one at any rate,' replied Nicholas.

'Third boy, what's a horse?'

'A beast, sir,' replied the boy.

'So it is,' said Squeers. 'Ain't it, Nickleby?'

'There is no doubt of that, sir,' answered Nicholas.

'Of course there isn't,' said Squeers. 'A horse is a quadruped, and quadruped's Latin for beast, as everybody that's learned Latin grammar knows, or what's the use of having grammars at all?'

'What indeed!' said Nicholas in disbelief.

'As you're perfect in that,' said Squeers turning to the boy, 'go and look after my horse, and rub him down well, or I'll rub you down – with my cane! The rest of the class go and draw water from the well until somebody tells you to stop. It's washing day tomorrow.'

So saying, he sent the class off to their work, and looked at Nicholas as though he was wondering what he thought.

'That's the way we do it, Nickleby,' he said after a pause, 'and a very good way it is too! Now, just take those fourteen little boys and hear some reading, because you must begin to be useful. Idling about here won't do.'

The children were soon arranged in a semicircle around the new teacher, and he was soon listening to their dull, drawling, hesitating recital of those dull as ditchwater stories which are found in old reading books.

The morning dragged slowly on in this tedious work, until, at one o'clock, the boys went to lunch in the kitchen where they were given some hard salt beef. After this, there was another hour of sitting in the classroom and shivering with cold.

Adapted from Nicholas Nickleby *by Charles Dickens*

VICTORIAN STORY CARDS

OBJECTIVES

UNIT	SPELLING/ VOCABULARY	GRAMMAR/ PUNCTUATION	COMPREHENSION/ COMPOSITION
WRITING FICTION Victorian Story Cards.	Extend vocabulary from reading. Use glossary.	Revise first- and third-person pronouns. Extend writing of dialogue.	Revise key writing skills and story structures. Write own story using story read as model.

ORGANIZATION (3 HOURS)

	INTRODUCTION	WHOLE-CLASS SKILLS WORK	DIFFERENTIATED GROUP ACTIVITIES	CONCLUSION
HOUR 1	Model oral story-telling activity using Victorian Story Cards.	Revise writing in first and third person.	1–4: All groups play with Victorian Story Cards. *Teacher supports Groups 1 & 4.	One child from each of Groups 1 & 4 tells their story.
HOUR 2	One child from each of Groups 2 & 3 tells their story.	Demonstrate how to transfer oral story onto Story Planner. Pupils plan own story.	All pupils turn oral story into written story. 1: Emulate language and style of Dickens, using words from glossary compiled in previous unit. 2 & 3*: As for Group 1. 4: Follow the Story Planner closely.	Good examples of beginnings written by pupils in Groups 2 & 3 read out.
HOUR 3	Read part of extract from previous unit from 'This is the first class...' to 'It's washing day tomorrow'. Discuss written form of dialogue.	All pupils write short dialogue between pupil and teacher.	1–4: All groups finish first draft. Teacher works with Group 4*.	Selected pupils read out first draft followed by discussion.

RESOURCES

Photocopiable pages 100–103 (Victorian Story Cards), 104 (Story Planner), 95 and 96 ('The First Class in English' from previous unit), OHP and acetate (optional), board or flip chart, sturdy card, lamination, scissors, writing materials.

PREPARATION

Photocopiable pagess 100–103 (Victorian Story Cards) should be printed onto card, laminated and cut into sets. One set per group of four or five children is needed. Make enough copies of the Story Planner (page 104) for one per child and, if possible, prepare it and the story from the previous unit as OHTs.

Introduction

The main aim of this unit is to revise key writing skills introduced in the 'Pleasant Afternoon' unit (Term 1), particularly skills of planning and structuring stories. The

Victorian Story Cards offer stimulus for ideas, and the Story Planner provides a template for some of the main story structures children have studied. The previous unit, 'The First Class in English' can be used as a model for an appropriate style.

Begin arranging the class into groups of four to five children, broadly according to ability, but overlapping where necessary to create groups of the required size. Then model the oral story-telling activity using the set of cards prepared from pages 100–103. Demonstrate the procedure by taking one group of children through the following process while others watch.

■ Shuffle each set of cards (CHARACTER, PLACE, OBJECT and SITUATION) separately and place the sets face down in the middle of the table.

■ The first player takes the top card from each set and places them face up in front of him/her.

■ The player must make up an oral story using all the cards (the teacher should do this during the demonstration session). The story should be told in the *first person*. (Remind the children what a story in the first person means. In this case, it means that the storyteller – the child – is a key character in the story, and he or she will tell the story from his or her point of view, using 'I'.)

■ Continue the game clockwise around the table.

■ When everyone has had a turn, decide whose was the best story.

■ The rest of the group should then help that person to prepare the story for presentation to the class or other groups.

Explain that by playing the game the children are preparing story structures with a beginning, middle and end, and that each story should have characters, a plot and setting.

Whole-class skills work

Use the following table to help children understand the difference between first and third person:

Personal pronouns

	SINGULAR	PLURAL
First person	I	we
Second person	you	you
Third person	he/she/it	they

A story in the first person might begin as follows:

I walked into the gloomy schoolroom and sat down on a wooden bench. The teacher gave **me** a slate to write on.

The same story in the third person would begin like this:

He walked into the gloomy schoolroom and sat down on a wooden bench. The teacher gave **him** a slate to write on.

A story written in the first person gives the impression of personal experience but the point of view is limited to one person. A story in the third person gives the author the freedom to write about anything, even things the main character does not know about.

Differentiated group activities

1–4*: All groups play the Victorian Story Cards game and tell their orally-composed stories to each other. The teacher works with Groups 1 and 4.

Conclusion

Choose one child from each of Groups 1 and 4 to tell his/her oral story to the whole class. The rest of the class should listen carefully and positive comment should be invited. For example, ask the class: 'What did you like about that story? What indications were there in the story that it was set in Victorian times?'

Introduction

Choose one child from each of Groups 2 and 3 to tell his/her oral story to the whole class. Discuss and evaluate the stories as described above.

Whole-class skills work

Explain that the oral stories are going to be developed into written stories. The first step is to plan a story with a good beginning, middle and end.

Give a copy of the Story Planner to all children. Remind them of the different stories they have studied. Explain that the boxes in the planner are to help them plan their story. Help children to do this by taking one of the oral stories from the Introduction and demonstrating how it could be transferred onto the Story Planner.

Ask children to plan their own stories. Children in Group 1 should be encouraged to adapt the structure freely, or to write a plan in a completely different way, if they wish. Children in Groups 2 and 3 should be encouraged to follow the basic structure, but write several paragraphs in each section. Children in Group 4 should follow the planner closely, writing one paragraph for each section. Explain to all children that they can develop or change their oral stories in any way, and can borrow ideas from the stories they heard at the end of Hour 1 or the beginning of this hour.

Differentiated group activities

Children in all groups begin to turn their oral story into a written story.
1: If the previous unit has been done recently, children should try to emulate the language and style of Dickens by borrowing some of his vocabulary (see the glossary compiled when reading the extract from *Nicholas Nickleby* on photocopiable pages 95 and 96) and trying to imitate his long sentences.
2 & 3*: As for Group 1, but concentrating on the vocabulary.
4: Children should follow the Story Planner closely.

Conclusion

Good examples of beginnings written by children in Groups 2 and 3 should be read out to the class. Invite the other children to say what they liked about them. Comment on effective features and encourage other children to use them. Children from the same groups (who will have heard the oral version of the story) could be invited to comment on the differences between the oral and written versions.

Introduction

Read 'The First Class In English' from 'This is the first class...' to 'It's washing day tomorrow.' (photocopiable pages 95 and 96). Discuss:
■ how dialogue is set out on separate indented lines for alternate speakers
■ how dialogue is punctuated
■ how Dickens writes interesting reporting clauses using synonyms of 'said', adverbs and phrases of description
■ how Dickens tries to make the dialogue sound true to life.

Whole-class skills work

Model dialogue writing by developing with the class a short dialogue between a pupil and a teacher. They should aim to consolidate what they know at whatever level they are working and go one step further on the following hierarchy of skills.
■ Place speech marks before and after words.
■ Begin direct speech with a capital letter.
■ Use additional punctuation when necessary.
■ Use synonyms of 'said' in the reporting clause where appropriate.
■ Use adverbs and phrases of description in the reporting clause where appropriate.

Differentiated group activities

1–4: Children in all groups finish the first draft of their stories, taking particular care with the writing of dialogue. *The teacher works with Group 4.

Conclusion

Ask selected children from all groups to read out their first draft. Follow up each reading with discussion and suggestions for further revision.

VICTORIAN STORY CARDS 1

Character

Mr Fortesque

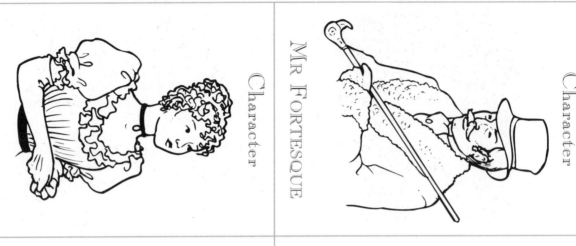

Character

Mrs Fortesque

Character

Master Fortesque

Character

Miss Fortesque

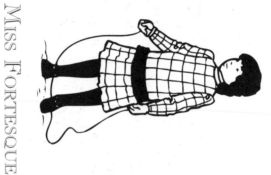

Character

Tom

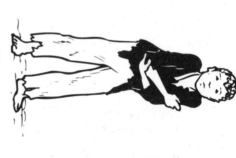

Character

Molly

Character

Sam

Character

Sally

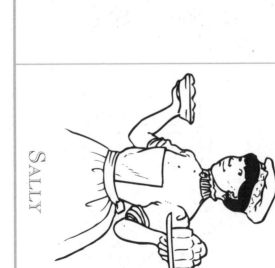

VICTORIAN STORY CARDS 2

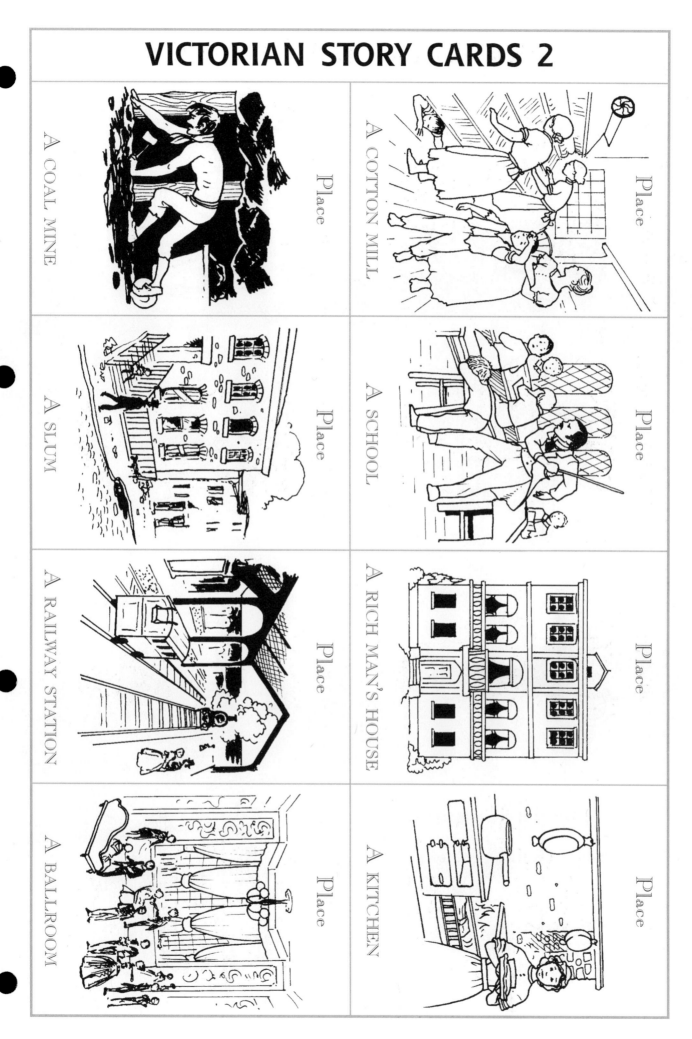

A COAL MINE — Place

A COTTON MILL — Place

A SLUM — Place

A SCHOOL — Place

A RAILWAY STATION — Place

A RICH MAN'S HOUSE — Place

A BALLROOM — Place

A KITCHEN — Place

VICTORIAN STORY CARDS 3

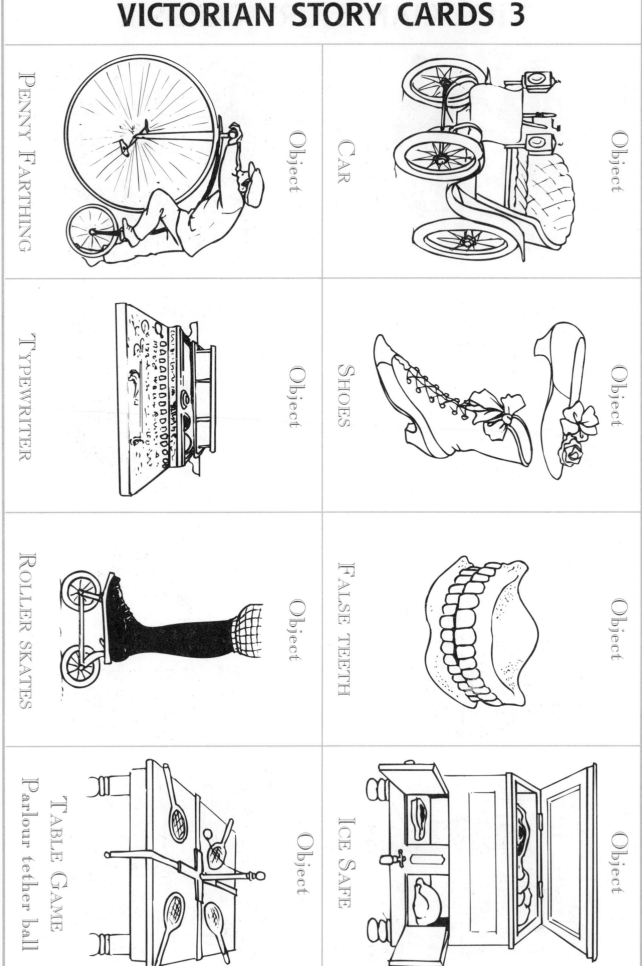

Object

PENNY FARTHING

Object

CAR

Object

TYPEWRITER

Object

SHOES

Object

ROLLER SKATES

Object

FALSE TEETH

Object

TABLE GAME
Parlour tether ball

Object

ICE SAFE

VICTORIAN STORY CARDS 4

Situation

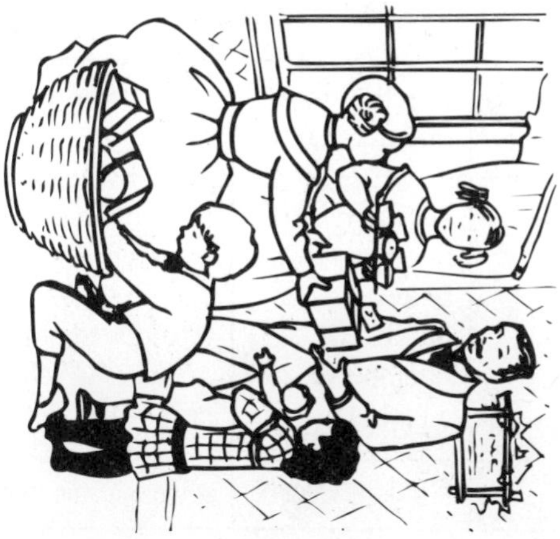

A RUNAWAY CHILD

Situation

CHRISTMAS DAY

Situation

A RAINY DAY

Situation

A FIRE

Situation

TROUBLE AT T'MILL

Situation

A CHOLERA OUTBREAK

CHOLERA
WARNING
Cleanse Everything
Daily

Situation

A HOLIDAY

Situation

A JOURNEY

STORY PLANNER

■ Study this grid to remind you of some of the different kinds of plot you have studied.

Beginning	Description of main character	Description of a place	Dialogue	Action
Middle	Description of a place. Describing a problem. Attempts to solve a problem.	Description of the main character. Describing a problem. Dialogue about a problem. Attempts to solve a problem.	Description of place or character. Describing a problem. Dialogue about the problem. Build up the suspense.	Description of place or character. Describing a problem. Attempts to solve the problem. Two different approaches to the problem by two characters.
End	Problem solved.	A twist in the tale.	Anti-climax.	Main character succeeds.

■ Use this grid to plan your new story.

Beginning	
Middle	
End	

GOLDEN ARROW PUBLICATIONS

OBJECTIVES

UNIT	SPELLING/ VOCABULARY	GRAMMAR/ PUNCTUATION	COMPREHENSION/ COMPOSITION
REDRAFTING SIMULATION 'Golden Arrow Publications'.	Identify misspelled words in own writing.	Revise structure and paragraphing. Revise all parts of speech, verb tenses and first- and third-person viewpoints. Revise punctuation, including that for dialogue.	Review, edit and evaluate own writing. Redraft content and format.

ORGANIZATION (3 HOURS)

	INTRODUCTION	WHOLE-CLASS SKILLS WORK	DIFFERENTIATED GROUP ACTIVITIES	CONCLUSION
HOUR 1	Explain purpose of simulation and read text 'Golden Arrow Publications' on photocopiable page 108.	Revise work on structure.	1–4*: All pupils work collaboratively to write a version of the Young Writers' Guide, appropriate to their individual level.	One style guide topic from each group read out in full. Rest of the class evaluates.
HOUR 2	Re-read style guide, emphasizing publisher's brief.	Revise all parts of speech, verb tenses and first- and third-person viewpoints.	1–4*: All pupils write story to fit brief.	One pupil from each group reads out story. Rest of the class evaluates.
HOUR 3	Recap on important points raised in the guides of each group. Explain how to use guides as redrafting checklist.	Revise basic and advanced punctuation, including punctuation of dialogue.	1–4*: All pupils work in pairs to redraft their work, using own guides as checklist.	Each group selects one story which best fits publisher's criteria. These are read out.

RESOURCES

Photocopiable pages 108 ('Golden Arrow Publications') and 109 (Redrafting Checklist), OHP and acetate (optional), board or flip chart, writing materials.

PREPARATION

Make enough copies of photocopiable page 108 ('Golden Arrow Publications') for one for each child and enough of photocopiable page 109 (Redrafting Checklist) for one between two.

Introduction

The text on photocopiable page 108 ('Golden Arrow Publications') is based on the style guides often circulated by publishers to prospective authors. Its purpose is to set up a simulation which will lead to children writing their own guides to content and presentation in story writing, thus enabling them to articulate and consolidate, at their own level, what they have already learned. The children will then use their own guides as a basis for story writing and redrafting.

Begin by explaining the purpose of the simulation, and then share the text on photocopiable page 108 ('Golden Arrow Publications').

Whole-class skills work

Use this session to revise previous work on story structures. Depending on the needs of your pupils, you might, for example, choose to focus on one or several of the following aspects:
- different ways of beginning a story
- how setting and characters are established
- how the middle of a story is told – for example chronologically, as a flashback, as a dream
- how the paragraphs in a story are linked
- different ways of ending a story.

Differentiated group activities

1–4*: All children, working in their groups and at their own level, write their own version of the Young Writers' Guide, the content outline of which is indicated in the last section of 'Golden Arrow Publications' (photocopiable page 108). Give each child a copy of the photocopiable page and provide also at least one copy between two children of photocopiable page 109 (Redrafting Checklist).
- Begin by choosing topics from the headings listed in the Young Writers' Guide on photocopiable page 108 (children in Group 1 should choose the more challenging topics, and children in Group 4 should choose easier topics, but all should try to provide a wide enough range of information to help a young writer).
- The Redrafting Checklist should be available for reference.
- Children can discuss ideas in their groups and help each other, but each child should produce his or her own version of·the guide.

Conclusion

Ask each group to report back on the topics it has chosen. Select one of these topics to be read out in full. The rest of the class should be asked to evaluate the following:
- Has the group included a wide enough range of information?
- Is the information accurate?
- Is it expressed in a clear and helpful way?

Introduction

Re-read the style guide from 'Golden Arrow Publications' (photocopiable page 108) with a particular focus on the brief given by the publisher. Ask the children to pick out the crucial bits of information and list these on the board or flip chart.

Whole-class skills work

Use this session to revise previous work on grammar. Depending on the needs of your children, you might, for example, focus on one or several of the following aspects:
- parts of speech, particularly those used to enhance description (adjective, adverb), and those used to extend sentences (conjunctions, prepositions and connectives)
- verb tenses
- narrative viewpoints: such as first and third person.

Differentiated group activities

1–4*: All children should write a story to fit the publisher's brief on photocopiable page 108. They should follow their own helpful advice which they wrote in the previous hour!

Conclusion

Aim for one child from each group to read out their stories, or as much of the story as they have written so far. The rest of the class should evaluate how closely the story meets the publisher's brief.

Introduction

Invite one or two children from each group to read out their Young Writers' Guide in full. Highlight some of the important points raised in the guides and, if you feel it necessary, fill in any serious gaps. Explain that the children have, in fact, created their own redrafting checklists by writing these guides and that the guides should be used in that way for redrafting their own stories.

■ First, each child checks through his/her story using his/her own guide as a redrafting checklist.

■ Then stories should be exchanged and the children help each other to check. Ideas from both guides can be consulted.

Whole-class skills work

Use this session to revise previous work on punctuation. Depending on the needs of your pupils, you might, for example, choose to focus on one or several of the following aspects:

■ basic punctuation (use of commas, apostrophes, and so on)

■ more advanced punctuation (use of colon, semi-colon, dash, hyphen, and so on)

■ punctuation of dialogue.

Differentiated group activities

1–4*: Children should work in pairs within groups to help each other to redraft their work, using their own guides as a redrafting checklist.

Note: it does not matter if stories are not finished at this stage.

Conclusion

Explain to the class that they are now going to role-play the publisher's selection process. This should be done as follows.

■ Each group shares its stories and selects one which *best fits the publisher's criteria.*

■ These are then read out to the whole class.

FURTHER IDEA

Each child could produce a one-page summary of his/her guide which could be pasted inside his/her exercise book as a redrafting checklist for regular use.

GOLDEN ARROW PUBLICATIONS

SHORT STORIES BY YOUNG PEOPLE: STYLE GUIDE

We are inviting contributions to a short story anthology which will be entitled: *Short Stories by Young People*. The following notes will help you to prepare your submission in an appropriate way. Your completed manuscript should be sent to the address on the accompanying letter by the deadline stated in the final paragraph.

CONTENT

We are looking for stories based on the everyday experiences of young people between the ages of 10 and 14. Here are some examples of the things you might write about:

- a problem at school
- a family argument
- a new friendship
- an adventure
- a holiday that went wrong
- a strange experience.

The characters should be true-to-life, and of the kind that young readers of today can identify with. The settings can be anywhere in modern Britain, either town or country, but in all cases they should seem real to the reader. Stories can be written in either the third or first person, but personal anecdote is unlikely to be suitable. Therefore if you decide to use the first person, make sure that the characters and events are fictional. Length of stories should be between 200 and 500 words.

THE MANUSCRIPT

Usually, we request that manuscripts be prepared using a word processor, but because of the age range of the contributors for this project, we will accept hand-written submissions.

However, the text must be double-spaced (leave alternate lines blank) to allow space for proof-reader's corrections. If you are able to send an electronic version of your manuscript, this should be supplied on disk or via e-mail. In this case, however, a printed hard copy should also be submitted. While Golden Arrow Publications will take every care of your manuscript, we can accept no responsibility for its loss – so please ensure that you *keep a copy*. Golden Arrow Publications will proof-read and correct your manuscript; however, manuscripts which contain many errors of grammar, spelling, punctuation and layout will be placed immediately in File 13 (the wastepaper bin!).

THE YOUNG WRITERS' GUIDE

We recognize that young writers may need more help than our established authors, and therefore enclose a copy of 'The Young Writers' Guide'. This includes help on many aspects of content and presentation, for example:

- how to make up an effective plot
- how to write vivid descriptions of people and places
- how to write interesting beginnings
- how to write satisfying endings
- how to write effective dialogue
- how to write correct sentences
- how to divide your story into paragraphs
- how to use capital letters and punctuation correctly
- how to avoid some common grammatical errors
- how to check and improve your spelling.

REDRAFTING CHECKLIST

■ Work through this checklist first by yourself, then with a partner.

PART 1: CONTENT

■ Find descriptions of people and places. Is there enough detail to help the reader imagine what they look like?

■ Find the action in the story. Is it described in enough detail? Investigate synonyms for some of the verbs to find better alternatives. Could adverbs be added to good effect?

■ Is the reader kept informed about how the characters feel?

■ Find the nouns. Add adjectives where appropriate.

■ Is there a place where a simile or metaphor would make description more vivid?

■ Look at the dialogue. Would a synonym of 'said' be more effective? Would it be effective to add an adverb to the reporting clause?

PART 2: GRAMMAR, PUNCTUATION & SPELLING

■ Is the story written in sentences and paragraphs?

■ Is the sentence construction clear? Would it be better to break up a part of the story into statements and put it back together again using appropriate conjunctions?

■ Have capital letters been used for beginning sentences, names, places, days, months, and special occasions?

■ Are speech marks used before and after words actually spoken?

■ Does speech begin with a capital letter?

■ Is there a comma, full stop, question mark or exclamation mark before final speech marks?

■ Have apostrophes been used to show missing letters in contractions?

■ Is 's used to show ownership?

■ Check the spelling.

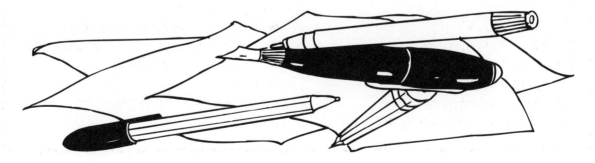

SHAKESPEARE'S THEATRE

OBJECTIVES

UNIT	SPELLING/ VOCABULARY	GRAMMAR/ PUNCTUATION	COMPREHENSION/ COMPOSITION
READING NON-FICTION 'Shakespeare's Theatre'.	Develop new vocabulary from reading.	Understand use of past tense in text. Identify sequencing words. Understand features of formal language.	Read and understand information text. Revise features of non-fiction recount. Interpret visual information. Write public information leaflet.

ORGANIZATION (3 HOURS)

	INTRODUCTION	WHOLE-CLASS SKILLS WORK	DIFFERENTIATED GROUP ACTIVITIES	CONCLUSION
HOUR 1	Read Part 1 of 'Shakespeare's Theatre' on photocopiable page 113.	Identify non-fiction genre of text and its characteristic features.	1–4*: Work in pairs to compare Globe Theatre and modern theatre, according to ability.	Share comparisons.
HOUR 2	Re-read Part 1 and read Part 2 of 'Shakespeare's Theatre'.	Examine formal, impersonal style of text.	1–4*: Work in groups of three or four to complete Globe reconstruction activity outlined in Part 2 of 'Shakespeare's Theatre'.	Display OHT of reconstructed Globe and compare with children's own.
HOUR 3	Re-read Part 1 of 'Shakespeare's Theatre'. Discuss rebuilding of Globe theatre.	Discuss stylistic and presentational features of a leaflet informing public of re-opening of Globe theatre and its amenities.	1-4*: Work in groups of three or four to write public information leaflet.	Share examples of leaflets and evaluate their effectiveness.

RESOURCES

Photocopiable pages 113 and 114 ('Shakespeare's Theatre: Parts 1 and 2') and page 1115 (New Globe Yard Level Plan), board or flip chart, OHP and acetate (optional), examples of leaflets about local amenities, tourist attractions, leisure facilities and so on (of the sort found in tourist information offices), writing materials.

PREPARATION

Prepare enough copies of photocopiable pages 113 and 114 ('Shakespeare's Theatre: Parts 1 and 2') for one between two children. If possible, prepare those pages and page 115 (New Globe Yard Level Plan) as OHTs or A3 photocopies to use as posters for focusing whole-class work.

Introduction

Read Part 1 of the reference text 'Shakespeare's Theatre' on photocopiable page 113. Then re-read it, telling pupils to listen very carefully to the description and asking them to imagine what Shakespeare's Globe would have looked like. Briefly discuss the differences between the Globe and a modern theatre.

Whole-class skills work

Discuss what type of text 'Shakespeare's Theatre' is and establish that it is non-fiction. What kind of non-fiction text is it? (It has features of both report and recount genres, but is predominantly the latter.) Revise the relevant key features (introduction to orientate reader; chronological sequence; supporting illustrations; degree of formality adopted; use of connectives and so on) and find examples in the text.

Differentiated group activities

All children work in pairs according to their ability to compare the Globe with a modern theatre.

1*: Write an essay about the differences between Shakespeare's Globe theatre and a modern theatre.

■ Begin with a brief description of the Globe (this could be a summary of the first three paragraphs of the text).
■ Take each key point and explain how a modern theatre would be different.
■ Explain the reasons for reconstructing the Globe when a modern theatre is so much more comfortable.

2 & 3: As above, but omitting point 3.

4*: Make a list of the differences between Shakespeare's Globe theatre and a modern theatre.

Conclusion

Discuss the differences between the Globe and a modern theatre – have the pupils missed anything (for example women's parts were played by boys in Shakespeare's time, but by women today)?

Introduction

Re-read Part 1 and read Part 2 of 'Shakespeare's Theatre'. Look at the illustrations and sketch and discuss what information can be gained from them. Discuss the following points.

■ Picture 1 shows the Globe as a smooth circular building. How do we know this picture is not completely accurate? How was the Globe shaped, and what is the evidence for this?
■ Picture 2 is a sketch of the inside of the Swan theatre. Compare this with Picture 1. How do we know that the Swan was smaller than the Globe? (The Tiring House of the Globe has a double roof.)

Whole-class skills work

Examine the use of impersonal style in reference texts by discussing the following questions.
■ Who wrote this text? (We don't know; the author's name is not given. This is often the case in encyclopaedias and so on. Even when the author's name is given, the style is not much different and we usually don't recognize the name.)
■ Is the style of this text different in any way from similar reference texts? (No – it is written in a 'standard' impersonal style in which the author never refers to himself/herself or his/her personal views and opinions.)
■ Why is the impersonal style effective for reference texts? (Because the reader wants information not personal opinion.)
　Conclude by pointing out that pupils should try to adopt this impersonal style for their own information writing.

Differentiated group activities

1–4*: Tell all the children to work in small groups of three or four, following the instructions on photocopiable page 114 ('Shakespeare's Theatre: Part 2') to reconstruct the Globe theatre.

Conclusion

Display the OHT or enlarged photocopy of photocopiable page 115 (New Globe Yard Level Plan). Compare and contrast with the children's own reconstructions and with the pictures of Shakespeare's original Globe.

Introduction

Re-read Part 1 of 'Shakespeare's Theatre' and discuss with the children why they think the Globe theatre was recently reconstructed. What would have been the arguments for reconstruction and who might have put those forward? What might the arguments have been against it and who might have disagreed with the reconstruction plans? You might wish to list these in grid form on the board or flip chart.

Whole-class skills work

Explain to the children that, in the group activities session, they are going to write an information leaflet, of the sort that might be found in a tourist information office, that explains to the public about the reconstruction of the theatre, its importance to the community and its amenities. Distribute the examples you have collected and discuss their characteristic features.

Ask the children to bear these features in mind when they write their own leaflets.

Differentiated group activities

1–4*: All children should work in small groups of three or four to write a public information leaflet about the reconstructed Globe theatre.

Conclusion

Selected explanations are read out, discussed and evaluated.

FURTHER IDEAS

■ Find out more about the Globe theatre and its reconstruction. Make a simple model of the Globe theatre.
■ Read a re-telling of a Shakespeare play and discuss how it might have been performed in the original Globe theatre.

SHAKESPEARE'S THEATRE: PART 1

Shakespeare's theatre, the Globe, was very different to a modern theatre. In *Henry the Fifth*, written for the Globe, Shakespeare called the theatre a 'wooden O'. First opened in 1599, it was a large, circular, wooden building with space in the middle that was open to the sky, allowing light to fall on the stage. All plays took place in daylight as artificial light was neither bright enough nor safe enough to use in a theatre. The roof covered only the outside galleries and part of the stage. If it rained, then part of the audience simply got wet! On the roof was a flagpole, and a flag would be flown to show that a play was about to start.

Most of the audience stood on the ground around the stage. They were called 'groundlings'. They were often rowdy and noisy, so Shakespeare filled his plays with action and humour to keep their attention. People who could afford higher prices went in the galleries where they had a bench to sit on and a roof to keep off the rain.

There was no scenery and very few props. However, the front of the 'tiring house' – the building at the back of the stage – had doors and a balcony and could be used to represent both the inside and outside of most buildings. For costumes, the actors wore either their everyday clothes or whatever they could find. So there was often a very odd mix of styles and periods of dress on stage! Women were not allowed on stage in Shakespeare's time, so all women's parts were played by boys.

In 1613 the old Globe theatre burned to the ground after being set on fire by a spark from a cannon during a performance of *Henry VIII*. It was soon rebuilt, but was pulled down in 1644 to make room for houses. But that was not the end of the Globe! In 1989 the remains of the Globe were discovered under Anchor Terrace, a nineteenth-century listed building. It was possible to excavate only 5 per cent of the Globe's foundations; the rest had to be mapped by radar. The little that was dug up, however, showed that the Globe was a 20-sided building of approximately 30 metres (100 feet) in diameter. The rest of the reconstruction was based on a few old engravings.

The campaign to rebuild the Globe was led by an American, Sam Wanamaker. After painstaking work on reconstructing the original accurately enough to draw up plans, the new Globe was built. As Anchor Terrace could not be pulled down, the new Globe was built on a site as near as possible to the original. Every attempt has been made to make the new Globe as authentic as possible: there are none of the lighting or acoustic elements of modern technology and everything has been designed to replicate as closely as possible the theatre of Shakespeare's time. Even the walls are of wood and plaster and the roof is thatched with Norfolk reed. It is the first building in London to have a thatched roof since the Great Fire of London in 1666!

The new Globe theatre staged its first production, *The Two Gentlemen of Verona*, in 1996, and since then over 300,000 visitors from all over the world have seen Shakespeare's plays in the theatre they were written for.

SHAKESPEARE'S THEATRE: PART 2

Can you reconstruct the Globe? Do this by following the guide below.

■ Look at Picture 1. This gives some idea what the outside of the Globe looked like.

■ Look at Picture 2. This is a picture of the inside of a theatre that existed about the same time as the Globe. It had features similar to the Globe and can be used to reconstruct the Globe. Try to estimate the width and height of the theatre and the size of the stage by assuming that the standing figure is approximately 2 metres tall.

■ Look at Picture 3. This is a design for a similar stage, but showing more detail than Picture 2.

From your study of the pictures, try to produce the following:

■ a plan view of the new Globe theatre with dimensions

■ a sketch of the inside

■ a sketch of the outside.

Finally, compare your work with the plan of the reconstructed new Globe.

Picture 1
The Globe theatre (after engraving by Hollar)

Picture 2
Inside of Swan theatre
▼

Picture 3
Rhetoric stage
▼

NEW GLOBE YARD LEVEL PLAN

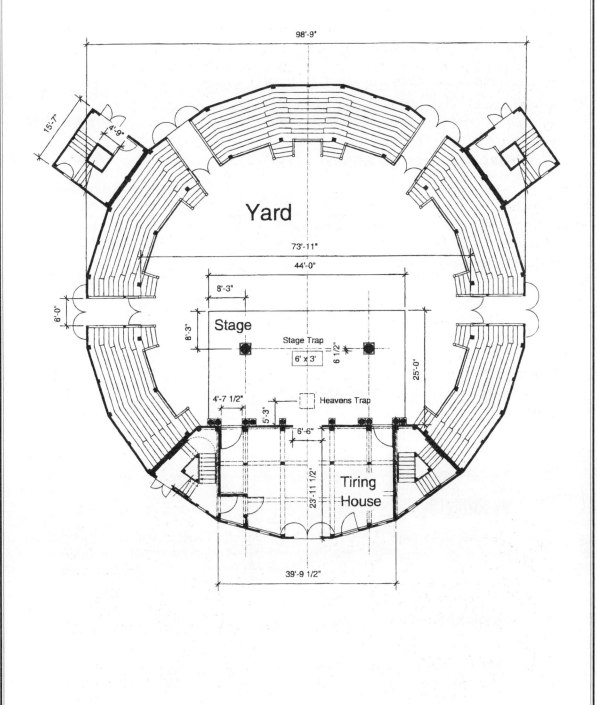

98'-9"

15'-7"

4'-9"

Yard

73'-11"

44'-0"

8'-3"

6'-0"

8'-3"

Stage

Stage Trap

6 1/2"

6' x 3'

25'-0"

4'-7 1/2"

Heavens Trap

5'-3"

6'-6"

23'-11 1/2"

Tiring
House

39'-9 1/2"

Reproduced by kind permision of Jon Greenfield (architect) for Pentagram Design

DESIGN A CD-ROM PAGE

OBJECTIVES

UNIT	SPELLING/ VOCABULARY	GRAMMAR/ PUNCTUATION	COMPREHENSION/ COMPOSITION
WRITING NON-FICTION Design a CD-ROM page.	Develop IT-related vocabulary. Develop and extend knowledge of acronyms.	Compare layout features of print and IT information texts.	Compare features of non-fiction texts in print and IT. Write text for a CD-ROM encyclopaedia page.

ORGANIZATION (2 HOURS)

	INTRODUCTION	WHOLE-CLASS SKILLS WORK	DIFFERENTIATED GROUP ACTIVITIES	CONCLUSION
HOUR 1	Display and read the example CD-ROM page on photocopiable page 119. Discuss features and specific vocabulary related to CD-ROM encyclopaedias. Compare print and IT versions of information texts.	Discuss and extend knowledge of acronyms.	1–4*: Research and plan information for a CD-ROM page.	Share information and planning ideas.
HOUR 2	Re-read photocopiable page 119. Discuss the layout of information.	Revise characteristic features of information texts and related vocabulary.	1: Design and write CD-ROM page including 'pop-up' screens. 2 & 3*: As for 1 with teacher support. 4: Design and write main page only.	Share and discuss CD-ROM pages.

RESOURCES

Photocopiable page 119 (CD-ROM Encyclopaedia Page), a selection of books and CD-ROM encyclopaedias (if available) giving background information on William Shakespeare, computers with CD-ROM drives (optional), dictionaries, board or flip chart, writing materials.

PREPARATION

Make enough copies of photocopiable page 119 (CD-ROM Encyclopaedia Page) for one each. Additionally, prepare writing templates for children in Group 4, by covering over the specific 'Article', 'See also' and 'Caption' text on the photocopiable page and making sufficient copies for the children in Group 4. Ideally, enlarge these to A3 size as this gives pupils more space in which to write.

Introduction

Begin by finding out how much the children already know about CD-ROM encyclopaedias. They have become a fairly standard resource for information both in the classroom and home, but different CD-ROMs have different ways of allowing you to access the information.

Distribute and display the example page on photocopiable page 119. Explain that it is a simplified facsimile. Read it through. Examine the text and illustration features and layout of the page. Discuss the options available by clicking on certain buttons, for example:

■ What do these buttons indicate?

(the 'minimize', 'maximize' and 'quit' buttons)

■ What would happen if you clicked on these buttons?
Home (returns to main menu)
Find (displays general index)
Options (displays copy, print, setting, customizing features)
Help (displays help index)
■ What would happen if you clicked on a heading in the 'See also' box? (The article about the related topic would be displayed.)

Discuss the differences between an information text in a book and on a CD-ROM. Make a list of the differences on the board or flip chart.

Whole-class skills work

Write 'CD-ROM' on the board or flip chart and ask the children if they know what the letters stand for (**C**ompact **D**isc-**R**ead **O**nly **M**emory). Revise or introduce the term 'acronym' – a word that is formed from the initial letters of other words. Ask the children for other examples of acronyms that they know, for example: RAM (**r**andom **a**ccess **m**emory), laser (**l**ight **a**mplification by **s**timulated **e**mission of **r**adiation), radar (**ra**dio **d**etection **a**nd **r**anging), NATO (**N**orth **A**tlantic **T**reaty **O**rganization), ASH (**A**ction on **S**moking and **H**ealth).

Make up some acronyms for words that have relevance to the children's own life – for example: school (**s**afe **c**omfortable **h**aven **o**f **o**ccasional **l**earning).

Differentiated group activities

1–4*: All children should work within their groups to research and plan a CD-ROM page on William Shakespeare. If units 'A Midsummer Night's Dream' (Term 1) and 'Shakespeare's Theatre' (previous unit) have already been undertaken, remind the children of the information they may already have from these. Other topics could include:
■ more information about his plays
■ information about his poems
■ his life
■ Stratford-upon-Avon.

Explain to the children that, because they are producing a CD-ROM page, each topic should consist of concise information. Children in Group 1 may be able to work with longer passages, subdividing them into smaller sections which can be viewed as 'additional' or 'pop-up' screens. Some illustrations should be chosen (these can be sketched or photocopied) but not every text entry needs an accompanying illustration.

Conclusion

Encourage the children to share their research and planning ideas for the CD-ROM page. Help them to collectively solve any problems that have arisen.

Introduction

Re-read photocopiable page 119 and discuss its layout. Explain to the children that they will be writing the information they have researched into a similar format.

Whole-class skills work

Revise the key features of information texts: formal, impersonal language; non-chronological (unless of an historical or sequence-sensitive nature); mostly use of present tense, but past tense when dealing with historical topics; extensive use of illustrations and helpful layout features such as subtitles, bullet points, captions and so on. Ensure that the children understand the following terms and can identify them in information texts: title, subtitle, headline, subheading, illustration, caption, columns, text boxes, bullet points, typeface, font, bold, italic, upper case, lower case, serif, sans serif, body text.

Ask the children to find examples in the reference material you have made available.

Differentiated group activities

All children should write their CD-ROM pages. Except for Group 4, these should be designed and drawn by the children.
1: Write a CD-ROM page including additional 'pop-up' screens and related pages.
2 & 3*: As for Group 1 with teacher support.
4: Write the main CD-ROM page only directly onto the template.

Conclusion

Invite the children to share and discuss their CD-ROM pages.

FURTHER IDEAS

Some children could design their CD-ROM pages on computer. There are a number of ways to do this.
■ Design a 'dead' (for example, no hypertext links) CD-ROM page in a DTP or art program.
■ Design a simulated CD-ROM page on a word processor which has hypertext links (for example, Microsoft 'Word').
■ Design an actual CD-ROM page in a hypercard-type package (for example, Microsoft 'Powerpoint').

CD-ROM ENCYCLOPAEDIA PAGE

CD-ROM REFERENCE

Home   Find   Options   Help

Article

THE ELIZABETHAN PERIOD

The Elizabethan period was one of the most glorious periods of English history. Elizabeth was born in 1558 and was queen from 1558 to 1603. She was the daughter of **Henry VIII**, and the last **Tudor** monarch of England.

During Elizabeth's reign, England developed industrially and economically. England grew to be a great seapower due to the achievements of great sailors such as **Sir Francis Drake** and **Sir Martin Frobisher**. The arts flourished. There were many great playwrights such as **Christopher Marlowe** and **William Shakespeare**, and many great musicians such as **Thomas Tallis** and **John Dowland**.

Through her skilled diplomacy, **Queen Elizabeth** managed to avoid war with Spain for many years, but when war did come, with the expedition of the **Spanish Armada** in 1588, her excellent sea captains gave her a resounding victory.

See also

- SPANISH ARMADA
- WILLIAM SHAKESPEARE
- CHRISTOPHER MARLOWE
- THE GLOBE THEATRE
- TIMELINE
- STRATFORD-UPON-AVON
- THOMAS TALLIS
- JOHN DOWLAND

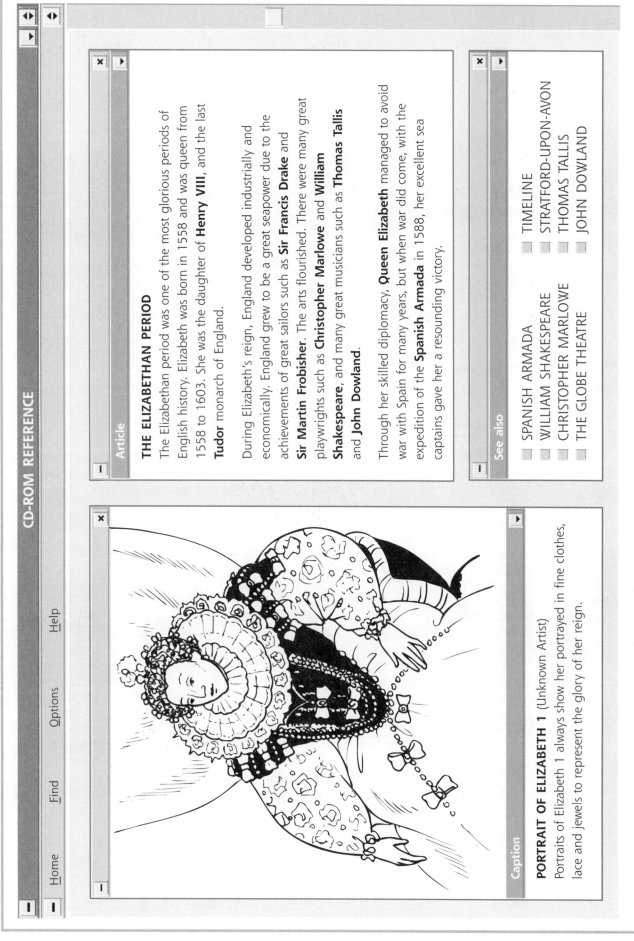

Caption

PORTRAIT OF ELIZABETH 1 (Unknown Artist)

Portraits of Elizabeth 1 always show her portrayed in fine clothes, lace and jewels to represent the glory of her reign.

ESTABLISHING ROOTS

OBJECTIVES

UNIT	SPELLING/ VOCABULARY	GRAMMAR/ PUNCTUATION	COMPREHENSION/ COMPOSITION
REFERENCE AND RESEARCH SKILLS Establishing roots.	Use personal reading, a range of dictionaries and previous knowledge to investigate words with common prefixes, suffixes and root words.	Understand that words can be changed by adding prefixes and suffixes.	Know how to use alternative strategy when meaning is not clear from context.

ORGANIZATION (1 HOUR)

INTRODUCTION	WHOLE-CLASS SKILLS WORK	DIFFERENTIATED GROUP ACTIVITIES	CONCLUSION
HOUR 1 Revise the terms 'root word', 'prefix' and 'suffix'. Introduce the term 'affix'. Read a passage and identify words with affixes.	Use activity on photocopiable page to practise identifying root words and affixes.	1–4: Use own reading books to find words with affixes and to identify root words, prefixes and suffixes. *Teacher works with Groups 1 & 4.	Share findings of group work. Reinforce idea that learning even a few common prefixes and suffixes gives helpful clues to the meanings of a large number of words.

RESOURCES

Photocopiable page 122 (Establishing Roots), a range of dictionaries appropriate to the abilities of the children in the class, fiction and non-fiction books that the children are currently reading, board or flip chart, OHP and acetate (optional), writing materials.

PREPARATION

Make enough copies of photocopiable page 122 for one between two children. If possible, prepare the page also as an OHT or A3 enlargement.

Introduction

Write the word 'illogically' on the board or flip chart. Ask the children: If you needed to find the meaning of this word in the dictionary, which headword would you look for? (*Logic.*) Remind the children that a word from which other words are made is called a *root word*. The meaning of the root word may be changed by adding a syllable or syllables to the beginning of the word (a *prefix*) or to the end of the word (a *suffix*). Sometimes a word comprises a root word with both a prefix and a suffix, as does 'illogically'. Introduce the term *affix* which is the generic term for additions to the root word (ie covering both prefixes and suffixes). Explain that most headwords in the dictionary are root words; however, very often the words they will need to look up in the dictionary are words with affixes. Therefore it is important to be able to identify root words. Remind them that sometimes the spelling of a root word changes when an affix is added.

Distribute copies of photocopiable page 122, and/or display the page on an OHP or flip chart. Read through the paragraph with the children and then ask them to identify those words which have affixes. Underline these.

Whole-class skills work

Now complete the rest of the activities on the photocopiable page. This can be done with the whole class working together from the outset on the displayed page – or you

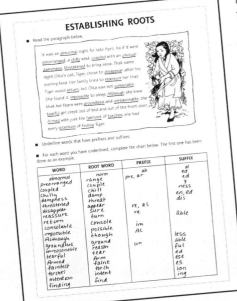

may prefer to have the children work in pairs on their own copies, coming together after five or ten minutes to complete the chart as a class.

Differentiated group work

All children should work within their groups, using fiction or non-fiction texts they are currently reading in other areas of the curriculum, and using dictionaries appropriate to their ability.

1*: Children should choose a page or two from their book and find words that have affixes. For each one, they should identify the root word and the prefixes and suffixes, and write these down. They should then use a dictionary to find the word's meaning as it is used in the sentence in the book. For one of the words identified, ask them to list other words that can be made from the root word.

2 & 3: As for Group 1, but give a set number of words to find – for example five – so that they are able to accomplish each of the tasks in the time.

4*: As for Groups 2 and 3, but omitting the last task.

Conclusion

Ask the children to share some of the words they have found. List them on the board, placing them in a grid like the one on the photocopiable page. Have the children discovered any new prefixes and/or suffixes? How does their addition to the root word change its meaning?

Conclude by emphasizing that the same prefixes and suffixes can be used in many different words. Learning even a few common prefixes and suffixes gives helpful clues to the meanings of a large number of words.

ESTABLISHING ROOTS

■ Read the paragraph below.

It was an abnormal night for late April. As if it were prearranged, a chilly wind, coupled with an unusual dampness, threatened to bring snow. That same night Gita's cat, Tiger, chose to disappear after his evening feed. Her family tried to reassure her that Tiger would return, but Gita was not consolable. She found it impossible to sleep. Although she knew that her fears were groundless and unreasonable, the tearful girl crept out of bed and out of the front door. Armed with just the faintest of torches, she had every intention of finding Tiger.

■ Underline words that have prefixes and suffixes.

■ For each word you have underlined, complete the chart below. The first one has been done as an example.

WORD	ROOT WORD	PREFIX	SUFFIX
abnormal	norm	ab	al

NIASSAN CREATION MYTH

OBJECTIVES

UNIT	SPELLING/ VOCABULARY	GRAMMAR/ PUNCTUATION	COMPREHENSION/ COMPOSITION
READING POETRY Extract from 'Niassan Creation Myth'.	Use phonetic knowledge to pronounce unfamiliar and foreign words. Understand the meaning of 'creation', 'myth', 'literature'.	Consider the impact of the use of active verbs.	Read a myth in poetic form. Recognize how words in poetry are manipulated to create rhythms. Analyse how mood and feeling are reflected in poetry. Extend knowledge of the oral tradition.

ORGANIZATION (1 HOUR)

	INTRODUCTION	WHOLE-CLASS SKILLS WORK	DIFFERENTIATED GROUP ACTIVITIES	CONCLUSION
HOUR 1	Introduce and read extract from 'Niassan Creation Myth' on photocopiable page 125.	Examine the use of repetition. Consider the use of active verbs	1: Memorize as much of first verse as they can. 2 & 3*: Write a description of what they imagine the Niassan ceremony to be like. 4: Plan and prepare a group presentation of the myth with percussion instruments.	Share and present ideas. Discuss the fact that the oral tradition consists of similar stories that have developed through generations and across cultures.

RESOURCES

Photocopiable page 125 ('Niassan Creation Myth'), OHP and acetate (optional), world map or globe (optional), percussion instruments (for Group 4), writing materials.

PREPARATION

Make enough copies of the poem for at least one between two children. If possible, prepare it also as an OHT or A3 enlargement.

Introduction

Begin by explaining to the children that they are going to be reading an extract from a creation myth in poetic form. Discuss what the children understand by both the terms 'creation' (in this context, how the world and man began) and 'myth' (a story usually involving supernatural beings and explaining natural phenomena). Explain that this poem has been passed on orally for centuries by the people of the Niassan tribe in Indonesia. (If you wish, use a map or globe to locate this area for the children.) It was only written down when heard by an anthropological researcher. Explain that once a story is written down, it becomes 'literature'.

Read the poem through once to give the children a feel for its content and rhythm. Explain that this creation myth is chanted at the funeral ceremonies of Niassan chiefs. Discuss this rather paradoxical juxtaposition of life and death. Ask whether the children know of any other similar creation myths. Then share the re-reading of the poem with the class. Explain that all names should be pronounced phonetically.

Whole-class skills work

Examine the use of repetition in the text. Explain that repetition is a powerful device used in many poems and songs to provide rhythm and pattern. Repetition is a characteristic feature of the oral tradition of poetry because it allowed people who had no written language to remember the patterns and the words. Work with the children to find and underline all repeated phrases. Discuss the effect of the repetition.

Explore also how, alongside of the repetition, the poem uses strong active verbs to tell what the 'he' of the poem did. Discuss the appropriateness of this in relation to the meaning of the poem – ie the 'he' of the poem is the powerful 'creator', the one who acts rather than is acted upon: he *arose*, he *took*, he *carried*, he *brought*, he *weighed*, and so on. Then contrast this with the use of the passive towards the end of the extract when 'man' is being described: 'A house *was built* for him of tree-fern...'

Differentiated group activities

1: Ask the children to work individually and, using both the 'story' and the repetition to help, memorize as much of the first verse as they can in the time allowed.
2 & 3*: Ask the children to work in pairs. Discuss the context in which this poem was recited and write a description of what they imagine the ceremony to be like.
4: Plan and prepare a group presentation of the myth with percussion instruments. The extensive repetition in the myth provides a good opportunity to share the lines out.

Conclusion

Ask the class to share their ideas. Organize the presentations so that at least one example of each group is seen or heard. Discuss whether or not the children in Group 1 found the poem easy to memorize. If they could not remember it word for word, could they remember the gist? Emphasize the fact that stories told in the oral tradition often experienced change as they went down through generations and across cultures, but that many of them are very similar. Remind children to look out for these in their reading.

NIASSAN CREATION MYTH

He arose, Uwu Lowalangi,
He arose, high Luo Zaho.
He went to bathe, to paint his body,
He went to bathe and to reappear again
Up there by the spring that is like a piece of mirror,
Up there by the spring that is like a piece of glass.
He took earth, one handful,
He took earth, the size of an egg,
When he saw his shadow in the water,
When he saw his shadow in the deep water.
He carried it to the village, under the council house,
He carried it to the village, under the dwelling house,
His earth, one handful,
His earth, the size of an egg.
He shaped it like the figure of an ancestor,
He shaped it in the form of a child,
His earth, one handful,
His earth, the size of an egg.
He brought out the pans of the balance,
He brought out the pans for weighing,
He brought out the weight shaped like a hen,
He brought out the weight in the likeness of a cock.
He laid it in the pan of the balance,
He laid it in the pan for weighing,
He weighed the wind like gold,
He weighed the wind like gold-dust.
When he laid it in the pan of the balance,
When he laid it in the pan for weighing,
He laid it on the lips of its mouth,
He laid it by the breath of its breathing,
Thereupon it spoke like a man,
Thereupon it spoke like a child,

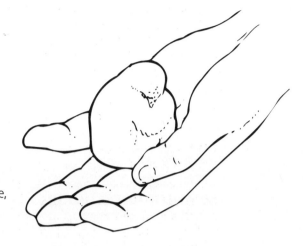

Up there before Uwu Lowalangi,
Up there before high Luo Zaho.
He gave him a name,
He gave him a name there:
Sihai, up there, who has no offspring,
Sihai, up there, who has no children.
And he arose, Uwu Lowalangi,
He arose, high Luo Zaho,
He gave a place to what he had made,
He gave a place to his handiwork,
To Sihai, who has no offspring,
To Sihai, who has no children.
And he thought, he reflected,
He thought, he began to move,
Up there, Uwu Lowalangi,
Up there high Luo Zaho,
Having now one like him in shape,
Having now one like him in body.
There was yet no sun, to guide the thousands,
There was yet no moon, to guide the many.
It was still dark, the land of Uwu Lowalangi,
It was still dark, the land of high Luo Zaho,
And Uwu Lowalangi established him,
High Luo Zaho established him,
Sihai, up there, who has no offspring,
Sihai, up there, who has no children:
"Walk upon the earth, which is shaken by the northwind,
Walk upon the earth, which is shaken by the blast."
A house was built for him of tree-fern,
A house was built for him of tuhu-wood,
Uwu Lowalangi had established him,
High Luo Zaho had established him,
Tuha Sihai, who has no offspring,
Tuha Sihai, who has no children...

Niassan Creation Myth

METAPHOR POEMS

OBJECTIVES

UNIT	SPELLING/ VOCABULARY	GRAMMAR/ PUNCTUATION	COMPREHENSION/ COMPOSITION
WRITING POETRY Metaphor poems: 'The Beach' by William Hart-Smith and 'What is . . . the sun?' by Wes Magee.	Understand the terms 'imagery' and 'metaphor'.	Demonstrate awareness of parallel grammatical structures in writing own poems.	Recognize figurative language and use in own writing.

ORGANIZATION (1 HOUR)

INTRODUCTION	WHOLE-CLASS SKILLS WORK	DIFFERENTIATED GROUP ACTIVITIES	CONCLUSION
Read and discuss metaphor poems on photocopiable page 128.	Revise and develop understanding of imagery and metaphor.	1–4*: All groups work at their own ability level to write metaphor poems based on models.	Share poems and evaluate effectiveness of metaphors. Discuss how to 'publish' class anthology.

HOUR 1

RESOURCES

Photocopiable page 128 (Metaphor Poems), board or flip chart, OHP and acetate (optional), writing materials.

PREPARATION

Make enough copies of photocopiable page 128 (Metaphor Poems) for one between two children. If possible, prepare the page also as an OHT or A3 enlargement.

In preparation for the 'Whole-class skills work' session, write the following poem scaffolds on the board or flip chart:

> **What is . . . a kitten?**
> A kitten is a fluffy ball
> A miaowing powder puff
> _____
> _____
> _____
>
> **A guitar**
> A guitar is a big tennis racket
> _____
> _____
> _____

Introduction

Read the first poem ('The Beach') on photocopiable page 128 aloud to the children. Then read it again and ask them to sketch very roughly the picture they 'see' in the words of the poem. Ask them: What does the poet imagine when he sees the sand and trees beyond the beach? How does he picture the sea?

Now do the same with the second poem, 'What is . . . the sun?'. Ask the children: What is the poet's answer to his own question? Have the children sketched one image or several? Discuss the fact that in the first poem the poet has created one visual image whereas in the second the poet has compared the sun to several different things.

Whole-class skills work

Revise the term 'imagery' – the use of words and phrases to create a vivid sensory image. Choose two or three familiar objects or experiences and ask the children to brainstorm words or phrases that might describe them in terms of their various sensory impressions, for example:

Object or experience	Sight	Sound	Touch	Taste	Smell
Loaf of bread	golden rectangle		soft springy warm	doughy	wafting inviting
candle	flickering flame translucent stalk	'hiss' when lit 'flapping' of the flicker	hot		smokey waxy
reading	black marks on white page	'whoosh' of the page turning	smooth paper hard cover slickness of laminated cover		musty (old book) fresh (new book)

Discuss how imagery makes the object or experience more real to the reader.

Now revise the term 'metaphor'. Ask the children if they can remember the definition. A *metaphor* is a direct comparison between two things. Instead of saying a thing **is like** another it says that a thing **is** another, for example:

■ My feet are icebergs.
■ The wind is a howling beast.
■ He has cast iron nerves.

Because metaphors are direct comparisons, they are more powerful than similes. They are also harder to recognize when studying a text.

Display the metaphor poem scaffolds that you prepared on the board or flip chart (see 'Preparation' above). Read them through and invite the children to suggest suitable metaphors to fill the gaps. The first scaffold is similar in format to 'The Beach' and the second scaffold is similar in format to 'What is . . . the sun?'

Differentiated group activities

All the children should write their own metaphor poems based on the models provided.
1*: Children should work individually and be encouraged to try to use the more complex model provided by 'The Beach' in which the metaphor is extended and composite.
2 & 3: Children should work with 'What is . . . the sun?' as their model and could work in pairs for support.
4*: Children should work in pairs or small groups of three to four using 'What is . . . the sun?' as their model, and using only the first line of each verse, for example:

What is . . . a ghost?
A ghost is a gust of wind
It is an uneasy feeling in the bones
It is a shiver down the spine
(...and so on)

Conclusion

Invite the children to share their poems. While listening to others, they should listen for examples of fresh and striking metaphors.

Discuss how the poems might be 'published' in a class anthology.

FURTHER IDEAS

Children could spend some time collecting examples of metaphors from poetry anthologies. They could then share the most interesting examples and say what they like about them.

METAPHOR POEMS

METAPHOR POEMS

The Beach
The beach is a quarter of golden fruit,
a soft white melon
slice a half-moon curve,
having a thick green rind
of jungle growth;
and the sea devours it
with its sharp,
sharp white teeth.

William Hart-Smith

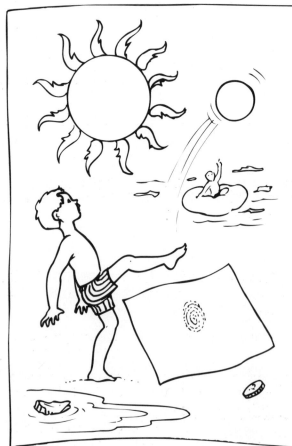

What is . . . the sun?
The sun is an orange dinghy
    sailing across a calm sea.

It is a gold coin
    dropped down a drain in heaven.

It is a yellow beach ball
    kicked high into the summer sky.

It is a red thumb-print
    on a sheet of pale blue paper.

It is the gold top from a milk bottle
    floating on a puddle.

Wes Magee

THE RED-HEADED LEAGUE

OBJECTIVES

UNIT	SPELLING/ VOCABULARY	GRAMMAR/ PUNCTUATION	COMPREHENSION/ COMPOSITION
READING FICTION 'The Red-Headed League' by Sir Arthur Conan Doyle (a Sherlock Holmes story).	Use and understand vocabulary related to mystery genre.	Investigate the use of hyphens and dashes.	Read a mystery story by a well-established author. Identify characteristic features of mystery genre.

ORGANIZATION (3 HOURS)

	INTRODUCTION	WHOLE-CLASS SKILLS WORK	DIFFERENTIATED GROUP ACTIVITIES	CONCLUSION
HOUR 1	Introduce mystery genre and features. Read 'The Red-Headed League', photocopiable pages 132–134.	Investigate the use of hyphens and dashes in the text.	1 & 2: Reading Comprehension, all parts. 3 & 4*: Reading Comprehension, Part A.	Share and discuss answers to Reading Comprehension.
HOUR 2	Re-read 'The Red-Headed League'.	Revise features of non-fiction report genre.	1–4*: Pupils work in pairs in their groups to solve mystery and write solutions as crime report.	Share and discuss solutions. Compare with real explanation.
HOUR 3	Recap on story. Plot storyline and discuss need for ending or resolution.	Discuss 'red herring' device used in mystery stories. Add feature to web.	1–4*: Draft an ending to the story.	Selected pupils read out draft endings. Read Conan Doyle's ending and compare.

RESOURCES

Photocopiable pages 132–134 ('The Red-Headed League'), 135 (Reading Comprehension), a copy of *The Adventures of Sherlock Holmes* by Sir Arthur Conan Doyle (optional), board or flip chart, writing materials.

PREPARATION

Make enough copies of photocopiable pages 132–134 for one set between two children. If possible, prepare the following web (for use in the introductory session to Hour 1) as an OHT. Alternatively, copy it onto the board or flip chart.

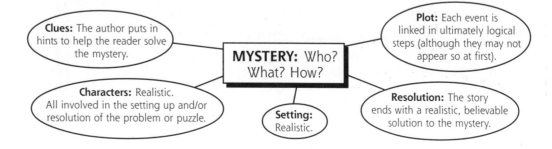

Introduction

Ask the children if any of them have enjoyed any mystery stories recently (either read or seen on television or in a film) and to say what these are. Discuss what makes them mysteries. Explain that the mystery story usually has the component features of realistic fiction, but with a significant change of emphasis: everything centres round a puzzle or an unusual problem that needs solving. Show the children the mystery features web that you have written on the board or flip chart (see 'Preparation' above) and discuss the various components.

Now, explain to the children that they are going to read a specially adapted version of a Sherlock Holmes detective story which allows them to solve the mystery themselves. To help them, the main clues have been marked in the text. If they aren't already familiar with Sherlock Holmes, explain that he is a fictional character famous for making deductions from seemingly unimportant observations about people and places. (Sir Arthur Conan Doyle (1859–1930), the author of the Sherlock Holmes stories, was a British doctor!)

Read 'The Red-Headed League' on photocopiable pages 132– 134 together.

Whole-class skills work

Discuss the differences between a 'dash' and a 'hyphen'.

■ A dash is a short line with a space before and after it. It is used to mark a sudden change of direction in a sentence or an expectant pause. Two dashes can be used like brackets to add extra information in the middle of a sentence.

■ A hyphen is usually shorter than a dash and has no space before or after. It is used to show that a word has been split at the end of a line, or to link two words together to make one.

Ask the children to find examples of both dashes and hyphens in the text. They should note that different authors use punctuation in slightly different ways, and that in this story the dash has been used where another author might have placed semi-colons.

Differentiated group activities

All children should work on the Reading Comprehension questions on photocopiable page 135. As well as being a valid exercise in itself, the comprehension activity will help the children to read the text carefully and get the basic facts of the case clear in their minds.

1 & 2: All parts.

3 & 4*: Part A only.

Conclusion

Share and discuss answers to the Reading Comprehension activity.

Introduction

Re-read the text.

Whole-class skills work

In a question-and-answer session, revise the key features of report genre:

■ written mainly in the present tense

■ often contains passages of recount written in the past tense

■ includes many facts, figures, dates and so on

■ written in formal, impersonal language.

Explain to the children that they will need to bear these features in mind when writing their reports in the next session.

Differentiated group activities

1–4*: All children should work in pairs within their groups to try to solve the mystery using the prompts at the end of the story on photocopiable page 134 to help them. When they have solved the mystery, they should write out their solution in report form. They could use a format similar to that shown.

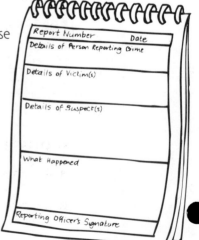

They should include a diagram of the crime showing the approximate position of the buildings (Groups 1 and 2 could refer to the sketch maps made earlier when doing part C of the Reading Comprehension).

Conclusion

Discuss the children's solutions to the crime, then explain what really happened:

Spaulding wanted to get Jabez Wilson out of his shop so that he could dig a tunnel to the bank in the next street. He therefore invented the idea of the Red-Headed League. Holmes found this out from the following clues: Spaulding spent a lot of time in the cellar; there was a hollow sound when he knocked on the street outside the pawnshop; and Spaulding had dirty knees.

Introduction

Recap on the story and the solution. Explain that, at this point, we know what Sherlock Holmes knows when he says, 'A great crime has been planned, but I think that we can prevent it'. But the story still needs an ending – how does Sherlock Holmes prevent it? Discuss suitable endings with the class.

Whole-class skills work

Now that the children have an overview of the whole story, it is possible to study the key narrative device used in this and many other detective stories. This device is called a 'distraction' or (more poetically) a 'red herring'. A red herring is something that the author introduces deliberately to distract the attention of the reader from the real solution. The Red-Headed League in this story is a good example. It is so unusual, and the author spends so long telling us about it, that we focus our attention on this, and not what was happening at the shop.

Ask how many children were distracted by the red herring when they were trying to solve the crime. Can they think of any other examples of red herrings in crime stories in books or on TV?

Add the red herring feature to the web on the board or flip chart:

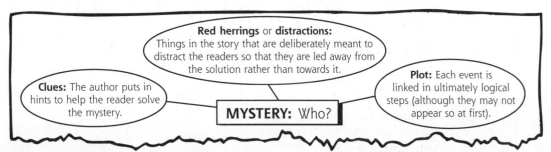

Differentiated group activities

1–4*: Ask all children to draft an ending to the story. The children could work individually, in pairs or in small groups according to ability. Children of higher ability should be encouraged to imitate the style of the author and keep the characters' manners and style of speaking consistent.

Conclusion

Ask selected children to read out their endings while the rest of the class evaluates how well they follow on from the first part of the story and incorporate the style.

Finally, see how Sir Arthur Conan Doyle finished the story. Read his ending from the version you have available. Discuss the similarities and differences with the children's versions.

FURTHER IDEAS

■ A number of other Sherlock Holmes stories could be adapted for study in the same way, or simply read for enjoyment.
■ Undertake a character study of Sherlock Holmes.

THE RED-HEADED LEAGUE

One Saturday morning in autumn, I went to see my friend Sherlock Holmes in Baker Street. But he already had a visitor – a man with unusually bright red hair and a red face.

'I will go away, Holmes – you are busy.'

'You could not possibly have come at a better time, my dear Watson,' he said welcomingly.

Holmes turned to his other visitor. 'Dr Watson has helped me in many of my most successful cases, Mr Wilson. Watson, this is Mr Jabez Wilson. Do not leave out any of the details which are all very interesting.'

Mr Wilson took a dirty old newspaper out of his pocket. 'There it is, sir,' he said to me.

I took the paper, which was two months old, and read the following advertisement:

THE RED-HEADED LEAGUE

A man is needed for a new post in this League which was started by the late Ezekiah Hopkins, of Lebanon, Pennsylvania, who left money to the society in his will. The wages are four pounds a week and the work is very easy. Any man who has red hair and good health, and is at least twenty-one years old, may apply for this post. Come to the Red-Headed League's offices, 7 Pope's Court, Fleet Street, London, at eleven o'clock on Monday morning.

Duncan Ross

'What does it mean?' I said.

Holmes laughed happily. 'It is rather unusual. And now, Mr Wilson, please tell us everything about yourself, your house and servants, and this "Red-Headed League".'

'Well gentlemen, I am a pawnbroker in Saxe-Coburg Square, here in London. I have a man to help me in my shop. His name is Vincent Spaulding. He is an excellent worker, Mr Holmes. He could easily earn much more money in another shop. But I am not going to tell him so!'

'Of course not!' said Holmes. 'But has this wonderful person no faults?'

'His only fault is a love of photography. He spends too much time in the cellar, busy with his developing and printing.'

'And have you any servants?' asked Holmes.

'Only a fourteen-year-old girl, who cooks and cleans the house. My wife is dead and I have no children.

'One Monday morning about two months ago, Spaulding came into my office. He had that newspaper in his hand and he said:

'"What a pity my hair isn't red! Here is a new advertisement from the Red-Headed League. If I had red hair I could get a nice easy job and a lot of money. Here's a society for men with red hair. You could apply for the post yourself!"

'"What are the wages?" I asked him.

'"Four pounds a week: and the amount of work would be very little. You could easily continue your work here too."

'"Well two hundred pounds a year would be very useful to me." He showed me the advertisement, saying:

'"I think the society's money came from a very rich American, Ezekiah Hopkins. He had red hair himself, and when he died all his money went to this Red-Headed League. In his will he gave orders that the money was to be used to give easy jobs to men with red hair. The Red-Headed League gives its posts only to men who were born in London. Ezekiah Hopkins was born here himself, and he loved the old place. Only men with really bright red hair can get these posts. The society does not accept men with light red hair or dark red hair. You would get the post easily if you applied for it!"

'I decided to take Spaulding's advice. I shut up the shop and we were soon on our way to Pope's Court.

'Mr Holmes, that little street looked like a basket of oranges! It was completely full of men with red hair. I could see hopeful men there going in, and disappointed men coming out. Soon we were in the office ourselves.

'A small man was sitting at the table. His hair was even redder than mine.

'"This is Mr Jabez Wilson," said Vincent Spaulding, "and he is willing to accept a post in the Red-Headed League."

'"...His hair is certainly very fine!" the other man said. "I will give you the post. Congratulations on your success! My name is Duncan Ross," he said. "I am the Secretary of the League."

'He told me the hours of work were from ten until two in the afternoon. Well, Mr Holmes, most of a pawnbroker's business is done in the evenings. So I could easily work for Mr Ross in the mornings. Besides, I knew that Spaulding was an excellent shopman, and that he would be able to deal with all business matters during the day. I agreed on the hours and was surprised to find out that all I had to do was stay in the office and copy out the *Encyclopaedia Britannica*. I was to start in the morning.

'Spaulding and I went back home. I felt thoroughly delighted at my own good fortune.

'Next morning, I bought some paper and returned to Pope's Court, though I had begun to suspect this "Red-Headed League" was only a joke. Mr Ross showed me the beginning of the letter A in the encyclopaedia, and then he left. At two o'clock he came back, congratulated me on the amount I had written, and then locked the door of the office after me.

'This continued for more than eight weeks, Mr Holmes. This morning, I went to my work as usual at ten o'clock, but the door was still locked. There was a card nailed to it – a little notice. Which I pulled down and here it is.'

On it somebody had written:
THE RED-HEADED LEAGUE DOES NOT EXIST ANY LONGER. 4TH OCTOBER.

'I knocked on the doors of all the other offices. But nobody had heard of Mr Duncan Ross. So I went to see the owner of the building, but he too told me that he had not heard of either the Red-Headed League or its Secretary, Mr Ross.

'I went home to Saxe-Coburg Square and asked Vincent Spaulding to advise me. But he could not give me any useful advice. But I was not satisfied, Mr Holmes – I did not want to lose my four pounds a week.'

'You must not complain, Mr Wilson,' said Holmes. 'You have really gained thirty-two pounds. And do not forget that you have also gained knowledge about subjects beginning with the letter A! Now, let me ask you a few questions. First of all, how long has Vincent Spaulding been your shopman?'

'For about three months.'

'And why did you choose him?'

'Because he seemed to be a sensible young fellow, and he was willing to accept half wages.'

Holmes stood up. 'Well Mr Wilson,' he said. 'I will think about this matter.'

When Mr Wilson had gone, Holmes asked me:

'What is your opinion of this Red-Headed League, Watson?'

'It is a complete mystery to me.'

'Yes,' he said. 'I must work hard, Watson. I want to look at Saxe-Coburg Square before we go to the Stainway Hall. And we must also have some lunch. Come along!'

Saxe-Coburg Square was a dull, poor sort of place, with some dirty grass in the middle, and a few bushes. I noticed a smell of smoke. The four rows of small brick houses had two floors each and a cellar. One of them had a shop window and shop door as well as a house-door. Above the window we saw a brown board with the name 'JABEZ WILSON' painted on it in white letters. There were also the three golden balls which are the sign of a pawnbroker's shop.

CLUE 3 Holmes stopped in front of Mr Wilson's house and looked at it for a moment. Then he knocked loudly several times on the large stones of the street with his stick. Finally he went up to the door and knocked.

The door was opened immediately by a young man.

'Can you tell me the way to the General Post Office, please?' Holmes asked.

The pawnbroker's man did not hesitate for a second. 'Go along that street,' he said, pointing. 'Then go down the third street on the right. After that, the General Post Office is in the fourth street on the left.'

'A clever man!' said Holmes, as we walked away.

'Did you recognize his face?' I asked.

'My dear Watson, I did not look at his face!'

'Oh! Why then did you knock at the door?'

'Because I wanted to look at the **CLUE 4** knees of his trousers. We have seen Saxe-Coburg Square. Now let us look at the streets behind it.'

We left the little square and were soon in one of the noisiest main roads in London. Some of the houses and shops in this main road, however, were separated only by gardens and yards from the quiet little square behind. There was a sweet shop, a newspaper shop, a branch of the City and District Bank, an **CLUE 5** Italian restaurant, and a small factory where carriages were made.

'We have done our work now, Watson,' said Holmes.

'A great crime has been planned, but I think that we can prevent it. I shall want your help tonight. And, Watson, there may be some danger – so please bring your gun.' He waved his hand and disappeared into the crowd.

Sir Arthur Conan Doyle (adapted from the original by Chris Webster)

Can you solve the mystery of the Red-Headed League?

To help you to solve the mystery of the Red-Headed League, keep these questions in mind: What crime is planned? How is it to be carried out? Discuss the clues in this order:

5. Jabez Wilson's pawn shop is just behind the City and District Bank.

2. The Red-Headed League job took Jabez Wilson away from his shop from ten until two in the afternoon.

1. Spaulding spent a lot of time in the cellar.

4. When Holmes looked at Vincent Spaulding's knees, he saw that they were covered with soil.

3. When Holmes knocked on the ground in front of Jabez Wilson's pawn shop, he heard a hollow sound.

READING COMPREHENSION

PART A

■ What was the name of the red-headed man who owned the pawnshop?

■ What was the name of his assistant?

■ Who else lived in the building?

■ What was the Red-Headed League?

■ Why did Jabez Wilson get a job with the Red-Headed League?

■ What were his working hours?

■ What did he have to do?

■ How much did he earn?

■ What was the name of the Square where the pawnshop was situated?

■ What was in the next street?

PART B

■ Why did Jabez Wilson consult Sherlock Holmes about the Red-Headed League?

■ How does Jabez Wilson describe Vincent Spaulding?

■ What was strange about the job he was given to do?

■ What kind of a place was Saxe-Coburg Square?

■ How did Sherlock Holmes go about solving the crime?

PART C

■ Read the description of Saxe-Coburg Square, the streets behind it, and the different businesses that are to be found there. The layout of this area is an important clue. Draw a sketch map of the area.

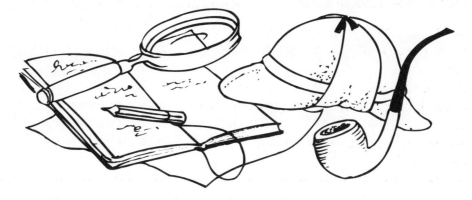

WRITE A DETECTIVE STORY

OBJECTIVES

UNIT	SPELLING/ VOCABULARY	GRAMMAR/ PUNCTUATION	COMPREHENSION/ COMPOSITION
WRITING FICTION Write a detective story.	Identify misspelled words in own writing. Develop vocabulary related to mystery/ detective genre.	Demonstrate grammatical awareness and knowledge of punctuation in own writing.	Write a story in a genre similar to one read.

ORGANIZATION (2 HOURS)

	INTRODUCTION	WHOLE-CLASS SKILLS WORK	DIFFERENTIATED GROUP ACTIVITIES	CONCLUSION
HOUR 1	Revise characteristic features of mystery genre. Investigate Detective Story Planner on photocopiable page 138.	Develop key terms and vocabulary related to detective stories.	1–4: All pupils plan detective stories. *Teacher works with Groups 1 & 4.	Share and discuss plans.
HOUR 2	Discuss how story beginnings can indicate genre.	Revise key skills of story writing.	1–4: All pupils start writing their stories. *Teacher works with Groups 2 & 3.	Selected pupils read their stories so far, followed by class evaluation.

RESOURCES

Photocopiable page 138 (Detective Story Planner), board or flip chart, OHP and acetate (optional), the mystery genre web from the previous unit, writing materials.

PREPARATION

It is assumed that the previous unit ('The Red-Headed League') will have been undertaken prior to this unit and that this unit will follow on immediately.

Make enough copies of photocopiable page 138 (Detective Story Planner) for each child. If possible, prepare the page also as an OHT or enlarged photocopy. You should also have to hand the mystery genre web prepared in the previous unit (either as an OHT or written on the board or flip chart).

Introduction

Display both the mystery genre web from the previous unit and photocopiable page 138 (Detective Story Planner) from this unit. Revise the former and read through and discuss the latter. At the end of each section there is a question which should be used as the basis for discussion. Encourage the children to refer to the characters, settings and plots of their favourite TV and film detectives as well as to those they've read about in books. Discuss how these apply to the characteristic features outlined on the web.

Remind the children that they should base their own plots on the key principle underlying all detective stories that there are sufficient clues for the reader to solve the crime. The challenge for the writer is to make this possible without making it too easy. This is where the 'red herring' or distraction comes in, as it can distract the reader's attention from the clues pointing to the real villain. Remind the children that this feature was added to the web in the previous unit.

Whole-class skills work
Revise key detective story terms and their role in the story's structure, for example:

clue	red herring	deduction
alibi	villain	mystery
motive	alias	detective

Model the process of completing the Detective Story Planner.

Differentiated group activities
1–4: All children should plan their detective stories using the Detective Story Planner. Children could work individually or collaboratively in pairs or small groups.
    *The teacher works with Groups 1 and 4.

Conclusion
Ask selected children to read out and talk about their story plans. Ask the rest of the class to comment and evaluate.

Introduction
To consolidate the children's understanding of what makes an effective mystery, contrast the beginning of a mystery with that of other genres. Write the following sentence on the board or flip chart: Once upon a time there was a princess in a high tower. Discuss what kind of story this beginning sentence indicates and why (for example fairy tale; use of 'once upon a time' and princess). What genre would they expect if they saw or heard:

In a tower way up high
I saw a girl as I was passing by.

They should expect poetry (indicated by rhyme, rhythm, layout). Discuss how the idea could be transformed to indicate a news report (for example *Yesterday afternoon a young girl was discovered living in the old derelict tower on the edge of town*); an autobiography (for example *For many years I lived by myself in what was once a castle tower*); a mystery (for example *Everyone assumed that the derelict tower was empty, so imagine my surprise when I saw a young girl's face at the window*). Encourage the children to be as creative and imaginative as they can, but to bear in mind the characteristic features of the genre.

Whole-class skills work
Recap on key skills of story writing, for example:
■ paragraphing
■ writing effective descriptions
■ writing convincing dialogue.
    Ask the children to think about their intended audience and possible adjustments they may need to make in the difficulty of solving the crime. For a younger audience, for example, this may mean that clues should be made more obvious, and/or the red-herring played down. The best way to find out how difficult the crime is to solve is to try the story out on a partner.

Differentiated group activities
1–4: All children should start writing their story. Some will begin and finish in this session, while others may only get through the beginning. Remind the children about the importance of an effective beginning that gives a clue to the genre.
    *The teacher works with Groups 2 and 3.

Conclusion
Ask selected children to read out their detective stories so far. The rest of the class should listen carefully for the clues to see how easy or difficult it is to solve the crime. Ask them to give their opinion about the strong points of the stories, including the story beginning. Ask the writers to say what they found most difficult in writing their stories.

DETECTIVE STORY PLANNER

NOTES	PLAN
CHARACTER Try to create a vivid character with a distinctive appearance, personality and method of working, eg: **Sherlock Holmes:** Wears a deerstalker hat, plays the violin, solves crimes by observation and deduction. **Poirot:** A Belgian detective with an odd-shaped moustache and immaculate dress. Solves crimes by careful reasoning. **Brother Cadfael:** A medieval Benedictine monk with an impish sense of humour. He solves crimes through wisdom, common sense and by applying his sharp intellect. What other detectives can you think of? What are they like? How do they operate?	**DESCRIBE YOUR CHARACTER**
SETTING Think of a setting in which your detective will usually operate, and be prepared to describe it in detail, eg: **Sherlock Holmes:** Victorian London. **Poirot:** Exotic locations such as country houses or the Orient Express. **Brother Cadfael:** England in the Middle Ages. What other settings can you think of?	**DESCRIBE YOUR SETTING**
PLOT There are many ways to plot a detective story. Here is one suggestion: ■ The victim, or friend or relative of the victim, comes to see the detective. ■ The detective examines the scene of the crime and interviews witnesses and suspects. *Clues* should be included in the description. ■ One of the suspects could be set up as a *red herring*. He or she will be an unpopular character who has an excellent *motive* for the crime and a weak *alibi*. The police may well arrest this person. ■ The detective, by employing his special method, finds out the real villain. ■ A dramatic scene in which the real villain is confronted and captured. There may be a fight or a car chase. ■ At the end of the story the detective should explain to the police, or to a friend or relative of the victim, how he discovered the real villain. What other kinds of detective story plot can you think of?	**OUTLINE OF YOUR PLOT**

LIGHTS

OBJECTIVES

UNIT	SPELLING/ VOCABULARY	GRAMMAR/ PUNCTUATION	COMPREHENSION/ COMPOSITION
READING NON-FICTION 'Lights', from *The RoSPA Bicycle Owner's Handbook*.	Study vocabulary in text. Revise *bi-* prefix and investigate words that include it.	Investigate conditional clauses. Understand features of formal official language.	Read a public information text and explore characteristic features of language and format.

ORGANIZATION (3 HOURS)

	INTRODUCTION	WHOLE-CLASS SKILLS WORK	DIFFERENTIATED GROUP ACTIVITIES	CONCLUSION
HOUR 1	Shared reading of 'Lights' text on photocopiable pages 142–143. Discuss unfamiliar and technical vocabulary.	Investigate use of conditional clauses in 'Lights' text.	1*: Guided reading and discussion. 2 & 3: Reading Comprehension, parts A & B. 4*: Guided reading and discussion.	Discuss the 'Lights' text in relation to pupils' bicycles.
HOUR 2	Shared re-reading of 'Lights' text. Identify characteristic features of style.	Explore the use of the modal verb 'must' in 'Lights' text.	1: Reading Comprehension, all parts. 2 & 3*: Guided reading and discussion. 4: Reading Comprehension, part A.	Discuss answers to the Reading Comprehension exercise.
HOUR 3	Discuss different ways of presenting the text.	Revise the *bi-* prefix and explore words which include it. Work in pairs to check word meanings and make a list of appropriate examples.	1*: Write article about bicycle safety. 2 & 3*: Write leaflet on bicycle safety for younger children. 4*: Design poster to encourage cyclists to follow the law on lights.	Share examples of articles, leaflets and posters.

RESOURCES

Photocopiable pages 142 and 143 ('Lights'), 144 (Reading Comprehension), dictionaries (one between two), board or flip chart, OHP and acetate (optional), writing materials.

PREPARATION

Prepare enough copies of photocopiable pages 142–143 ('Lights') for one set per pair, and enough of photocopiable page 144 (Reading Comprehension) for one per child. In addition, prepare OHTs or A3 enlargements of the 'Lights' article.

Introduction

Display the 'Lights' article on the OHP. Explain that the text is taken from a double-page spread in *The RoSPA Bicycle Owner's Handbook*. Read the text and discuss its purpose. Who is it aimed at? (General public.) What is it trying to do? (Persuade and advise on bicycle safety.) Discuss any difficult spellings and technical vocabulary in the article (for example, *British Standard, visibility, unobscured, conform, LED, axle-mounted, drivewheel, dynamo* and so on).

Whole-class skills work

Investigate conditional clauses. Explain to the children that conditional clauses are used to talk about possible situations and their consequences. They are easily recognized because they usually begin with 'if' or 'unless'. Write this example from the 'Lights' text on the board or flip chart:

> If they do not meet this standard, they may only be used in addition to normal lights that do conform to BS 6102/3.

Note the pattern: the 'if' clause, followed by a comma, followed by the consequence clause (main clause). When an 'if' clause is put first, 'then' is sometimes put at the beginning of the main clause (for example *If you clean my car, then I will give you some money*). In the example above from the 'Lights' text, 'then' is understood rather than stated. Explain that the 'if' clause does not always come at the beginning.

Give each pair of children their own copy of the 'Lights' text and ask them to find more examples of conditional clauses. They should underline the 'if' clause in one colour and the 'consequence' clause in another.

If they arise, you might wish to discuss these issues with the children:
- The second sentence of the piece (*You will also be breaking the law*) is an *implied* conditional sentence because 'if you ride in the dark without lights' is understood but not stated.
- Sentences using 'only if' are conditional sentences where one situation is necessary for another situation.
- The sentence beginning 'To see if the light is working...' (under 'Dynamo lights') is not a conditional sentence. The 'if' means 'whether' in this sentence.

Differentiated group activities
1*: Guided reading and discussion of the 'Lights' text. The following questions can be used as a starting point.
- Who in the group has a bike? What sort of lights does your bike have? Does it fulfil the legal requirements?
- If someone gave you an old bike without any lights, what would you have to do to make it legal?
- What else could you add to make the bike really safe?
- Who is addressing the reader in the text? (We don't know; it is an example of 'impersonal' style.)
- In what tense are most of the verbs? (Present tense.)

The children should refer closely to the text, as appropriate, in their replies.

2 & 3: Complete parts A and B of the Reading Comprehension exercise on photocopiable page 148.

4*: Guided reading and discussion, as for Group 1.

Conclusion
Consolidate the children's understanding of the text by discussing it in relation to their own bikes. How well do they conform to the safety advice and laws described in the text?

Introduction
Re-read 'Lights'. Discuss the language and format features that characterize it as a public information document – use of: impersonal voice, imperative verbs, formal vocabulary, present tense, 'windows of text' and subheadings for easy access, pictorial and diagrammatic information and so on. Identify examples of each.

Whole-class skills work
Explore the use of the auxiliary modal verb 'must'. Explain to the children that the verb 'must' is added to the simple present tense to indicate necessity or obligation, for example *'You must wash your hands before cooking'*. The 'Lights' text uses the modal 'must' a great deal because it is explaining the obligation to comply with the law, for example *'By law, you must have a red rear reflector when riding at night'*.

Ask the children to find more examples of the use of 'must' in the text. Get them to make up their own examples. Write their suggested sentences on the board or flip chart.

Differentiated group activities
1: Complete all parts of the Reading Comprehension exercise.

2 & 3*: Guided reading and discussion as in Hour 1.
4: Complete part A of the Reading Comprehension exercise.

Conclusion
Discuss the answers to the Reading Comprehension exercise.

Introduction
Discuss what you would have to do to the 'Lights' text to:
- express the same information on a poster
- express the same information in a leaflet for younger children
- write a magazine article based on the information provided.

Prompt the children with questions such as: What essential information would need to be included? How would the language and style need to change? What layout features could be used? How useful or appropriate would illustrations be?

Whole-class skills work
Revise the prefix *bi-*, and explore more words which include it. Remind the children that '*bi*' is from a Latin word meaning 'two' or 'twice'. Provide them with some examples, listing them on the board or flip chart:

bicycle: a cycle with two wheels
bifocals: spectacles with two different focal lengths (one for reading, one for long distance)
bigamist: a man with two wives
bikini: could be a swimming costume in two pieces, but this is a 'false derivation', as bikinis are named after Bikini Atoll!
bilingual: someone who can speak two languages
binary: counting with two numbers, 0 and 1

Now ask the children to work in pairs looking through the dictionary in the following way.
- Find words beginning with *bi-*.
- Ask yourself if there is anything to do with 'two' in the meaning of the word. If there is, add it to the list on the board or flip chart along with the dictionary definition. If not, do not add it to the list.

Differentiated group activities
1*: Write an article explaining the dangers of riding bicycles without proper lights. Outline the law on bicycle safety and give advice persuading people to make their bicycles safer.
2 & 3*: Design a short, simple leaflet on bicycle safety aimed at younger children.
4*: Design a poster to encourage bicycle owners to follow the law on lights.

Conclusion
Share examples of the children's articles, leaflets and posters.

FURTHER IDEA

Leaflets or booklets of this kind (such as providing public information) are often available free. Try to get a class set for further detailed study.

The law on bicycle lights

Riding in the dark without lights puts you at great risk. You will also be breaking the law. Lighting-up time is sunset to sunrise and when visibility is seriously reduced. Any bicycle being ridden on public roads in the dark must be fitted with:

- a white front light
- a red rear light
- a red rear reflector

It should also be fitted with:

- a white front reflector
- amber pedal reflectors
- white or amber wheel reflectors

Lights must be kept lit and unobscured, and must conform to the British Standard BS 6102/3. Reflectors must be kept clean and unobscured, and should conform to BS 6102/2.

Exceptions

Bicycle lights that meet a Standard approved by a Member State of the European Union may be used, but **only if** they provide the same level of safety as the British Standard. However, RoSPA only recommends lights that meet BS 6102/3.

Rear lights fitted to bicycles that were made or first used before 1 October 1995 may conform to an older British Standard, BS 3648.

LED lights

It is against the law to fit flashing LED lights to a bicycle. Non-flashing LED lights may be used **IF** they conform to BS 6102/3. If they do not meet this standard, they may only be used **in addition to** normal lights that do conform to BS 6102/3.

Fitting your lights

The diagram illustrates the best places where you can fit your lamps.

1. Rear of carrier
2. Seat stay
3. Handlebar bracket
4. Headset bracket
5. Fork bracket — brazed on
6. Axle-mounted bracket

- The rear lamp and reflector must be securely fitted to the bicycle centrally or on the right-hand side of the bicycle. They must be fitted to point straight behind.
- The front lamp should be fitted centrally or on the right-hand side. It should shine slightly downwards.
- Make sure you adjust the lamp to the correct angle on your bicycle before tightening nuts.
- Most important of all, check regularly that lamps are fastened securely and nuts are tight. Loose lamps can fall into spokes and cause a nasty accident.
- When fitting lights follow the manufacturer's instructions.

Keeping your lights shining brightly
Battery lights

Check that your lights are shining brightly when you set out, if you know you are going to need them by the end of a ride. If the light is getting weak, it means that your batteries are running down. Replace the batteries regularly, and carry a spare set with you. Occasionally check and clean contacts inside the lamps and keep the lens clean. Remove them when leaving your bicycle if they can be easily stolen.

Dynamo lights

Check that the drivewheel of your dynamo rests fully on the side of the tyre when you put it on. To see if the light is working before you set out, hold the wheel and make it go round. Check wires and terminals which can work loose or get rusty. Keep them clean and tightly attached to get a good light. Clean lamp glasses regularly.

LIGHTS

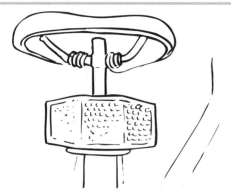

Reflectors

There are many different reflectors you can fit to your bicycle. Reflectors, in the same way as reflective clothing, shine the light straight back to where it comes from. This means that they only show up at night to a driver whose vehicle headlights are shining directly onto them. By law, any reflector or light attached to a bicycle must shine or reflect red to the back (except pedal reflectors) and white to the front, and apart from pedal reflectors and spoke reflectors, must not move or swivel.

Pedal reflectors

They must be amber (orange) and marked BS 6102/2. They can be fitted to most pedals if you don't already have them. They show up very well in the dark, as they are low enough to pick up the beam from vehicle headlights, and move while you ride.

Wheel reflectors

Spoke reflectors or reflective tyres are now fitted to bicycles, and they can show up well in car headlights when you are side-on. Keep them clean.

White front reflector

Many new bicycles will have a white reflector on the front but of course lights **must** also be fitted before you use your bicycle at night.

Red rear reflector

By law, you must have a red rear reflector when riding at night.

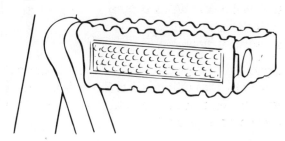

'Bike spacer' flags or rods

These are horizontal rods with a flag or reflector attached. They are fitted to the rear of the bicycle to encourage drivers to leave more space when overtaking cyclists. If you use a bike spacer, make sure it is fixed securely and check the nuts and bolts for tightness regularly.

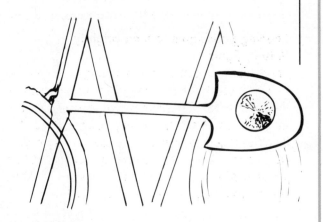

Bulbs

Always carry spare bulbs, and keep a note of the number of bulb which fits your light. Although the same bulb usually fits both front and rear battery lights of the same make, the front and rear bulbs for dynamo lights are different. Make sure you wrap the bulbs up well, or keep them in a box, to prevent breakage.

READING COMPREHENSION

PART A

■ Give two reasons why you must have at least one front and back light and back reflector in good working order.

■ When must you switch your lights on?

■ Why is it dangerous to wait in the middle of the road to turn right if you only have dynamo-powered lights?

■ What should you do if your lights stop working at night?

■ List the different kinds of reflectors you can fit to a bicycle. Which ones must you have by law?

■ What is a 'bike spacer' rod or flag used for?

PART B

■ Find examples of the following, and explain how they help the reader: columns, sub-headings, illustrations, diagram, bullet points.

■ Which sections of the text explain the law about lights, and which sections give advice? How can you tell which is which? Is the difference always clear?

■ Which section gives advice on maintenance of lights? How is it made to stand out from the rest?

■ If you have a bicycle, state how well it meets the requirements explained in the text.

PART C

■ Write about the language of the text. For example, comment on the use of conditional clauses, the tense of verbs, the authorial voice and the intended audience.

THE HOVER-BIKE OWNER'S HANDBOOK

OBJECTIVES

UNIT	SPELLING/ VOCABULARY	GRAMMAR/ PUNCTUATION	COMPREHENSION/ COMPOSITION
WRITING NON-FICTION 'The Hover-bike Owner's Handbook'.	Identify misspelled words in own writing. Use independent spelling strategies. Use vocabulary appropriate to content and style.	Revise use of conditionals. Use conventions of official language: imperatives and the auxiliary modal verb 'must'.	Use features of official language to produce a public information booklet.

ORGANIZATION (2 HOURS)

	INTRODUCTION	WHOLE-CLASS SKILLS WORK	DIFFERENTIATED GROUP ACTIVITIES	CONCLUSION
HOUR 1	Display and discuss 'The Hover-bike Owner's Handbook' on photocopiable page 147.	Revise imperatives, conditionals and the auxiliary modal verb 'must' in preparation for writing activity.	Pairs of pupils produce a spread for 'The Hover-bike Owner's Handbook'. 1*: Pupils cover as much of the contents as possible. 2 & 3: Pupils choose a topic from contents list. 4*: Pupils write about 'Lights and reflectors', using photocopiable pages 142 and 143 from previous unit as a model.	Selected examples of the different spreads from Groups 1 & 4 are shared and discussed.
HOUR 2	Examples of different spreads from Groups 2 & 3 are discussed. Show how to use page 147 to finish booklet.	Revise key redrafting skills.	1-4*: All pupils redraft their work and write on folded A4 paper, attaching the cover on photocopiable page 147 to create an A5 booklet.	The final booklets are displayed and discussed.

RESOURCES

Photocopiable pages 147 ('The Hover-bike Owner's Handbook'), 142 and 143 ('Lights') from previous unit, public information documents (such as booklets/leaflets on health, safety and so on), board or flip chart, OHP and acetate (optional), writing materials.

PREPARATION

Make one copy of photocopiable page 147 ('The Hover-bike Owner's Handbook'). Cut it out and photocopy it to make an A4 cover to wrap around an A5 booklet. Make enough copies for one per child in Groups 2–4, and a single copy for Group 1. In addition, prepare an OHP or A3 enlargement of this page. Have available from the previous unit enough copies of photocopiable pages 142 and 143 ('Lights') for one between two. **Note:** It is assumed that the previous unit 'Lights' will have been undertaken prior to this unit. If not, prepare for this unit by reading pages 142 and 143 ('Lights').

Introduction

Display 'The Hover-bike Owner's Handbook' on OHP. What kind of text do they think would be included in the booklet itself? (The contents list is a clue!) Who would it be aimed at? What purpose would it serve? Show the children other documents giving advice and information. How/why might these be helpful? Try to identify common features such as the use of official or 'impersonal' language (including imperatives and conditionals), and layout devices such as boxes, bullet points, headings and so on.

Whole-class skills work

Explain to the children that they will be writing their own double-page spread for 'The Hover-bike Owner's Handbook'. For this, they will need to use a formal style of writing, similar to that in the 'Lights' text from the previous unit. Ask them what features of this style they can recall, then sum up by revising the following grammatical forms:

■ *Imperatives:* the form of the verb used for giving orders. It is the simple present without a subject, for example <u>Check</u> *the cable often for fraying.*

■ *Conditionals:* conditional clauses are used to talk about possible situations and their consequences. They are easily recognized because they usually begin with 'if' or 'unless'. eg <u>If</u> *your lights stop working, you must walk your bicycle;* <u>Unless</u> *approved lights are fixed, you will be breaking the law.*

■ *Auxiliary modal verb 'must':* the modal verb 'must' is added to the simple present tense to indicate necessity or obligation, for example *Pedal reflectors <u>must</u> be amber.*

Differentiated group activities

The children should work in pairs within their ability groups to produce a double-page spread for 'The Hover-bike Owner's Handbook'. Ask them to use one side of a sheet of A4 paper folded in half to make an A5 booklet (this will ensure that they write the correct amount of text). Emphasize that, at this stage, they should focus on the style of language rather than layout, incorporating the features of formal writing/official language revised in the skills section. Provide them with copies of the 'Lights' text (photocopiable pages 142 and 143) to refer to, or to use as a basic model in Group 4's case. They could also use the selection of documents you have collected as models.

1*: Children in this group should collaborate to cover as much of the contents list as they can. In this way, the group can combine their spreads to make as complete a version of 'The Hover-bike Owner's Handbook' as possible.

2 & 3: Children in these groups can choose any topic from the contents list. If they feel that it will not fill a double-page spread, suggest they combine it with one or two others.

4*: Children in this group should write a spread on 'Lights and reflectors', using the 'Lights' extract from the RoSPA booklet as a model.

Conclusion

Ask children from Groups 1 and 4 to share examples of their spreads. How clear is the information? How successfully have the features of a formal writing style been used?

Introduction

Start by sharing and discussing examples of the different spreads from Groups 2 and 3. Next, explain that the children will have the chance to redraft their spreads as part of the group activities. Then show them how to use 'The Hover-bike Owner's Handbook' cover on the photocopiable sheet to complete their booklets. Explain that the cover can simply be stapled onto the folded A4 page of their final redrafted spread.

Whole-class skills work

Go over the key skills of redrafting. Give the children guidance on organizing non-fiction texts, for example using paragraphs to make the text clear; grouping related points in the same paragraph; using boxes and bullets to make the layout clear; planning how diagrams and illustrations will be fitted in; using subheadings if appropriate.

Differentiated group activities

1–4*: Children work in ability groups to redraft their work, concentrating on the features in the skills section and writing on A4 paper folded to A5 size. Group 1 should plan which sections will appear on which pages. Groups 2–4 should attach their own covers.

Conclusion

Display the final booklets and choose selected ones to evaluate, commenting on the effect of the redrafting process and any problems encountered during this time.

THE HOVER-BIKE OWNER'S HANDBOOK

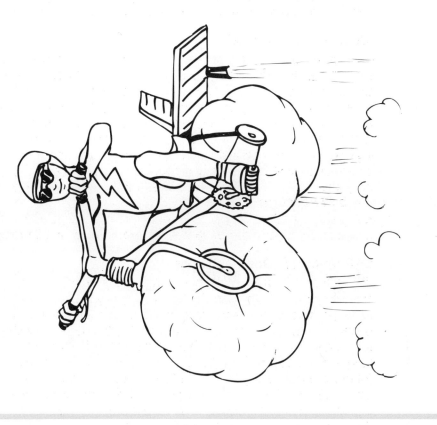

THE HOVER-BIKE OWNER'S HANDBOOK

The extraordinary hover-bike is the bike of the future. It is powered by compressed air and floats 6 cm above the ground, travelling at a maximum speed of 15 kph. It is capable of making a short vertical 'hop' – which is the recommended way of overtaking (except when passing under low bridges). Because of its low speed, children over the age of 10 are permitted to ride the hover-bike when they have passed the appropriate test. It is becoming an increasingly popular form of transport and as more users take to the road, safety is ever more important. This booklet outlines the law and major safety guidelines on the riding of hover-bikes. It also provides detailed advice on the care and maintenance of hover-bikes.

INCLUDES:

- The law and your hover-bike
- Caring for your hover-bike
- Carrying luggage
- What to wear
- Lights and reflectors
- Safety check and maintenance chart
- Hover-bike control
- The rules of the road
- Safe overtaking
- Road signs
- Taking your test
- Security and insurance

PARAPHRASING AND SUMMARIZING

OBJECTIVES

UNIT	SPELLING/ VOCABULARY	GRAMMAR/ PUNCTUATION	COMPREHENSION/ COMPOSITION
REFERENCE AND RESEARCH SKILLS Paraphrasing and summarizing.	Spell and understand meaning of words with prefix *para-*.	Revise work on contracting sentences by summarizing.	Develop key skills of paraphrasing and summarizing.

ORGANIZATION (1 HOUR)

	INTRODUCTION	WHOLE-CLASS SKILLS WORK	DIFFERENTIATED GROUP ACTIVITIES	CONCLUSION
HOUR 1	Introduce the term 'paraphrasing' and its importance as a key research skill. Model paraphrasing.	Use the words 'paraphrase' and 'paragraph' to initiate work on the prefix *para-*.	1*: Make notes on and paraphrase a text read aloud by teacher. 2 & 3: Work in pairs reading and paraphrasing paragraphs. 4*: As for Group 1, but with pupils paraphrasing individual sentences.	Recap on importance of key skill of paraphrasing.

RESOURCES

A collection of non-fiction texts (for example books, newspapers, magazines) appropriate to the various reading levels of the children (at least one between two children), dictionaries, board or flip chart, writing materials.

PREPARATION

From the collection of non-fiction texts, select those that can be used in the introductory and differentiated group activities sessions. Ideally they should be texts related to topics being studied in other areas of the curriculum and they should cater for all reading abilities in the class. If necessary, select appropriate pieces for children in Groups 1–3 to use in the differentiated group activities session. You will also need to select suitable sentences for use with Group 4.

Write the following paragraph on the board or flip chart, for use in the introductory session:

Undersea Life
The numerous seas of the world are home to an enormous variety of life. Seaweeds, sea grasses and microscopic phytoplankton make up the ocean's plant life. Plants generally live only in the photic zone, that is, in the ocean's sunlit surface waters. Where sunlight does reach the shallower ocean floor, plants and plantlike organisms, such as kelp and sea grass, grow anchored to the bottom.

Introduction
Read the paragraph about undersea life that you have written on the board or flip chart. Ask the children whether they found this easy to understand. Explain that sometimes an author's ideas can be difficult to understand, but that they can check their understanding by explaining the ideas in their own words. This is called paraphrasing: retelling what they've read in their own words without changing the meaning of the original.

Re-read the first sentence. Ask the children: What kind of picture does it create in your mind? What do you think the author is really trying to say? How would you paraphrase it? Explain that a helpful strategy for paraphrasing is to simplify the difficult words. For example, what would be a simple word for 'numerous', and for 'variety'?

Re-read the paragraph. Discuss with the children how they would paraphrase the whole paragraph. They should be aware of the following steps:

1. Reread the paragraph.
2. Think about its meaning, or what the author was trying to say.
3. Retell the paragraph in your own words. Don't change the meaning.

Reiterate that knowing how to paraphrase will help them to understand and remember what they read.

As time allows in this session, ask the children to practise the skill as you've modelled it, using paragraphs from newspapers, magazines or non-fiction books which you read aloud to them.

Whole-class skills work

Write the words 'paraphrase' and 'paragraph' on the board or flip chart. Ask the children to identify what the two words have in common. Revise the term 'prefix' and, together, compose a definition – for example:

prefix: an addition to a word made by joining one or more letters at the beginning. The addition has its own meaning but isn't a complete word. Prefixes usually have their own entry in the dictionary.

Remind the children that if they know the spelling and meaning of prefixes they can spell and understand many more words.

Tell the children to find the prefix 'para-' in the dictionary and ask for a volunteer or volunteers to give its various meanings: eg 'beside', 'beyond', 'protect'. Ask them to look up the word 'phrase' and to give its meaning: eg 'to express in words'. So, together, 'para' and 'phrase' give 'paraphrase', meaning an alternative way of expressing something in words. Analyse 'paragraph' in the same way, and then find other 'para' words in the dictionary to study – for example: *parable, parachute, paradise, paradox, paragon, parallel.*

Differentiated group activities

1*: Read a non-fiction text aloud and ask the children to write down three or four key words for each paragraph. If necessary, re-read the text to them. Then ask the children to paraphrase the piece using only their notes.

2 & 3: The children should work in pairs within their ability groups. Ask each one to find (or provide them yourself) a short non-fiction piece containing two or three paragraphs. One member of each pair reads aloud the first paragraph of his or her piece while the partner listens. The listening partner then writes down the ideas without looking at the text and without trying to capture the exact words. The reader continues, paragraph by paragraph, until the passage has been completed. Then the partners compare the new version with the original, to make sure key ideas were accurately reflected. The children then swap roles.

4*: Work with this group as with Group 1, but ask the children to paraphrase sentences.

Conclusion

Conclude by emphasizing that paraphrasing is a particularly valuable skill to use with non-fiction material. When the children successfully paraphrase what they have read, or restate the information in their own words while retaining the original meaning, they are more likely to remember what they have read.

INVESTIGATING HUMOROUS VERSE

OBJECTIVES

UNIT	SPELLING/ VOCABULARY	GRAMMAR/ PUNCTUATION	COMPREHENSION/ COMPOSITION
WORD PLAY Investigating humorous verse: Three poems by Charles Causley.	Use known spellings as a basis for spelling other words.	Revise work on contracting sentences.	Investigate humorous verse. Explore three poems by a significant poet.

ORGANIZATION (1 HOUR)

	INTRODUCTION	WHOLE-CLASS SKILLS WORK	DIFFERENTIATED GROUP ACTIVITIES	CONCLUSION
HOUR 1	Introduce the work of Charles Causley by reading 'Old Mrs Thing-um-e-bob' on photocopiable page 152. Respond to humour in the poem.	Read two other Charles Causley poems on photocopiable page 152. Compare and contrast poems and examine how humour is achieved.	1*: Write about preferred poem. 2: Take roles and prepare 'Old Mrs Thing-um-e-bob' for reading aloud. 3: Use dictionaries to find meanings of all 'cat' words in 'As I Went Down the Cat-Walk'. 4*: Use poetry books to find poem by same poet and humorous verse by different poet. Prepare a reading.	Selected members of each group share their work, followed by class discussion and evaluation. Sum up features and appeal of humorous verse.

RESOURCES

Photocopiable page 152 (Charles Causley poems), a collection of poetry books (including humorous and other poems by Charles Causley; if possible, include a copy of *Figgie Hobbin*, the collection from which the poems in this unit are taken), dictionaries, board or flip chart, OHP and acetate (optional), writing materials.

PREPARATION

Make enough copies of photocopiable sheet 152 for one between two children. Prepare the poems as an OHT or enlarge to at least A3 size.

Introduction

Explain to the children that during this hour they will be hearing and reading three humorous poems by the same poet, Charles Causley. If you know that they have read other poems by him, refer to these.

Read 'Old Mrs Thing-um-e-bob' aloud, giving emphasis to the colloquialisms. Then ask the children for their responses. Did they enjoy the poem? Why? Display the poem and read it again. Ask the children what specifically about the poem makes it humorous, or funny. Focus attention on the informal, conversational use of colloquial language. (Introduce the term 'colloquial' if this is new to the children.) Highlight in particular the almost nonsensical, hyphenated phrases used to name people, places or things we can't immediately think of. This is language we all use all the time, but it is not standard English!

Whole-class skills work

Now read 'I Saw a Jolly Hunter', and ask the children for their responses. Did it amuse them? Why? Is it funny in the same way as 'Old Mrs Thing-Um-E-Bob'? What are the differences? Display the poem and look more carefully at its structure and the poet's choice of words. The rhyme and rhythm of the poem are reminiscent of nursery rhymes, and the use of the word 'jolly' gives an impression of fun and frivolity. However, Causley juxtaposes this with the definitely unfunny theme of guns and hunting. The 'black' humour is achieved by this mismatch of language and format, and theme.

Next, read 'As I Went Down the Cat-Walk'. Ask the children to identify why this is a humorous poem – such as the poet has devised a story around words that begin with 'cat'. Choose some of the 'cat' words and ask the children to define them.

Differentiated group activities

1*: Consider the three poems and produce a short piece of writing about the poem they prefer. Give reasons and examples.
2: Prepare 'Old Mrs Thing-Um-E-Bob' for reading aloud. Work in groups of three, taking on the roles of narrator, Mrs Thing-um-e-bob and Mr What's-his-name.
3: Work in pairs. Identify all 'cat' words in 'As I Went Down the Cat-Walk'. Use dictionaries to find their meanings.
4*: Work in pairs. Look through the collection of poetry books. Find another poem by Charles Causley and another humorous verse by a different poet. Prepare one poem to read aloud.

Conclusion

Ask selected children from Groups 1 and 3 to share their work. Choose one group from each of Groups 2 and 4 to give their readings of a poem. Conclude by summing up the various ways that poets can play with language to create humorous verse and why these appeal.

OLD MRS THING-UM-E-BOB

Old Mrs Thing-um-e-bob,
    Lives at you-know-where,
Dropped her what-you-may-call-it down
    The well of the kitchen stair.

'Gracious me!' said Thing-um-e-bob,
    'This don't look too bright.
I'll ask old Mr What's-his-name
    To try and put it right.'

Along came Mr What's-his-name,
    He said, 'You've broke the lot!
I'll have to see what I can do
    With some of the you-know-what.'

So he gave the what-you-may-call-it a pit
    And he gave it a bit of a pat,
And he put it all together again
    With a little of this and that.

And he gave the what-you-may-call-it a dib
    And he gave it a dab as well
When all of a sudden he heard a note
    As clear as any bell.

'It's as good as new!' cried What's-his-name.
    But please remember, now,
In future Mrs Thing-um-e-bob
    You'll have to go you-know-how.'

Charles Causley

AS I WENT DOWN THE CAT-WALK

As I went down the cat-walk
    Where all the catkins blow,
I saw an old cat-burglar
    Beside a cattalo[1].
And O he miaowed and O he mewed
    Just like the cat-bird's call.
I said, 'Pray cease this catalogue
    Of scatty caterwaul.
I didn't catch your name, I fear,
    But how, my dear old chap,
Among such cataracts of tears
    May I take my cat-nap?'
He said, 'Of various cat-calls
    I'm running the gamut
Because upon my cat-fish
    No catsup has been put!
Such catchpenny behaviour
    It makes me ill, then iller.'
I said, 'Please don't excite yourself.
    Lean on this caterpillar.'
I plucked from off the apple tree
    A juicy, ripe cat's head.
He took it with some cat-lap
    And felt much better fed.
And then he played cat's-cradle
    And turned cat in the pan,
And sailed to Catalonia
    All in a catamaran.
He sailed away by Catalan Bay[2]
    That happy catamaran.

Charles Causley

[1]*A cross between a buffalo and a cow.*
[2]*in Gibraltar.*

I SAW A JOLLY HUNTER

I saw a jolly hunter
    With a jolly gun
Walking in the country
    In the jolly sun.

In the jolly meadow
    Sat a jolly hare.
Saw the jolly hunter.
    Took jolly care.

Hunter jolly eager –
    Sight of jolly prey.
Forgot gun pointing
    Wrong jolly way.

Jolly hunter jolly head
    Over heels gone.
Jolly old safety-catch
    Not jolly on.

Bang went the jolly gun.
    Hunter jolly dead.
Jolly hare got clean away.
    Jolly good, I said.

Charles Causley

Term 3

POEMS BY WILLIAM BLAKE

OBJECTIVES

UNIT	SPELLING/VOCABULARY	GRAMMAR/PUNCTUATION	COMPREHENSION/ COMPOSITION
READING POETRY Poems by William Blake.	Develop vocabulary to talk about poems. Understand that language changes over time.	Understand and demonstrate when reading aloud how punctuation signposts meaning. Identify and use contrastive connectives.	Read, describe, compare and evaluate poems by significant poet. Investigate meaning conveyed through figurative language. Write summaries.

ORGANIZATION (3 HOURS)

	INTRODUCTION	WHOLE-CLASS SKILLS WORK	DIFFERENTIATED GROUP ACTIVITIES	CONCLUSION
HOUR 1	Introduce William Blake. Read 'The Tyger' on photocopiable page 158. Discuss vocabulary and meaning.	Analyse form. Investigate imagery.	1–4*: Write a short essay about the poem using given headings as a guide to structure.	Share and discuss ideas written in essays, particularly personal response to poem.
HOUR 2	Read 'The Chimney Sweeper' on photocopiable page 158. Discuss its historical context and its meaning.	Revise summary writing. Collaborate on writing a summary of the 'story' in the poem.	1*: Write the poem as an extended story. 2 & 3: Write the poem as a story. 4*: Work with a partner to retell the poem as a story.	Share stories and story ideas and evaluate how accurately they reflect the meaning of the poem.
HOUR 3	Read 'The Blossom' and 'The Sick Rose' on photocopiable pages 158–159. Discuss how these are 'paired'.	Use contrastive connectives to compare two poems.	1–4*: Write an essay on the poems of William Blake using template adapted according to ability.	Discuss personal responses to the work of William Blake.

RESOURCES

Photocopiable pages 158 and 159 (William Blake Poems) and 160 (William Blake: Essay Template), a copy of the complete works of William Blake (optional), OHP and acetate (optional), board or flip chart, dictionaries, writing materials.

PREPARATION

Make enough sets of photocopiable pages 158 and 159 (William Blake Poems) for one set between two children. If possible, prepare the poems also as OHTs or enlarge to at least A3 size, ideally putting each poem on a separate sheet. Make enough copies of photocopiable page 160 (Essay Template) for one between two children in Group 1. Prepare simplified versions for Groups 2–4 as necessary (see below under Hour 3, Differentiated group activities). In preparation for Hour 1, write out on the board or flip chart the headings outlined for writing under Differentiated group activities.

Introduction

Explain to the children that during this unit they will be looking in depth at one poet, William Blake, and reading five of his poems. Provide them with a bit of biographical background information to set the poems in context:

William Blake was born in 1757 in London. In 1772 he was apprenticed to an engraver – and later illustrated his own and others' work with engravings and water colours. He had a very vivid imagination and radical religious and political beliefs. Both influenced his poems and other writings, but caused them to be unpopular with the public who thought them mystical and mysterious. As he could find no publisher for his work, he published them himself on engraved plates. However, they were not fully appreciated until long after his death. He died in 1827 and is now regarded as one of the finest poets of the period.

Display and read 'The Tyger' on photocopiable page 158. Explain that the poem is presented here exactly as Blake published it in 1789, but that they might find certain changes to spelling and punctuation in modern anthologies. What would they expect these to be? (For example 'Tyger' changed to 'tiger'; '&' changed to 'and'; 'Lamb' changed to 'lamb'; 'What dread hand? & what dread feet?' changed to 'What dread hand what what dread feet?')

Distribute copies of the poem and re-read it, asking the children to identify (by underlining, perhaps) any vocabulary they don't understand. Discuss some of the difficult vocabulary and lead children to an understanding that language changes over time. Not only do words come in and out of use, but often words which were once commonly used are still used but rarely, or words take on different meanings.

immortal = undying, long-lasting	frame = make
symmetry = well-proportioned body	deeps = seas
aspire = hope to achieve	thy/thine = your

Explore with the children what the poem is saying by going through it verse by verse and paraphrasing, for example:
- Verse 1: What 'hand or eye' (ie 'who') could make such a fearful creature as the tiger?
- Verse 2: Where did the fire of the tiger's eyes come from?
- Verse 3: Who had the strength and skill to make the tiger's heart and make it beat?
- Verse 4: Who dared to get hold of the terrors of a tiger?
- Verse 5: Did the creator of the tiger smile when he saw his work and was this the same being who created the lamb?
- Verse 6: This verse repeats the first with one difference: the word 'dare' instead of 'could'.

Whole-class skills work

Remind children that poetry is meant to be *heard* not just read silently. Poets know this, and set up the lines of their poems accordingly. Ask the children to re-read the poem themselves in pairs and then work together analysing the rhythm and rhyme, marking the stressed syllables with '/' and the rhyme pattern with letters of the alphabet.

```
     /      /      /       /
Tyger! Tyger! burning bright          a
    /      /      /      /
In the forests of the night,          a
     /       /      /      /
What immortal hand or eye             b
      /        /       /       /
Could frame thy fearful symmetry?     b
```

Revise the concept of imagery and figurative language, in particular metaphor, and explore how it is used in the poem. For example, in verse 4, God making the tiger is compared to a blacksmith working in his forge. Why is this effective? What are the images in the first two lines of verse 5?

Remind the children about the type of metaphor called personification where attributes of a human being are given to an animal, inanimate object or idea. A device closely related to personification is that called 'apostrophe', which consists in addressing someone absent, or something non-human, as if it were alive and present and capable of replying to what is being said. Discuss with the children how this applies to Blake's 'The Tyger'.

Differentiated group activities

1–4*: All children should write a short essay about the poem using the following headings as a guide:
- Explain what the poem is about.
- Briefly describe the verse form.
- Explain how the metaphors add to the power of the poem.
- What questions is Blake asking about God?
- Conclude by expressing your personal response to the poem. (Is it a good description of a tiger? What do you think about the views it expresses about God and so on?) Children in Groups 3 and 4 could be given a simplified version of the headings (for example they could be asked to write about the first three points only and explain only *one* metaphor).

Conclusion

Ask the children to share and discuss their ideas about the last three headings.

Introduction

Display and read aloud 'The Chimney Sweeper' on photocopiable page 159. On the surface this poem is easier to understand than the 'The Tyger'. Apart from the language being more familiar, it tells a simple story which involves a dream. However, as with most of Blake's poems, things are not that simple and this poem is both ironic and symbolic.

After reading the poem, explain to the children that in the 18th century, small boys were often employed to climb up narrow chimney flues and clean them, collecting the soot in bags. Such boys, sometimes sold to the master sweepers by their parents, were miserably treated by their masters and often suffered disease and physical deformity.

Read the poem again and then ask the children to characterize the boy who speaks in the poem. How do the children think his and the poet's attitudes toward his lot in life differ? Look, for example, at lines 7 and 8. What do they think Blake is trying to say when he puts these words into the boy's mouth? Does Blake really believe as he has the boy say in the last line 'So, if all do their duty, they need not fear harm'?

Ensure that the children understand that 'As Tom was a-sleeping, he had such sight!' means that what follows is what Tom saw in a dream. Ask the children if they think Tom's dream was a happy one and to support their ideas with reasons. If you feel the children are able, you could discuss possible symbolic interpretations with them.

Whole-class skills work

Revise summary writing:

> A *summary* is a re-written version of the text which has been shortened in length but which retains the meaning. A summary should not be confused with an *abridgement* which is a shortening of a text by cutting phrases and sentences.

Write a summary of the poem in about 80 words with the children contributing ideas and you acting as scribe on the board or flip chart. Brainstorm the appropriate ideas and sentences and don't worry initially about the length. Then go back and refine, deleting all but the most important details until the approximate number of words is achieved.

Differentiated group activities

1*–4*: All children should work on turning the poem into a short story. The story could begin with the events in the poem, and continue with a typical day in Tom's life.

*Encourage children in Group 1 to use as much information from the poem as possible, for example building up characters round all the names mentioned, using the 'moral' in the last line at the end of their story, and so on. Children in Group 4 could work in pairs and retell the poem as a story to their partner, swapping roles half way through the session.

Conclusion

Ask selected children to read out or talk about their ideas for their story version of the poem. Discuss how accurately they reflect the poem and, for those who have gone beyond the text, how appropriate their extended ideas are.

HOUR 3

Introduction

Explain that many of Blake's poems were written in pairs with one of the pair appearing in a collection called *Songs of Innocence* and its companion appearing in *Songs of Experience*. 'The Blossom' and 'The Sick Rose' are such a pair. Display and read them both. On first impressions, which poem do they think appeared in which collection?

Re-read 'The Blossom' and ensure the children understand it at a basic level: a 'merry sparrow' has nested near a 'happy blossom'. The blossom hears a robin, also nested nearby, sobbing. Ask the children why they think the robin is sobbing.

Re-read 'The Sick Rose'. Ostensibly this poem is about a flower and a garden pest which attacks it on a stormy night, but is that all? Discuss with the children how the language indicates that there is more meaning intended here. What do the children think Blake is talking about here if he is not talking about country gardens? Read the first line and draw the children's attention to the fact that the poet is addressing the rose directly (like he did the tiger in 'Tyger! Tyger!' The emotion is strong and the meaning expressed succinctly. Look at other uses of powerful language, for example 'sick' as applied to a flower, 'howling storm', 'crimson', 'dark secret', the rhyming of contrasting ideas in 'joy' and 'destroy' and so on.

What are the main differences between the two poems? ('The Blossom' is about the happy and beautiful side of nature; 'The Sick Rose' is about the corruption and destruction in nature.)

Whole-class skills work

Ask the children to study this list of contrastive connectives:

although	even though	nevertheless
however	in contrast (to)	on the other hand
this differs from	but	whereas

They should then experiment with using the connectives to compare the two poems, for example:

'The Blossom' is a happy tree *but* the rose in 'The Sick Rose' is dying because of an infection.
Although 'The Blossom' is a happy poem, there is note of sadness because the robin is sobbing.

Differentiated group activities

1–4*: All children use the Essay Template on photocopiable 160 to plan and write an essay on William Blake. The headings on the template are aimed at Group 1. Templates with fewer headings could be provided for other groups. For example, for Group 4, the template could be as follows:
■ Research and write a brief biography of William Blake.
■ Write about your favourite poem as follows:
　– Write a summary of the poem.
　– Describe the verse form.
　– Pick out one really striking metaphor and explain it.
　– Write your opinion of the poem.

Conclusion

Conclude the unit with a general discussion on William Blake. This could be focused around the personal responses and opinions expressed in the essays.

FURTHER IDEAS

Ask children to read more of Blake's poems and to look for the features already studied. The topic could be made cross-curricular by adding a detailed study of Blake's art.

WILLIAM BLAKE POEMS

THE TYGER

Tyger! Tyger! Burning bright
In the forests of the night,
What immortal hand or eye
Could frame thy fearful symmetry?

In what distant deeps or skies
Burnt the fire of thine eyes?
On what wings dare he aspire?
What the hand dare seize the fire?

And what shoulder, & what art,
Could twist the sinews of thy heart?
And when thy heart began to beat,
What dread hand? & what dread feet?

What the hammer? what the chain?
In what furnace was thy brain?
What the anvil? What dread grasp
Dare its deadly terrors clasp?

When the stars threw down their spears,
And water'd heaven with their tears,
Did he smile his work to see?
Did he who made the Lamb make thee?

Tyger! Tyger! Burning bright
In the forests of the night,
What immortal hand or eye,
Dare frame thy fearful symmetry?

William Blake

THE BLOSSOM

Merry, Merry Sparrow!
Under leaves so green
A happy Blossom
Sees you swift as arrow
Seek your cradle narrow
Near my Bosom.

Pretty, Pretty Robin!
Under leaves so green
A happy Blossom
Hears you sobbing, sobbing
Pretty, Pretty Robin,
Near my Bosom.

William Blake

THE CHIMNEY SWEEPER

When my mother died I was very young,
And my father sold me while yet my tongue
Could scarcely cry, ''weep, 'weep! 'weep 'weep!'
So your chimneys I sweep, and soot I sleep.

There's little Tom Dacre, who cried when his head,
That curled like a lamb's back, was shaved: so I said,
'Hush, Tom! Never mind it, for when your head's bare
You know that the soot cannot spoil your white hair.'

And so he was quiet, and that very night,
As Tom was a-sleeping, he had such a sight!
That thousands of sweepers, Dick, Joe, Ned, and Jack,
Were all of them lock'd up in coffins of black.

And by came an Angel who had a bright key,
And he opened the coffins and set them all free;
Then down a green plain leaping, laughing they run,
And wash in a river, and shine in the Sun.

Then naked and white, all their bags left behind,
They rise upon clouds and sport in the wind;
And the Angel told Tom, if he'd be a good boy,
He'd have God for his father, and never want joy.

And so Tom awoke; and we rose in the dark,
And got with our bags and our brushes to work.
Though the morning was cold, Tom was happy and warm;
So, if all do their duty, they need not fear harm.

William Blake

THE SICK ROSE

O Rose, thou art sick!
The invisible worm
That flies in the night
In the howling storm,

Has found out thy bed
Of crimson joy:
And his dark secret love
Does thy life destroy.

William Blake

WILLIAM BLAKE: ESSAY TEMPLATE

■ The introduction could be a *brief* biography of William Blake. Find out more about his life through research.

■ Write about the style and language of his poems, giving examples (simple rhyming verse, simple vocabulary, use of archaic words).

■ Write about his use of metaphor, including personification. Begin by explaining what a metaphor and/or personification is, then choose one example from each of the poems studied and explain what it means and why it is effective.

■ Write in detail about one of Blake's poems. Begin with a short summary of the poem, explain the verse form, explain the use of metaphor, and talk about the ideas in the poem. Finish the paragraph by saying why you liked the poem.

■ Write about how the other poems you have studied are similar or different to this poem.

THE POETRY MACHINE

OBJECTIVES

UNIT	SPELLING/VOCABULARY	GRAMMAR/PUNCTUATION	COMPREHENSION/ COMPOSITION
WRITING POETRY The Poetry Machine.	Develop vocabulary to talk about poetry.	Revise parts of speech.	Write poems linked by form. Revise features of different poetic forms.

ORGANIZATION (2 HOURS)

	INTRODUCTION	WHOLE-CLASS SKILLS WORK	DIFFERENTIATED GROUP ACTIVITIES	CONCLUSION
HOUR 1	Read 'The great pyramid' on photocopiable page 163. Discuss how the Poetry Machine works as a template.	Revise parts of speech.	1–4: All pupils use Poetry Machine to write poem according to ability. *Teacher works with Groups 1 & 4.	Volunteers share their poems, followed by class evaluation and discussion.
HOUR 2	Read the poems in various forms on photocopiable page 164.	Identify characteristic features of different poetic forms.	1–4: All pupils write a poem in the form of their choice, according to ability. *Teacher works with Groups 2 & 3.	Pupils who have not yet read out a poem should be selected to read theirs. Recap on the distinctive features of different forms of poetry.

RESOURCES

Photocopiable pages 163 (The Poetry Machine) and 164 (Examples of Poetic Forms), OHP and acetate, board or flip chart, writing materials.

PREPARATION

Make enough copies of both photocopiable pages for all children. If possible prepare OHTs of these sheets – or enlarge to at least A3 size.

Introduction

Read aloud the example poem 'The great pyramid' from photocopiable page 163 (The Poetry Machine). Tell the children that it is a poem written by a child using a particular poetic form. Display the OHT (or A3 enlargement) of photocopiable page 163 (The Poetry Machine) and explain to the children how the Poetry Machine works, using the example poem and working through it line by line.

Whole-class skills work

Revise the key skills and understanding necessary to make the Poetry Machine work, using a whole-class question-and-answer session, for example:
■ What is a noun? Give some examples. What is a proper noun?
■ What is an article? What is the difference between the article 'a' and the article 'the'?
■ What is an adjective? Give examples of different types of adjectives.
■ What is a simile? Give examples. How is a simile different from a metaphor?
■ What is a fact? How does it differ from an opinion?
  Write a class poem using the Poetry Machine.

Differentiated group activities

All children should experiment with writing their own poems using the Poetry Machine.
1*: Children in this group should be encouraged to develop their poems further and even to devise their own, more sophisticated poetry machines.
2 & 3: Children in this group should be encouraged to develop their poems further.
4*: Children in this group should write to the model provided. They may need particular support when trying to find 'the big idea' that arises from their noun.

Conclusion

Over this and the next hour, aim for each child to share one poem with the class. Ask for volunteers on this occasion. The volunteers should read out their poems while the rest of the class evaluates how effective they are, ie appropriate choice of adjectives, vivid similes, a thought-provoking idea at the end.

Introduction

Photocopiable page 164 includes examples of some of the poetic forms children will have studied in Key Stage Two. Display the OHT or enlarged sheet and ask for volunteers to them read aloud to the rest of the class. Encourage the readers to emphasize the rhythm patterns where there are such.

Whole-class skills work

Identify the features of each of the forms, outlining them on the board or flip chart – for example:
■ Haiku: A short poem in which economy of expression is the important thing. Three lines of 5 syllables, 7 syllables and 5 syllables.
■ Ballad: A four-line verse in which lines 2 and 4 rhyme. Three stresses in lines 1 and 3 and two in lines 2 and 4. These rules can be treated very freely.
■ Couplets: Two rhyming lines. Couplets are often grouped together to make longer verses.
■ Sonnet: Fourteen lines with five stresses in each line. The pattern is 12 lines of alternating rhyme scheme with a couplet at the end: ababcdcdefefgg.
■ Blank verse: A rhythm pattern of five stresses in each line, but no rhyme.
■ Free verse: No set scheme of rhyme or rhythm – but fairly short lines.

Differentiated group activities

1–4: All children should work towards building up their personal poetry collections by writing in whichever of the above forms appeals to them. Children who find they are struggling with a form should try a simpler form (such as a shorter form, or a form without rhyme). Children who find writing any kind of poetry difficult should continue to use the model provided by the 'Poetry Machine' on photocopiable page 163.
    *The teacher works with Groups 2 & 3.

Conclusion

Those who did not read at the end of Hour 1 should now read out their poems. Attempt to hear a variety of forms and recap on the distinctive features of each.

 # THE POETRY MACHINE

PROMPT	EXAMPLE
	The great pyramid
Write a noun (with article).	The great pyramid
Write a fact about the noun.	Built thousands of years ago
Write three adjectives to describe the noun.	Huge, mighty, soaring
Write a simile to describe the noun.	Like a mountain reaching to the sky
Write another simile.	Like a finger pointing at heaven
Write how you feel about it.	It makes me feel small
Write a simile about how you feel.	Like a tiny ant that no-one notices
Repeat the noun.	The great pyramid
Express an important idea that the noun makes you think of.	Reminds us how short our life is.

■ Try it yourself.

PROMPT	YOUR POEM
Write a noun.	
Write a fact about the noun.	
Write three adjectives to describe the noun.	
Write a simile to describe the noun.	
Write another simile.	
Write how you feel about it.	
Write a simile about how you feel.	
Repeat the noun.	
Express an important idea that the noun makes you think of.	

EXAMPLES OF POETIC FORMS

HAIKU

Haikus are icebergs
Three lines floating on the page
The rest unwritten.

FREE VERSE
Clouds

Clouds are countries in the sky
Countries with rolling hills
Huge mountains
Mighty cliffs
And an ocean of deepest, purest blue.

COUPLETS
Douglas the dentist

Douglas the dentist, bored with drilling,
Holes in teeth that needed filling,
Decided to take a holiday
As far as possible away
From teeth and dental miscellanea
And so he went to Transylvania...

BALLAD
Robin Hood

Robin Hood went to Nottingham town
With a link, a down and a day,
And there he met an old widow woman
Who was weeping on her way.

"What news? What news?" said Robin Hood,
"You are weeping – tell me why?"
Said she, "My sons in Nottingham town
This day are condemned to die."

"I'll help if I can," said bold Robin Hood
With a link, a day and a down,
And then he spied a ragged old man
On his way to Nottingham town.

Extract from English traditional ballad

SONNET
18

Shall I compare thee to a summer's day?
Thou art more lovely and more temperate.
Rough winds do shake the darling buds of May,
And summer's lease hath all too short a date.
Sometimes too hot the eye of Heaven shines,
And often is his gold complexion dimmed.
And every fair from fair sometimes declines,
By chance of nature's changing course untrimmed.
But thy eternal summer shall not fade,
Nor lose possession of that fair thou owest,
Nor shall Death brag thou wander'st in his shade
When in eternal lines to time thou grow'st.
So long as men can breath, or eyes can see,
So long lives this, and this gives life to thee.

William Shakespeare

BLANK VERSE
The Passing of Arthur

So all day long the noise of battle rolled
Among the mountains by the winter sea;
Until King Arthur's Table, man by man,
Had fallen in Lyonesse about their lord,
King Arthur. Then, because his wound was
   deep,
The bold Sir Bedivere uplifted him,
And bore him to a chapel nigh the field,
A broken chancel with a broken cross,
That stood on a dark strait of barren land:
On one side lay the Ocean, and on one
Lay a great water, and the moon was full.

From 'The Passing of Arthur' by Alfred, Lord Tennyson

CAPITAL PUNISHMENT

OBJECTIVES

UNIT	SPELLING/VOCABULARY	GRAMMAR/PUNCTUATION	COMPREHENSION/ COMPOSITION
READING NON-FICTION Persuasive writing: 'Capital Punishment'.	Develop vocabulary through reading.	Revise language conventions and grammatical features of persuasive texts.	Read and review characteristics of argument texts. Distinguish fact from opinion. Express personal responses to text.

ORGANIZATION (2 HOURS)

	INTRODUCTION	WHOLE-CLASS SKILLS WORK	DIFFERENTIATED GROUP ACTIVITIES	CONCLUSION
HOUR 1	Read 'Capital Punishment' on photocopiable pages 167 and 168. Identify different points of view.	Revise the difference between fact and opinion.	1*: Guided reading and discussion. 2 & 3: Reading Comprehension, parts B and C. 4*: Guided reading and discussion.	Discuss personal views on the issue, developing additional arguments for and against.
HOUR 2	Re-read 'Capital Punishment' on photocopiable pages 167 and 168, focusing on how the arguments are structured.	Examine the different types of argument used.	1: Reading Comprehension, all parts. 2 & 3*: Guided reading and discussion. 4: Reading Comprehension, part A.	Discuss answers to the Reading Comprehension exercise. Recap on different ways of supporting arguments.

RESOURCES

Photocopiable pages 167 and 168 ('Capital Punishment: For and Against 1 and 2'), 169 (Reading Comprehension), dictionaries, thesauruses, board or flip chart, OHP and acetate (optional), writing materials.

PREPARATION

Make enough copies of each of the photocopiable pages for one between two children. If possible, prepare photocopiable pages 167 and 168 ('Capital Punishment: For and Against 1 and 2') as OHTs or enlarge to at least A3 size.

Introduction

Read the two essays on photocopiable pages 167 and 168, 'Capital Punishment: For and Against 1 and 2'. Ensure that the children understand what is meant by capital punishment. Then work with them to determine both what the issue is (ie what the argument is about) and what are the different points of view. (Discourage 'taking sides' on the issue at this stage; this will come when the arguments presented have been analysed.) Work collaboratively to write on the board or flip chart a paragraph that follows this format:
- **1st sentence:** State what the issue is about.
- **2nd sentence:** Identify the groups that are debating the issue.
- **3rd sentence:** Summarize the point of view of one group.
- **4th sentence:** Summarize the point of view of the other group.

Whole-class skills work

Revise the difference between fact and opinion. Ask the children to find and share definitions of the word 'fact' using dictionaries and thesauruses. Write down a definition with which everyone agrees – for example:

Fact: something which is certainly known to have happened or to be true.

Invite the children to provide examples and write these under the definition.
    Repeat the activity for the word 'opinion' – for example:

Opinion: a personal belief not directly based on evidence.

Go through the two arguments in 'Capital Punishment: For and Against' and underline facts in one colour and opinions in another.

Differentiated group activities

1*: Guided reading and discussion of the text. The following questions may be used as a starting point:
■ What do we mean by 'capital punishment'?
■ What different kinds of arguments have the writers used?
■ Regardless of your personal views, which essay do you think presents the most powerful arguments?
■ Could you add any extra arguments to either essay?
■ Discuss your personal views on capital punishment.
2 & 3: Complete parts B and C of the Reading Comprehension on photocopiable page 169.
4*: Guided reading and discussion of the text. Use some of the above questions as appropriate.

Conclusion

Invite the children to discuss their personal views on capital punishment and to make additional arguments for or against.

Introduction

Re-read 'Capital Punishment: For and Against' asking the children to think about the different persuasive techniques the writers use to put forward their point of view. Ask them to look also at how the writers link the points of their argument together.

Whole-class skills work

Examine the different ways arguments can be supported. Some of the main ones are:
■ using facts and statistics
■ quoting the opinion of an important person or source
■ arguing that something is fair or unfair
■ giving a specific example, story or anecdote
■ appealing directly to the audience's emotions or feelings, for example with a personal question.
    Ask children to find examples of the above in the two essays presented in 'Capital Punishment: For and Against'.

Differentiated group activities

1: Complete all parts of the Reading Comprehension on photocopiable page 169.
2 & 3*: Guided reading and discussion (see above).
4: Complete part A of the Reading Comprehension on photocopiable page 169.

Conclusion

Discuss answers to the questions on the Reading Comprehension sheet. As well as ensuring that the children know what is an appropriate answer to each question, use questions as the basis for further discussion where appropriate.
    Recap on the different ways of supporting arguments.

CAPITAL PUNISHMENT: FOR AND AGAINST 1

FOR

I am going to argue the case for the reintroduction of capital punishment in Britain. I will base my argument on some highly convincing facts and statistics.

The death penalty was abolished in Britain in 1964. Since then the murder rate has roughly doubled to around 640 every year. What is worse is that, in the same period, there have been 71 murders committed by people who have been released after serving 'life sentences'. I found these statistics in a Home Office report, and anyone is free to check them. I think they speak for themselves. They prove that the death penalty deters criminals from committing murder. They certainly prove that the death penalty prevents criminals from murdering again, because dead people can't commit murders!

Another argument for the death penalty is that it is a just punishment. People who take the lives of others deserve to lose their own life. Even the Bible advocates 'An eye for an eye and a tooth for a tooth'. What kind of a punishment is life imprisonment? It is not even for life! After ten years, with 'good behaviour', the murderer can be let loose on society again.

Also, think of the cost of looking after all those prisoners. Home Office statistics say that it presently costs £550 per week to keep an ordinary, minimum-security prisoner – that's more than a luxury hotel! Just think of the money that could be saved for good causes if we didn't waste it on keeping murderers in luxury!

The abolition of the death penalty took place in the 'swinging' 1960s – a time of liberal values, when 'do-gooders' thought more about the welfare of the criminal than the victims, and we must not forget that as well as the person who has lost his or her life, there is a whole family and circle of friends who will also have suffered. We have learned that 1960s values do not work and have made major changes in areas such as education and health – why should criminal justice be left behind?

Opponents of the death penalty say that it is not a fitting punishment for a civilized society. But what is civilized about a society where children cannot go for a walk in a park without fear of being attacked, where old people are beaten to death for a few hundred pounds, and where even the police are stabbed and shot in the conduct of their duty?

In my opinion, Britain would be a happier and safer place if we had the courage to reintroduce the death penalty.

CAPITAL PUNISHMENT: FOR AND AGAINST 2

AGAINST

In this essay, I hope to convince you that capital punishment is wrong, and that the British Government was right to abolish it.

Many people argue about capital punishment by quoting statistics, but the suffering capital punishment has caused to real people is a far more powerful argument. A good example is the case of Ruth Ellis.

Ruth Ellis was the victim of a cruel boyfriend who abused her so badly that, on 10 April 1955, after a particularly bad period of abuse, she shot him. She was charged with murder and duly appeared at the Old Bailey. Her lawyer argued for a verdict of manslaughter because of the way her boyfriend had treated her, but the jury found her guilty and she was sentenced to death. This was clearly an unjust punishment. There was great public sympathy for Ruth and many people wrote letters of protest to their MPs. The case of Ruth Ellis, and a number of other doubtful executions led to the Homicide Act of 1957 which limited the types of murder that were punishable by the death penalty. Capital punishment was effectively abolished nine years later.

It is true that crime rates have risen since the 1960s, but we cannot simply blame this on the abolition of the death penalty. It is more likely that crime has risen because of changes in society such as the break-up of families, the decline of religion and social problems such as unemployment. If we need evidence of this, we have only to look to the United States and compare States which still have the death penalty with those which do not. States that have the death penalty seem to have a higher number of murders than States which do not have the death penalty. States that abolish and then reintroduce the death penalty do not seem to show a change in the murder rate. No change in the number of murders in a given city or State seems to take place following an execution.

There is no conclusive evidence to show that the death penalty is a more effective deterrent than long-term imprisonment. Critics of the death penalty have always pointed out the risk of executing the innocent. For example, there was one case in Britain where the victim was pardoned after he had been hanged! Human beings will always make mistakes and we cannot afford to make mistakes with something as precious as life.

The main objection to the death penalty is that it is bound to be used unfairly. For example, women are rarely executed in the United States, even though 20% of all murders have been committed by women.

Many eminent social scientists and psychologists say that the death penalty will not stop the increasing number of murders and violent crimes, and that we have to look for other ways to do this, such as reducing the violence shown on television, controlling firearms, and so on.

The above evidence shows that life imprisonment is a preferable alternative to the death penalty in a civilized society.

READING COMPREHENSION

PART A: 'FOR'

■ When was the death penalty abolished in Britain?

■ How many murders are committed each year?

■ Where did the writer of the essay get his evidence?

■ What does the Biblical saying 'An eye for an eye and a tooth for a tooth' mean?

■ What is the weekly cost of keeping an ordinary prisoner in prison?

■ What is the writer's opinion about the death penalty?

PART B: 'AGAINST'

■ Why did Ruth Ellis shoot her boyfriend?

■ Do you agree with the writer that her punishment was unjust?

■ What changes in the law were made as a result of the Ruth Ellis case and similar cases?

■ How does the writer explain the rise in crime since the 1960s?

■ Do you think this is a convincing explanation?

■ What does the evidence from America show?

■ What is the writer's main objection to the death penalty?

PART C: GENERAL

■ Make a list of the facts presented in each essay.

■ Compare the facts presented in each essay. Do any facts appear to be contradictory? Which facts seem to be the most reliable?

■ Pick out some statements that are opinions, not facts.

■ In one sentence, summarize the main argument in each paragraph.

CORPORAL PUNISHMENT

OBJECTIVES

UNIT	SPELLING/VOCABULARY	GRAMMAR/PUNCTUATION	COMPREHENSION/ COMPOSITION
WRITING NON-FICTION Persuasive writing: 'Corporal Punishment'.	Identify misspelled words in own writing. Develop vocabulary of argument.	Extend knowledge and use of connectives.	Write a persuasive argument in paragraphs with appropriate links. Secure control of impersonal writing.

ORGANIZATION (3 HOURS)

	INTRODUCTION	WHOLE-CLASS SKILLS WORK	DIFFERENTIATED GROUP ACTIVITIES	CONCLUSION
HOUR 1	Read and discuss 'Corporal Punishment' on photocopiable page 173.	Revise techniques for supporting arguments and apply to text.	1–4: All groups re-read and discuss 'Corporal Punishment', particularly questions in final paragraph. *Teacher works with Groups 3 & 4.	Spokespersons from each group report back. Identify and discuss strong, effective arguments.
HOUR 2	Re-read 'Corporal Punishment' and investigate different uses of connectives.	Examine oppositional connectives in text and develop list to use in own writing.	1–4: All pupils use one of the templates on photocopiable page 174 to write a discursive essay on corporal punishment. *Teacher works with Groups 1 & 4.	Selected pupils read out drafts of their essays.
HOUR 3	Use examples of children's writing to identify weak arguments.	Analyse why certain arguments are weak and counter-productive.	1–4*: All pupils work in pairs to evaluate each other's writing. Then all re-draft.	Discuss how re-drafting partners exercise helped to improve arguments.

RESOURCES

Photocopiable pages 173 ('Corporal Punishment: A Case Study'),174 (Writing Templates: 1 and 2), board or flip chart, OHP and acetate (optional), writing materials.

PREPARATION

Make enough copies of photocopiable page 173 ('Corporal Punishment') for one between two. If possible, also prepare an OHT or A3 enlargement. Make enough copies of photocopiable page 174 (Writing Templates: 1 and 2) so that each pair in Groups 1–3 has a copy of Template 1, and each child in Group 4 has a copy of Template 2.

Introduction

Read 'Corporal Punishment: A Case Study' on page 174. Ensure the children understand what is meant by 'corporal punishment' and any other unfamiliar words or phrases, for example *abolished, in-school suspension, resort to the strap, justified, controversy, coalition, spokesperson, empathy*. Discuss what the article is about. What is the issue? What was the incident that sparked off the controversy? Summarize the point of view of each side.

Whole-class skills work

Revise some of the main techniques for supporting an argument:

■ using facts and statistics
■ quoting the opinion of an important person or source
■ arguing that something is fair or unfair
■ giving a specific example, story or anecdote
■ appealing directly to the audience's emotions or feelings, for example with a personal question.

Discuss how each of them could be used to argue a case for or against corporal punishment.

Differentiated group activities

1–4: All children, working in ability groups, should re-read and discuss the text, particularly the questions posed in the final paragraph. Ask each group to appoint a 'spokesperson' to report back to the class on the opinions of the group.
    *The teacher should work with Groups 3 and 4.

Conclusion

The chosen spokesperson for each group should be invited to report back to the class. As he or she speaks, the rest of the class should listen carefully to the kinds of argument used as well as to the content of the argument. Ensure that you highlight the content and technique of effective arguments. Discuss whether there is any consensus of opinion (defining the term if necessary) or whether there is a split of opinion.

Introduction

Display the text of 'Corporal Punishment'. Read the first two sentences and ask the children to identify the connective word that shows how the ideas in the two sentences are linked or related. The word is 'however'. Now read through the rest of the piece, asking the children to look out for other words that signpost connections (for example, *but, in the end, then, after, finally, if*). Discuss how connecting words can serve different purposes – for example to indicate a connection of time (*then, after, finally*), of opposition (*however, but*), of cause (*so, then, because*), of addition (*and, also, furthermore*).

Whole-class skills work

A language feature of persuasive argument writing is the use of oppositional connectives. Write on the board or flip chart some connectives that writers use when they are presenting opposing ideas:

although	though	the reverse
but	unlike	while
however	yet	unless
in contrast	on the other hand	

Ask the children to think up some sentences using these words and phrases. You may wish to get them started by providing a couple of sentence frames and asking them to supply the connective, for example:

Some children in this school believe that having a school uniform is a good idea (connective) many pupils would rather wear their own clothes.
Watching too much television can be unhealthy (connective) television can be very educational.

If they can, ask the children to add to the list of oppositional connectives. Keep this list displayed as an aide-memoire for the children to use when writing their own arguments.

Differentiated group activities

All children should use one of the templates on photocopiable page 174 (Writing Templates: 1 and 2) to write a discursive essay on corporal punishment in which they argue for or against according to their own choice.
1*: Use Template 1 as a guide to be freely developed – for example add more arguments in the middle section of the essay.

2 & 3: Follow Template 1 closely. Note that the conclusion which links back to the example is a more effective, but more difficult way to end the essay, and is thus best suited to the more able children in these groups.

4*: Follow Template 2 closely. In the template the example also serves as an introduction.

Conclusion

Ask selected children to read out the first draft of their essays. Aim to hear an equal number for and against corporal punishment.

Introduction

Explain that the purpose of this lesson is to redraft the essays and that the main focus will be on the quality of the arguments presented.

Ask two selected children (one arguing for, and one against) to read their essays. Select these carefully so that they provide examples of different kinds of unsound or misleading arguments (see below).

Whole-class skills work

Examine some of the commonest types of unsound, misleading or diverting argument:
■ Abusive argument, for example 'Only a stupid idiot could think that corporal punishment would improve behaviour.' This is merely an insult, not an argument. It proves nothing, and simply leads to heightened tempers, especially in discussion.
■ Exaggeration: 'Corporal punishment is vicious, brutal and inhuman. Violent physical abuse is not a suitable form of punishment in schools.'
■ Emotional argument, for example 'Think of the pain, the humiliation, the sheer degradation of being punished in this way.' This argument plays on the emotions of the reader in a way that makes them forget to weigh the different arguments logically.
■ Misuse of statistics, for example '40% of children have reading difficulties.' Statements like this should be challenged. Where did the figure come from? What is meant by 'reading difficulties'?

Note that there are many other types of unsound or misleading argument which would be too technical to discuss with most children at this level. However, the following could be mentioned with some of the more able children:
■ Illogical argument, such as when the conclusion does not follow from the premise.
■ Generalizations, such as when one case is used to prove an argument rather than a representative sample.

Differentiated group activities

Ask the children to work in pairs within groups. They should read their essays to each other and help each other to look for unsound or misleading arguments. They should then redraft their essays.

Conclusion

Ask children to read out examples of some of the arguments they have improved.

Finally, select a few examples of essays for and essay against to be read out in their entirety.

FURTHER IDEA

Ask children to look out for examples of argument both in TV and radio discussion and in books, newspapers and magazines. Encourage them to get into the habit of evaluating arguments using the skills covered in this unit as a starting point.

CORPORAL PUNISHMENT: A CASE STUDY

Corporal punishment was abolished in British state schools in 1986. However, there are still some countries where corporal punishment is legal. Although the case described below really happened and was reported in a variety of media, all the names have been changed and are fictional.

Norton Primary School is not very different to a state primary school in the United Kingdom. Pupils belong to a similar age range, and follow a similar curriculum.

In the summer term of 1998, a group of older pupils were caught selling stolen goods. The headteacher, Mr Brooker, spent the better part of a morning interviewing the pupils, but all they did was to lie about what happened and to try to blame it on other pupils. In the end they had blamed about 100 other pupils. After lengthy questioning, Mr Brooker found overwhelming evidence that the pupils had stolen over 300 gemstones from a woman and given them to other pupils.

Mr Brooker then put nine of the pupils on in-school suspension, but they just ran up and down the corridor, throwing books and creating chaos. Teachers asked them to behave, but the pupils took no notice; they just made insulting gestures.

Finally, Mr Brooker decided that he would have to resort to the strap. He had used the strap so rarely in the past that it took him quite a while to even find it. He then called an assembly and strapped the three worse troublemakers on the hand in front of the whole school.

Mr Brooker subsequently justified his action by pointing out that things had been much better since the strapping and that it provided an example for all the pupils in the school. 'I believe that if everything else fails, the strap is needed,' he said.

The incident caused much controversy throughout the country, particularly the fact that the pupils were punished publicly. A spokesperson for The Coalition for the Protection of Children objected to the punishments. She said, 'It is our belief that not only are there more effective ways to shape children's behaviour, but the message that is sent through the use of this approach does little to contribute to the development of empathy and respectfulness in children.'

Due to this controversy, there is a possibility that a law will be passed similar to the law in the United Kingdom which bans corporal punishment. If this happens, will pupils at Norton Primary School be better off – or worse?

* * * * * * * * * * *

■ Think about your own school. What kind of bad behaviour takes place, and how is it controlled? Are there some kinds of behaviour, such as bullying, which need to be dealt with more severely? Would your school be a happier place if really badly behaved children were punished with the cane or strap, or would it be a place where you would live in fear?

WRITING TEMPLATES: 1 AND 2

TEMPLATE 1

■ Introduction: explain your views on corporal punishment and how you are going to support them.

■ Describe an example of serious bad behaviour that took place in your school recently. Explain how the pupils were punished. Explain how it affected them and how they behaved afterwards. This example should enable you to make the point that corporal punishment would have been more/less effective.

■ Think of two more reasons to support/oppose corporal punishment.

■ Think of the strongest argument that those who oppose/support corporal punishment might put forward and argue against it.

■ Conclusion: *either* sum up your main points, *or* refer back to the example of bad behaviour in paragraph 1, in a way that clinches your point of view about corporal punishment.

- -

TEMPLATE 2

■ Describe an example of serious bad behaviour that took place in your school recently. Explain how the pupils were punished. Explain how it affected them and how they behaved afterwards. This example should enable you to make the point that corporal punishment would have been more/less effective.

■ Think of two more reasons to support/oppose corporal punishment.

■ Conclusion: sum up your main points.

It's All Fantasy

OBJECTIVES

UNIT	SPELLING/VOCABULARY	GRAMMAR/PUNCTUATION	COMPREHENSION/COMPOSITION
READING FICTION Fantasy genre: *Fantasy Stories*, chosen by Diana Wynne Jones.	Develop vocabulary through text. Extend literary vocabulary for talking about texts.	Identify the language features of fantasy genre. Identify and understand complex sentences. Revise conditional clauses.	Examine different authors' treatment of same themes and genre. Look at contrasts and connections in the work of different writers. Write a brief synopsis of a text. Understand the use of paragraphs.

ORGANIZATION (5 HOURS)

	INTRODUCTION	WHOLE-CLASS SKILLS WORK	DIFFERENTIATED GROUP ACTIVITIES	CONCLUSION
HOUR 1	Introduce fantasy genre. Shared reading of 'The Peasant and the Devil' (pages 7–8, approximately 2 minutes).	Investigate common features found in fairy tale genre, focusing on language, characters and plot.	1*: Guided reading and discussion. 2 & 3: Write alternative ending for 'The Peasant and the Devil'. 4*: Guided reading and discussion.	Selected pupils from Groups 2 & 3 share their alternative endings. Discuss how well these fit fantasy genre.
HOUR 2	Shared reading of 'Ully the Piper' (pages 31–44, approximately 18 minutes). Discuss similarities with fairy tale genre.	Revise conditional clauses. Find examples on page 38 of 'Ully the Piper' story.	1: Turn 'Ully the Piper' story into a narrative poem using extract from 'The Pied Piper' as a model. 2 & 3: Guided reading and discussion. 4*: Write a simplified version of 'Ully the Piper' suitable for a young child.	Selected pupils from Groups 1 & 4 share their different versions of the story.
HOUR 3	Shared reading of 'Abu Ali Meets a Dragon', from page 96 to page 109. Discuss author's different treatment of traditional story elements.	Display Propp's Functions on photocopiable page 180. Explain how it works, then identify these functions in well-known fairy stories.	1*: Guided reading and discussion. 2 & 3: Identify Propp's functions in the story, using appropriate symbols. 4*: Guided reading and discussion.	Groups 1 & 4 report back on their discussion of the text. Class discussion on similiarities to and differences from other known fantasy stories.
HOUR 4	Recap on story so far of 'Abu Ali Meets a Dragon', and discuss what may happen next. Follow with shared reading of the story from page 109 to the end (page 115).	Revise the terms 'summary' and 'blurb'. Model the writing of a 100-word summary of the story. Pupils write 50-word blurbs for the story.	1: Work with a partner to identify Propp's functions in the story. Use appropriate symbols. 2 & 3*: Guided reading and discussion. 4: Work with a partner to find similarities and differences between the story and traditional tales.	The class discusses how many of Propp's functions they identified in the story.
HOUR 5	Read 'Jermain and the Sorceress' (pages 202–207, approximately 8 minutes).	Revise setting out and use of paragraphs. Work in pairs to analyse paragraphing in 'Jermain and the Sorceress'.	1–4*: All children work in their ability groups to write a plot for a full story about Jermain and the Sorceress. They use Propp's functions to help them.	Sum up the key features of fantasy genre and its relationship to fairy/folk tale genre.

RESOURCES

Fantasy Stories, chosen by Diana Wynne Jones (Kingfisher, ISBN 1-85697-209-7) – if possible, enough copies for half the class, photocopiable pages 180 (Propp's Functions) and 57–59 (extract from 'The Pied Piper of Hamelin' unit, Term 1), board or flip chart, an OHP and acetate, writing materials.

PREPARATION

Decide how you wish to manage the reading of the stories – whether they will be read as part of the Literacy Hour or outside the hour in previous reading sessions. The text is probably above the independent reading level of some Year 6 children.

Make enough copies of photocopiable page 180 (Propp's Functions) for one between two. In addition, prepare an OHT or A3 enlargement of this sheet. Provide one copy between two of photocopiable pages 57–59 (extract from 'The Pied Piper of Hamelin') for children in Groups 1–3 only. Make an OHT or A3 enlargement of the 'The Peasant and the Devil' story on pages 7–8 of *Fantasy Stories*.

HOUR 1

Introduction

Tell the children that they are going to do an in-depth study of a specific genre: fantasy. Ensure that they understand the meaning of the term 'genre'. (It means 'style' or 'kind', and when applied to writing refers to the different types of writing, each with its own specific features.) What other popular genres can the children think of? (Examples could include adventure, horror, science fiction, mystery and so on.) Now focus specifically on the fantasy genre, explaining that it has its roots in the fairy tale or folk tale and contains many of the same themes and characters. In fantasy writing, these are re-interpreted in new ways, often merging into the modern world, or even the future. Refer back to the 'Wizard of Oz' unit in Term 1 as an example of fantasy that they have read.

Display 'The Peasant and the Devil' (pages 7–8) on OHP. Introduce it as an example of the fantasy genre. Tell the children that it is taken from a collection of traditional fairy tales, written by the Grimm brothers in the 19th century. Explain that fairy tales arise from oral tradition and were in common circulation amongst people for a very long time before they were finally written down (that is why 'folk tales' is a better term).

Now read the story aloud.

Whole-class skills work

Investigate the traditional fairy tale genre, exploring its common features. Begin by looking at the type of language used in fairy stories. Establish that it is traditional, then ask the children to think of some popular phrases that frequently occur, especially at the beginning and end of these tales. Help them to identify phrases such as: 'once upon a time...', 'a long time ago...', and 'they all lived happily ever after'. Discuss the types of character that occur. Establish that there tends to be a hero or heroine (often either very poor, or very rich as in a prince or princess) whose various fortunes and misfortunes the reader follows. Other characters often include magical folk such as witches, fairies, elves, gnomes, dragons and so on. (Note that any discussion of the traditionally negative portrayal of step-mothers in fairy stories will need sensitive handling.)

Move on to look at plot – the usual structure consists of a hero or heroine who either hits misfortune or is faced with some great challenge. He or she overcomes the problem, and finds everlasting happiness (the 'moral' triumph of good over evil is a common theme). Happy endings sometimes revolve around poor people becoming rich, or the marriage of the hero or heroine after overcoming great obstacles to their love. Magic and spells are often a strong element in the fairy tale genre.

Finish by asking the children to briefly identify as many of these features as they can in 'The Peasant and the Devil' and a couple of other well-known fairy stories such as 'Snow White', 'Cinderella' and 'The Elves and the Shoemaker'. What do they think is the one most obvious distinguishing characteristic of fantasy from other genres? (Possibly that it is a narrative that is simply not possible in real life.)

Differentiated group activities

1*: Guided reading and discussion. Use the following questions as a starting point:
■ How can you tell from the first few lines that this is a fairy tale?
■ What bargain does the peasant strike with the devil?

- Who usually comes off best in such bargains in fairy stories?
- How does the peasant manage to trick the devil twice?
- Analyse the structure of the first paragraph which is all one complex sentence.

2 & 3: Write an alternative ending, appropriate to fantasy genre, in which the devil gets his own back by finding a way to trick the peasant.

4*: Guided reading and discussion, using the most appropriate questions outlined for Group 1 above as a starting point.

Conclusion

Invite children from Groups 2 and 3 to share their alternative endings. Ask the rest of the class for their responses. Discuss how appropriate to the fantasy genre these endings are.

Introduction

Read 'Ully the Piper' on pages 31–44. This story shares many similarities with traditional fairy tales, although it was written fairly recently. Ask the children to identify some of these, based on their work from Hour 1. They should notice that, though the language is more modern, the tiny village setting and character types are fairly traditional. The plot also shares similarities in that Ully, the hero, begins in a very unfortunate situation but ends up much more happily as his terrible injury is cured. A supernatural, magical element brings about this resolution. The 'moral' element of reward for good characters (Ully) and punishment for bad characters (Matt) is also a typical element of fairy tales.

Whole-class skills work

Investigate further the use of conditional clauses. Ask the children what they remember about this type of clause from previous work (see the 'Lights' unit, Term 2, page 139). Make sure they all understand that a conditional clause is used when the writer wants to talk about a possible situation and its consequence. Explain that there are many types of conditional clause. One common type begins with 'if' and uses 'were' (instead of 'was' in certain cases) as the main verb, as in this example on page 37 of 'Ully the Piper': *It was almost as if it were being guided.*

There are three more examples of this type of conditional clause on page 38. Ask the children to find these, telling them to look particularly for the 'if' which introduces the conditional clause, and the main verb 'were'. Finish by asking the children to suggest some similar examples of their own.

Differentiated group activities

1: Look again at 'The Pied Piper of Hamelin' poem on photocopiable pages 57–59 (from 'The Pied Piper of Hamelin' unit in Term 1). Now turn the story of 'Ully the Piper' into a narrative poem using 'The Pied Piper' as a model. The children can work in pairs.

2 & 3*: Guided reading and discussion. Use the following questions as a starting point:
- What do we learn about the setting from the first two pages?
- Do we know when the story is set?
- What do we learn about Ully from page 33?
- Explain how Ully comes to learn to play the pipe.
- What kind of person is Matt and how does he treat Ully at the dance?
- What happens to Ully in the glade?
- How is Matt punished for his behaviour?
- Compare this story with 'The Pied Piper' (see above).

4: Write a simpler version of 'Ully the Piper' suitable for a young child. Children could work in pairs, first re-telling the story orally in their own words and then transcribing it.

Conclusion

Ask selected children from Groups 1 and 4 to share their different versions of the story and discuss how well each one fufils the writing task set.

Introduction

Explain that you are going to read an extract from a longer story called *The Land of Green Ginger* by Noel Langley. Read 'Abu Ali Meets a Dragon' up to page 109, ending on *'Whoops!' roared the Dragon triumphantly. 'Gotcha!'*. Briefly discuss the children's personal responses. Have they enjoyed the reading so far?

Then look again at the introduction to the story where Abu Ali is referred to as 'the son of Aladdin'. Point out the names of the other characters and the mention of the place 'Samarkand'. Do the children recognize any links with the famous traditional tale of the 'Arabian Nights'?

Discuss how, although the setting, characters and plot are traditional, the author's overall treatment is very different. The language, for example, is completely modern (*'Whoops!' roared the Dragon triumphantly. 'Gotcha!'*). Most of all, a strong humorous element runs through the whole story, with the very untraditional portrayal of the dragon, the humorous character names and the repeated exaggerations in descriptions (*No one before, or since, has ever been so beautiful* and *Indeed, her voice so enraptured the already enraptured Abu Ali...,*) creating a parody. Compare the story with pantomime.

Whole-class skills work

Display photocopiable page 180 (Propp's Functions) on the OHP. Introduce it by reading the description provided about its background. Explain that Propp's lists of 'functions' provide a useful way of studying aspects of narrative structure and character in fairy and fantasy stories (and in several other kinds of stories such as Westerns).

Go through the two lists with the class, and ask them to identify examples of each function in well-known fairy stories, such as 'Sleeping Beauty', 'Snow White', and so on.

Differentiated group activities

1*: Guided reading and discussion. Use the following questions as a starting point:
■ How traditional is the portrayal of Silver Bud?
■ How is the plot similar to traditional fairy tales?
■ In what ways is Abu Ali a traditional 'hero'?
■ What is unexpected about the way the dragon is presented? How do we expect dragons to be presented in traditional fairy tales?
■ Does the humour appeal to you? Why?
■ How does the author achieve this humorous effect?
2 & 3: The children should go through the story with a partner and see which of Propp's functions they can identify. Ask them to write down the appropriate symbol next to their own brief description of a particular character or event.
4*: Guided reading and discussion (see above).

Conclusion

Ask selected children from Groups 1 and 4 to report back on their discussion of the text. Involve all the children in summing up how the story so far is both similar to and different from other fantasy stories with which they are familiar.

Introduction

Before reading the end of 'Abu Ali Meets a Dragon', briefly recap on what has happened so far. Ask the children what they think will happen next. Then read from page 109, line 19 to the end.

Whole-class skills work

Revise the terms 'summary' and 'blurb' with the children as follows:

A **summary** is a shortened version of a story in a specified number of words. It is rewritten and should not be confused with an abridgement which simply cuts out words, phrases and whole passages. A **blurb** is a summary written to interest the reader in the book. It therefore emphasizes what is interesting and exciting, while avoiding details of how the story ends which might spoil the reader's enjoyment.

Now use the children's suggestions to model the writing of a 100-word summary of the story. Ask the children each to spend a few minutes writing a 50-word cover blurb for the story. Then share some of these and highlight the most successful features.

Differentiated group activities

1: The children should go through the story with a partner and see which of Propp's functions they can identify. Ask them to write down the appropriate symbol next to their own brief description of a particular character or event.

2 & 3*: Guided reading and discussion, using the questions outlined in Hour 3. In addition, talk about the appearance of the Djinn who comes to rescue Abu Ali. How is this different from traditional tales?

4: Go through the story with a partner and make a list of all the things that are (a) the same as, and (b) different to those found in a traditional fairy tale.

Conclusion

Discuss with the class how many of Propp's functions the children found in the story. (Remind the children that this is only part of a longer story, so the plot is not complete.) Some functions may apply only partially, while others are much clearer. A list of possibilities is given below.

PLOT FUNCTIONS
- Function M: A difficult task is set for the hero (Abu Ali must go out and find the phoenix tail feathers).
- Function ↑: The hero leaves home (Abu Ali sets off on his journey).
- Function H: The hero and villain (the dragon) in combat.
- Function D: The hero is tested and receives magical help (the appearance of the Djinn frightens off the dragon).
- Function I: The villain is defeated (the cowardly dragon runs away!).

CHARACTER FUNCTIONS
- Function 1: Villain – the dragon fights the hero, Abu Ali.
- Function 2: Donor – the Djinn tries to give magical help (but fails!).
- Function 3: Helper – Abu Ali's friend, Omar Khayyam.
- Function 4: Princess – there is no princess, but Silver Bud fills the same role.
- Function 5: King – there is no king, but the rich jeweller Sulkpot Ben Nagnag fills the same traditional role.
- Function 6: Hero – Abu Ali.

Introduction

Read 'Jermain and the Sorceress' on pages 202–207. Discuss the children's ideas on Jermain. Why is he being chased? Is he a dangerous character? What do they think the Sorceress will do and how might things end?

Whole-class skills work

Analyse how individual paragraphs are structured. First, revise how to set out paragraphs. All paragraphs (except the first) should be indented by approximately 1cm. Do not leave blank lines between paragraphs.

Next, revise when to start new paragraphs in stories. The children should note that there are no absolute rules, only guidelines. These include starting a new paragraph for: a new idea/thought; a new scene; a new time; a new place; a new character; a different character speaking.

Now ask the children to analyse the paragraphing of 'Jermain and the Sorceress'. They should try to understand why the author has started each new paragraph.

Differentiated group activities

1–4*: All children work in their ability groups to write a plot for a full story about Jermain and the Sorceress, with a clear beginning, middle and ending. Give the children some helpful prompts:
- Why is Jermain fleeing from Leshiya?
- What might happen after the scene described in the extract?
- Keep the actions of the characters consistent with what we know about them from the story so far. Introduce new characters if necessary.
- Use Propp's Functions to help construct the plot, for example Jermain is the hero, the Sorceress is his magical helper. Who is the villain? What is the object of Jermain's search? When will the hero and villain meet in combat? How will the villain be punished? And so on.

Conclusion

Ask the children to share their ideas for plots. End the unit by summing up the key features of fantasy genre and its relationship to fairy/folk tale genre.

PROPP'S FUNCTIONS

In 1968, the Russian folklorist Vladimir Propp wrote a book comparing the plot and characters of a group of fairy tales. He found many similarities which he called 'functions'. He classified these functions and gave each one a symbol. The tables below give a simplified version of his functions for plot and character.

SYMBOL	PLOT FUNCTION
A	The villain causes harm or injury to a member of a family.
B	Misfortune is made known.
↑	The hero leaves home.
D	The hero is tested and receives magical help.
G	The hero is led to object of search.
H	The hero and villain in combat.
I	The villain is defeated.
↓	The hero returns.
Pr	The hero is pursued.
Rs	Rescue of hero from pursuit.
O	The hero, unrecognized, arrives home or in another country.
L	A false hero presents unfounded claims.
M	A difficult task is given to the hero.
N	The task is completed.
Q	The hero is recognized.
Ex	The false villain is exposed.
T	The hero is given a new appearance.
U	The villain is punished.
W	The hero is married and ascends the throne.

SYMBOL	CHARACTER	DESCRIPTION
1.	Villain	Fights with hero.
2.	Donor	Gives hero magical help.
3.	Helper	Helps hero to solve difficult tasks.
4.	Princess	Sought-after person.
5.	King	Gives difficult tasks.
6.	Hero	Searches for something or fights with villain.
7.	False hero	Claims to be hero, but is unmasked.

(Adapted from: Propp, Vladimir, *Morphology of the Folktale*, University of Texas Press, 1973.)

WRITING FANTASY STORIES

OBJECTIVES

UNIT	SPELLING/VOCABULARY	GRAMMAR/PUNCTUATION	COMPREHENSION/ COMPOSITION
WRITING FICTION: Writing fantasy stories.	Check spelling in own writing. Use vocabulary appropriate to fantasy genre.	Demonstrate grammatical awareness and check grammar in own writing.	Write a story based on fantasy genre. Revise key plot structures. Revise redrafting skills.

ORGANIZATION (2 HOURS)

	INTRODUCTION	WHOLE-CLASS SKILLS WORK	DIFFERENTIATED GROUP ACTIVITIES	CONCLUSION
HOUR 1	Display Propp's Functions on photocopiable page 180. Use it to create an outline plot and characters for a story.	Revise key plot structures using the Story Planner on photocopiable page 104.	1*: Experiment with fantasy genre, writing a story with a twist on a traditional fairy tale, a parody, or weaving in modern elements. 2 & 3: Write a traditional fairy tale with traditional plot and characters. 4*: Write a short, simple fairy tale based on a well-known fairy tale.	Selected pupils from Groups 1 & 4 share the first drafts of their stories. Discuss how content and structure relate to Story Planner and Propp's Functions.
HOUR 2	Pupils from Groups 2 & 3 share the first drafts of their stories, followed by discussion and evaluation.	Revise the key areas/skills for redrafting stories. Display the 'Redrafting Checklist' on photocopiable page 109 and recap on the main points.	1–4*: All pupils work on finishing and re-drafting their stories.	Discuss possible titles for class anthology of fantasy stories. Collaborate on writing an introduction.

RESOURCES

Photocopiable pages 104 (Story Planner from 'Victorian Story Cards' unit, Term 2), 109 (Redrafting Checklist from 'Golden Arrow Publications' unit, Term 2) and 180 (Propp's Functions from previous unit), board or flip chart, OHP and acetate (optional), writing materials.

PREPARATION

The children must have studied the previous unit 'It's all fantasy' before covering this unit. Provide one copy each of photocopiable page 104 (Story Planner). Provide one copy between two of photocopiable pages 109 (Redrafting Checklist) and 180 (Propp's Functions). In addition, prepare OHTs or A3 enlargements of all three sheets if you have not already done so for work in previous units.

Introduction

Tell the children that they will be using the fantasy genre as a model for writing their own stories. Recap on the basic characteristics of this genre from the previous unit. Then display an OHT of Propp's Functions (photocopiable page 180) and discuss how they can be used as the basis for planning a story. Explain that, because the 'functions' were

derived from a group of tales, they contain several types of beginning, middle and end. Model on the OHP how to use the functions to plan a story plot:
- Use three different coloured highlighter pens to sort out the functions in the first list into beginnings, middles and ends.
- Select a function from each colour (such as beginnings, middles and ends) to create a plot for a story.
- Choose at least four types of character from the second list and give each a name.

Whole-class skills work

Revise the key plot structures covered in previous work. Write three headings on the flip chart as follows: 'Beginning', 'Middle', 'End'. Ask children to suggest some different ideas for how to approach these parts of a story (for example a beginning which includes a description, dialogue or action, an ending which involves a problem being solved, a twist in the tale, an anti-climax and so on). Write these on the board or flip chart.

Then display the Story Planner on photocopiable page 104. Go through the different kinds of plot outlined on the sheet and ask the children to provide examples of stories that correspond to the different kinds of plot.

Now give out one copy to each child of the Story Planner, and one copy between two of Propp's Functions. Ask the children to use ideas from Propp's Functions to help them build up a story plot and then to write an outline on their Story Planner sheet.

Differentiated group activities

All children work in their ability groups to produce their outline and first draft of a story:
1*: Experiment with fantasy genre, such as writing a story which gives a twist on a traditional fairy tale, or which weaves traditional fairy tale themes with the modern world, or a science fiction world and so n. More confident children may wish to attempt a parody, in a similar style to 'Abu Ali Meets a Dragon' studied in the previous unit.
2 & 3: Write a fantasy story, with a traditional fairy tale plot and characters.
4*: Write a short, simple fairy tale based on a well-known fairy tale, but with different characters and/or setting. Suggest, perhaps, a modern version.

Conclusion

Ask selected children from Groups 1 and 4 to share the first drafts of their stories. Discuss how the various elements of structure and content relate to those on the Story Planner and Propp's Functions sheets.

Introduction

Continue on from the concluding session Hour 1 by inviting children from Groups 2 and 3 to share the first drafts of their stories followed by discussion and evaluation. Focus the discussion particularly on aspects of the stories which would benefit from revision.

Whole-class skills work

Explain to the children that they will be finishing and redrafting their stories in the group activities. First, however, they are going to revise redrafting skills. Write up two headings on the board or flip chart: 'Content' and 'Grammar, punctuation and spelling'. Invite the children to suggest the main points to go under each heading. Jot down their ideas, then display an OHT of the Redrafting Checklist (photocopiable page 109). Briefly go through the list to remind the children of any points they left out.

(NB If the children have previously done the work in 'Golden Arrow Publications' unit (Term 2), they might like to refer also to the 'Young Writer's Guides' they produced.)

Differentiated group activities

1–4*: All children should work in their ability groups to redraft and finish off their stories, using the Redrafting Checklist on photocopiable page 109. Some children may benefit from working with a 'redrafting partner', where they read their stories to each other and the partner asks questions and makes redrafting suggestions.

Conclusion

Suggest that the stories be made into a class anthology. Discuss possible titles. Suggest that the anthology should have an introduction explaining what fantasy genre is and why it is so popular. Draft this together as a summing up of this and the previous unit.

A PURPOSE FOR READING

OBJECTIVES

UNIT	SPELLING/VOCABULARY	GRAMMAR/PUNCTUATION	COMPREHENSION/COMPOSITION
REFERENCE AND RESEARCH SKILLS Setting a purpose for reading.	Understand and differentiate the terms 'scanning', 'skimming' and 'studying'.		Set purposes for reading so that research is fast and effective. Use reading style appropriate to purpose.

ORGANIZATION (1 HOUR)

INTRODUCTION	WHOLE-CLASS SKILLS WORK	DIFFERENTIATED GROUP ACTIVITIES	CONCLUSION
Read the article 'Lighten Up' on photocopiable page 185. Try to answer questions without looking back at text. Establish need for setting purpose for reading.	Devise a class poster defining the terms 'skimming', 'scanning' and 'studying' and outlining for what purposes each reading style is appropriate.	1–4: Pupils work individually to write about their past week's reading: the purposes they had and the reading styles they used. *Teacher works with Groups 3 & 4.	Share and discuss outcomes of group activities session. Recap on differences between the three reading styles outlined. Suggest each child keeps a similar record for coming week.

RESOURCES

Photocopiable page 185 ('Lighten Up'), board or flip chart, OHP and acetate (optional), writing materials.

PREPARATION

Make enough copies of photocopiable page 185 ('Lighten Up') for one for each child. If possible, prepare it also as an OHT or enlarged A3 photocopy.

Introduction

Display the article 'Lighten Up' and read it all the way through once. Remove the displayed text and ask the children to tell you, without looking back at the text, what two things changes in light may explain.

Could they do it, or did they have trouble remembering? Suggest that if they had trouble this might be because they didn't have that question (or any other) as a purpose for reading. Explain that it is easier to remember what you read when you know what your purpose for reading is and you keep that purpose in mind while reading.

Whole-class skills work

Distribute copies of the article to the children and ask them to read it again, this time with the purpose of finding the answer to the question you asked. Tell them to mark the section of text that gives the answer and to underline the two things changes in light may explain. Give them a few minutes to complete this.

Now ask for their answers and mark the appropriate passage and lines on your display copy. Ask the children how they read to find the answer. Did they read the whole article over again very carefully, or did they scan it quickly to find the information they wanted?

It should have been the latter! Emphasize that their purpose for reading should help them decide on a reading style.

Through class discussion, establish definitions and uses for the three reading styles of skimming, scanning and studying. Write these on a flip chart so that they can be used as a classroom reference poster along the lines of the one below:

WHAT'S YOUR STYLE?

SKIMMING: When you want a general idea of what an article is about, you **skim** it. When you skim, you quickly read the title, headlines, highlighted words or phrases and topic sentences. You also look at visual aids, such as photographs, illustrations, graphs, maps and diagrams, and read captions. If the passage has an introduction or summary, you read that too.

SCANNING: When you want to find a specific piece of information, you **scan** an article. When you scan, you start at the beginning of the passage and run your eyes over the lines as quickly as possible until you find what you are looking for.

STUDYING: When you want to understand and remember the information, you **study** it. When studying, first skim the material for an overview. Then read it slowly and carefully. Look for main ideas and supporting details. Take notes to record key words, dates and facts.

Differentiated group activities

1–4: Ask all the children to work individually and to think about things they have read in the past week, both at school and at home. They should write these down and for each one say what their purpose for reading was, what reading style they used and why. Finally, they should indicate whether, for any of the items they list, they would choose a different reading style based on what they have learned in this lesson.

*The teacher supports children in Groups 2 and 3.

Conclusion

Share and discuss the outcomes of the group activities session. Did the children have difficulties in writing down what their purpose for reading was? Why might this be? (No purpose was set!) Ensure they all understand the differences between the three reading styles outlined. Suggest that each child keep, for the coming week, a similar record to find out if they are getting better at setting purposes for reading and using the appropriate reading style.

LIGHTEN UP

When winter sweeps across the country, it can bring freezing temperatures, chilly winds and snow. It can also bring the 'winter blues'. Experts say almost everyone feels a little less energetic in winter. But some people can get very depressed. They may feel, unhappy, have trouble concentrating, eat more sweets and want to spend more time alone.

Doctors have named these serious winter blues SAD. This stands for Seasonal Affective Disorder. About 10 million get SAD each year. SAD can strike both children and adults. It usually lasts from the end of autumn through the end of winter. The happy news is that doctors have found an easy cure for SAD. It's light!

SAD in the dark
Scientists believe people get SAD because there is less daylight in winter than in other seasons. During winter in our hemisphere, the northern part of the Earth is tilted away from the sun. It gets less light and is colder than in summer, when it is tilted toward the sun. This lack of light can play havoc with the body's natural rhythms and routine ways of working.

Every living thing has what scientists call a 'biological clock'. It is not a clock you can see, but a system your body has for keeping up certain activities. A biological clock is like an alarm clock inside the body. It sounds off at about the

Sitting under a light box can cure SAD, or a serious case of the winter blues

same time each day to let you know that it's time to eat, get up or go to sleep.

When clocks stop
Scientists have been studying how light affects the biological clocks of living things, including people. If there is a change in the time that people get light each day, their biological clocks can be thrown off schedule.

Changes in light may explain why some animals hibernate. They may also explain why people feel different in winter. Doctors say when winter shortens daylight hours, the biological clocks of people with SAD are thrown off schedule.

Lighten up
People who get SAD can put their biological clocks back on schedule by getting more light. Doctors encourage people with SAD to sit in front of a special light box every day. Some SAD sufferers even have light boxes at home! Others beat SAD by wiring their bedroom lights to timers. The timers make the lights go on little by little as a person is waking up.

Doctors have also found that getting outside and exercising as much as possible can chase away anyone's winter blues. Exercise keeps people's energy levels up and passes the time until the end of winter. By the time spring has sprung, most people who get the winter blues feel much happier. With more hours of daylight, the world looks a lot brighter.

(Adapted from 'Light Makes Winter Blues Glow Away' by Courtney Silk from *Scholastic News*, 14.2.92, copyright Scholastic Inc.)

THE SILVER SWORD

OBJECTIVES

UNIT	SPELLING/VOCABULARY	GRAMMAR/PUNCTUATION	COMPREHENSION/ COMPOSITION
READING FICTION *The Silver Sword* by Ian Serraillier.	Revise and consolidate work during past year by learning and inventing spelling rules. Use independent strategies by applying knowledge of rules and exceptions. Practise and extend vocabulary through crosswords.	Revise the language conventions and grammatical features of narrative text. Consolidate work on complex sentences.	Read a work by a significant children's author and compare it (in next unit) with a poem by same author. Describe and evaluate the style of an individual writer. Write a summary, deciding on priorities relevant to purpose.

ORGANIZATION (5 HOURS)

	INTRODUCTION	WHOLE-CLASS SKILLS WORK	DIFFERENTIATED GROUP ACTIVITIES	CONCLUSION
HOUR 1	Shared reading of Chapters 1–3, approximately 20 minutes.	Revise the conventions and grammatical features of narrative genre.	1*: Guided reading and discussion. 2 & 3: Produce a storyboard of Joseph's escape. 4*: Guided reading and discussion.	Groups 2 & 3 share their storyboards. The rest of the class highlights effective aspects.
HOUR 2	Shared reading of Chapters 4 and 5, approximately 15 minutes.	Revise and consolidate spelling rules and conventions. Secure vocabulary to talk about spelling and vocabulary.	1: Write Joseph's diary entry after meeting Jan. 2 & 3*: Guided reading and discussion. 4: Write Joseph's diary entry after meeting Jan.	Selected pupils read out their diary entries to the rest of the class. Discuss how effectively the entries reflect Joseph's feelings.
HOUR 3	Shared reading of Chapters 6 and 7, approximately 15 minutes.	Identify difficult words in text, find meanings and devise a crossword.	1*: Guided reading and discussion. 2 & 3: Design brochure for Ruth's school. 4*: Guided reading and discussion.	Some pupils read out their diary entries for discussion and evaluation by the rest of the class.
HOUR 4	Shared reading of Chapters 8–10, approximately 20 minutes.	Revise sentence construction.	1: Write list of personal treasures for treasure box. 2 & 3*: Guided reading and discussion. 4: Write list of personal treasures for treasure box.	Pupils from Groups 1 & 4 share ideas of what to put in a treasure box. Whole-group discussion of what to put in a class treasure box.
HOUR 5	Shared reading of Chapters 11–13, approximately 20 minutes.	Revision of the term 'summary'.	1*: Guided reading and discussion. 2 & 3: Write diary of the journey from Jan or Ruth's point of view. 4*: Guided reading and discussion.	Selected pupils read their diary entries to the rest of the class. Explain how rest of book will be read.

RESOURCES

Class set of *The Silver Sword* by Ian Serraillier (Puffin, ISBN 0-14-030146-1) – it is possible to manage with a half-class set if children share, photocopiable page 190 (Spelling Checklist), wall map of Europe, board or flip chart, OHP and acetate (optional), class dictionaries, A4 paper cut in half lengthwise (enough for one strip per pair of children), writing materials.

PREPARATION

The study of this book can be planned in several ways. The recommended model is to study Chapters 1–13 in detail in five consecutive hours, then to read Chapters 14–26 during the next week outside literacy hours. Finally, Chapters 27–29 should be studied as the basis for two literacy hours which focus on an overview of the whole book (ideas for this will be found in the two-hour follow-up grid on page 190). Photocopy enough copies of the Spelling Checklist (photocopiable page 190) for one for each child.

SYNOPSIS

This remarkable novel, written in 1956, is one of the most popular children's novels of this century – and well deserves to be called a 'classic'. It tells the story, based on fact, of four children who, having survived the Second World War, make an epic journey from their home in Poland to Germany and then on to Switzerland to find their parents, who were carried off to prison camps during the war. Ruth and Bronia, along with their brother Edek, are joined by another boy, Jan, in their seemingly doomed quest. The silver sword of the title is only a paper knife, but it becomes a symbol of the hope and courage displayed by these children in a time of incredible deprivation and danger.

Introduction

Explain that the story you are about to read is a narrative fiction and, although the characters are fictitious, the story is based upon historical fact. Provide some background to the story by reading the frontispiece of the book, but do not give away the ending! Show a map of Europe pointing out Poland, Germany and Switzerland and explain that most of the place-names in the story can be found on the map. Read Chapters 1–3.

Whole-class skills work

Revise the conventions and grammatical features of narrative genre:
- Narrative texts tell a story. They have characters, plot and setting.
- They are usually written in the past tense.
- They are usually written in the first or third person.
- Narrative texts often feature dialogue.

Ask children to identify the above features in *The Silver Sword*.

Differentiated group activities

1*: Guided reading and discussion. Use the following instructions as a starting point:
- Pick out words and phrases which describe Joseph and make a note of them.
- In your own words, explain Joseph's plan of escape.
- Pick out words and phrases which describe Joseph's feelings during his escape.

2 & 3: Produce a storyboard version of Joseph's escape.

4*: Guided reading and discussion (see above).

Conclusion

Ask selected children from from Groups 2 and 3 to share their storyboards with the rest of the class. Invite positive comments such as 'Sam's storyboard was effective because...'.

Introduction

Read Chapters 4 and 5. Ask the children to think about the significance to the plot of the story of the meeting of Joseph and Jan.

Whole-class skills work

Revise and consolidate spelling rules and terms covered during the past year. Display the Spelling Checklist (photocopiable page 190) and read it through with the children. Point out that it includes some of the most important rules and guidelines but that there is not space for all the rules, terms and spelling investigations they have encountered.

Ask the children to *find* examples from the text for each of the rules and write these on the board or flip chart. Then *give* them examples from the text of the terms on the list and ask them to say what they are. For example, *their* and *there* are homophones, *building* and *buildings* are singular and plural. And so on.

Differentiated group activities

1: Write Joseph's diary entry after meeting Jan.

2 & 3*: Guided reading and discussion. The following questions can be used as a starting point:
- What did Joseph do when he got to Warsaw?
- What did he find in the ruins of his old home?
- Who did he meet there?
- What are the hazards of 'jumping a train'?
- Why did Joseph want to get on a train? What was his plan?

4: Write Joseph's diary entry after meeting Jan.

Conclusion

Ask selected children from Groups 1 and 4 to share their diary entries with the rest of the class. Invite others in the class to comment on how effective the diary entries are in conveying Joseph's *feelings*.

Introduction

Read Chapter 6 and 7. As you read, ask the children to think about the strategy the author has used to provide the information in these chapters. How effective do they think it is?

Whole-class skills work

Brainstorm about 20 long or difficult words from *The Silver Sword*. Write these up on the board or flip chart. Assign one word to each pair of children and ask them to look up as quickly as they can the meaning in the dictionary. Give each pair a half-A4 strip of paper on which to write the word and its meaning in fairly large print. Display the strips at the front so everybody can see them. Then collaborate to make a class crossword puzzle using the words and meanings. It may not, of course, be possible to use all the words.

Differentiated group activities

1*: Guided reading and discussion. Use the following questions as a starting point:
- What plot device is used in Chapters 6 and 7? (Flashback.)
- Briefly describe the other members of Joseph's family.
- What happened when the storm troopers came?
- How did they live for the rest of the winter?
- How did war change Edek and Ruth? Make notes about these changes.
- Why did Ruth start a school and what was it like?

2 & 3: Design a brochure for Ruth's school using information from the book. Include a timetable. Children could work collaboratively on this, either in pairs or small groups.

4*: Guided reading and discussion (see above).

Conclusion

Ask children from Groups 2 and 3 to share their school brochures with the class. Ask the rest of the class to say how well they fit the context, for example, do any of the brochures offer lessons which need resources that were not available to Ruth?

Introduction

Read Chapters 8–10. Ask the children to think about why Chapter 10 is such an important one in the story.

Whole-class skills work

Examine sentence construction in the first two paragraphs of Chapter 8. Begin by revising the following:
- **A simple sentence** is a sentence in which one statement (main clause) is made.
- **A compound sentence** is a sentence in which two or more simple sentences of equal weight are joined by **coordinating conjunctions** such as *and, but*.
- **A compound sentence** is a sentence in which two or more statements (clauses) are made, but one (the main clause) is more important than the others (the subordinate clauses). The statements are joined by **subordinating conjunctions.**

Ask children to examine each sentence in the first two paragraphs and to say which type it is. Groups 1–2 could also identify conjunctions in complex and compound sentences.

> **Sentence 1:** simple. **Sentence 2:** compound: the use of 'and'; 'they went' is implied in the second statement. **Sentence 3:** simple. **Sentence 4:** simple. **Sentence 5:**

simple. **Sentence 6**: compound; the use of 'and'; the repetition of the phrase 'From the distant city they could hear' is implicit rather than explicit. **Sentence 7**: simple. **Sentence 8**: complex; the use of 'though' to introduce the subordinate clause; there is also an adverbial clause at the end. **Sentence 9**: compound: the use of the colon shows that what follows is of equal value. **Sentence 10**: simple. **Sentence 11**: simple.

Most children should be able to identify the large number of simple sentences. Explain that this is a noticeable feature of Ian Serraillier's writing in this book. It is appropriate because it is a children's book and simple sentences are easier to understand.

Differentiated group activities
1: Children should make a list of items to keep in a personal box of treasures like Jan's. They should give reasons why these are treasured items.
2 & 3*: Guided reading and discussion. Use the following questions as a starting point:
■ The time and place have switched again. Where are we now?
■ Discuss and make notes on how Jan has changed since we first met him.
■ How does Jan react to the soldier?
■ Why does he react in this way?
■ What words and phrases are used to describe him?
■ What important decision is made at the end of Chapter 10?
4: Children should make a list of items to keep in a personal box of treasures like Jan's.

Conclusion
Ask children from Groups 1 and 4 to share their ideas about what they would put in a box of treasures and why they have chosen certain items. Suggest there is a class treasure box and ask for ideas for what should go in it and why.

Introduction
Read Chapters 11–13. As you read ask the children to jot down the names of places that are mentioned. When you have finished reading, plot the journey of the children so far. If you have a map with a scale, try to estimate how far the children travelled.

Whole-class skills work
Revise the term summary. A **summary** is a shortened version of a text, often to a specified number of words. It involves re-writing the text not merely cutting words, sentences and paragraphs, which is termed **abridgement.**

Explain to children that that they will continue reading the book, but not in literacy hours, and that they will return to the book to write about it as a whole in about a week's time. It is therefore important to produce a summary of what has been read so far so that this can be used as a basis for further study.

Write collaboratively a class summary of Chapters 1–13 in about 250 words.

Differentiated group activities
1*: Guided reading and discussion. Use the following questions as a starting point:
■ How do you think the children felt about leaving Warsaw?
■ Describe how they meet Edek.
■ How did Edek manage to get out of Germany?
2 & 3: Write a diary of the journey so far from Warsaw to Berlin from the point of view of Jan or Ruth.
4*: Guided reading and discussion (see above).

Conclusion
Ask children from Groups 2 and 3 to read out their diary entries. Invite comments from the rest of the class on how the diaries highlight the feelings of Jan or Ruth. Explain how the rest of the book will be read (see below).

FOLLOW-UP

Read Chapters 14–26 during the next week outside literacy hours. Then Chapters 27–29 should be studied as the basis for two literacy hours which focus on an overview of the whole book. The ideas for this will be found in the two-hour follow-up grid on page 191.

SPELLING CHECKLIST

SPELLING TERMS

■ VOWELS AND CONSONANTS
A E I O U are *vowels*. All other letters are *consonants*.

■ SINGULAR AND PLURAL
Singular means 'one', *plural* means 'more than one'.

■ PREFIX
A *prefix* is a beginning added to a word to change its meaning. When a prefix is added to a word, the spelling of the word itself remains the same.

■ SUFFIX
A *suffix* is an ending added to a word to change its meaning.

■ HOMOPHONES
Words with the same sound but different meanings usually have different spellings. Learn them!

■ SYNONYMS
Words of similar meaning. Use a thesaurus to help you find which has just the right shade of mean for your needs.

SPELLING RULES AND GUIDANCE

■ 'I' BEFORE 'E'
Write 'i' before 'e' except after 'c' when the sound is 'ee'. Common exceptions: seize, weird, weir, neither, foreign.

■ -FUL/ -LESS SUFFIXES
When adding suffixes '-ful' or '-less' to words ending in 'y' change 'y' to 'i'. Other words do not need to be changed.

■ -ED/ -ING SUFFIXES
Drop the final 'e' before a suffix beginning with a vowel, eg '-ed', '-ing'.

■ '-Y' SINGULAR/ '-IES' PLURAL
Words ending in y when the sound is short 'i' have a plural ending '-ies'.

■ '-F' SINGULAR/ '-VES' PLURAL
The ending of words ending in '-f' changes to '-ves' in the plural. Common exceptions: dwarfs, roofs, chiefs.

TIP! Make a list of any words you often get wrong and then try to learn them. Work with a partner to test each other.

■ IRREGULAR PLURALS
There are two groups of irregular plurals:
1. Those from old English, eg sheep, sheep, mouse, mice, woman, women.
2. Those from Latin, eg formula, formulae.
Irregular plurals have to be learned individually.

■ SILENT LETTERS
The following letters are silent when in certain positions in words: B, E, G, H, K, L, N, P, S, T.
Some examples: bomb, late, gnome, rhythm, knife, calm, autumn, pneumonia, island, castle.

■ CONTRACTIONS
An apostrophe is used to show where letters are missed out.

■ SPELLING BY SYLLABLES
Breaking up long words into separate syllables which can be pronounced by themselves will often help.

THE SILVER SWORD: FOLLOW-UP

OBJECTIVES

UNIT	SPELLING/VOCABULARY	GRAMMAR/PUNCTUATION	COMPREHENSION/ COMPOSITION
READING FICTION The Silver Sword by Ian Serraillier.	Use independent spelling strategies. Revise and consolidate work during past year.	Revise language conventions and grammatical features. Revise formal styles of writing.	Overview The Silver Sword. Describe and evaluate the style of the author. Write summaries. Write an introduction to a school edition of the book, tailored for a real audience.

ORGANIZATION (2 HOURS)

	INTRODUCTION	WHOLE-CLASS SKILLS WORK	DIFFERENTIATED GROUP ACTIVITIES	CONCLUSION
HOUR 1	Shared reading of Chapter 27 (approximately 10 minutes).	Study description of storm. Investigate use of adjectives and adverbs; descriptive details; length of sentences; reactions and feelings of the children. Establish author's 'documentary' style with extensive use of simple sentences and little use of figurative language.	1*: Guided reading and discussion. Sum up story. Recap on the main characters and how war changes them. Describe the events on the lake. How is Jan changed by this? 2 & 3: Write an introduction to a school edition of the book. Include brief facts about the setting, a summary of the plot and notes on the main characters. 4*: Guided reading and discussion (see above).	Children from Groups 2 & 3 read their introductions to the book. The rest of the class evaluate how helpful the introductions would be to children of their own age.
HOUR 2	Shared reading of Chapters 28 and 29 (approximately 12 mintues).	Revise conventions of writing a literary essay. Remind pupils how to support points with evidence: • an indirect reference to the text; • using a short quotation; • using a longer quotation which should be set out on indented lines.	1: Write essay on Ruth or Edek, focusing on how they change from beginning to end of story. 2 & 3*: Guided reading and discussion: • Summmarize story. • Describe how each of the children develop in their new home. 4: Write a report on Jan for the International Tracing Society – see page157.	Discuss the text as a whole. Ask children if they enjoyed the text, what they liked and disliked about it, which characters they liked best, which scenes they found most interesting.

AFTER EVER HAPPILY

OBJECTIVES

UNIT	SPELLING/VOCABULARY	GRAMMAR/PUNCTUATION	COMPREHENSION/ COMPOSITION
WRITING FICTION 'After Ever Happily' by Ian Serraillier.	Appreciate poet's use of language to create humour. Use independent spelling strategies when writing own poem and fairy tale.	Revise language conventions and grammatical features of different types of text.	Compare works by a single writer. Investigate humorous verse. Revise and extend writing of free verse. Write own story using flashback structure.

ORGANIZATION (2 HOURS)

	INTRODUCTION	WHOLE-CLASS SKILLS WORK	DIFFERENTIATED GROUP ACTIVITIES	CONCLUSION
HOUR 1	Use title for 'before reading' prediction. Shared reading and discussion of the poem 'After Ever Happily' on photocopiable page 194.	Examine different types of writing by same author and identify characteristic features.	1–4: All groups write own backward fairy-tale poem. *Teacher supports Groups 1 & 4.	Selected pairs of pupils from Groups 1 & 4 share their poems.
HOUR 2	Relate 'narrative in reverse' to 'flashback' technique. Discuss how this can be used to structure stories.	Use Flashback: Story Planners on photocopiable page 195 to plan a story with a flashback.	1–4: All groups write their stories with flashbacks. *Teacher supports Groups 2 & 3.	Selected pupils from Groups 2 & 3 share their plans and stories so far. Discuss what advantages/ disadvantages using flashback device has.

RESOURCES

Photocopiable pages 194 ('After Ever Happily') and 195 (Flashback: Story Planners), OHP and acetate (optional), board or flip chart, writing materials.

PREPARATION

Make enough copies of the poem 'After Ever Happily' for one between two children. If possible, prepare the poem as an OHT or enlarge to at least A3. Make enough copies of photocopiable page 195 (Flashback: Story Planners) for one per child. Practise reading the poem aloud, with different voices for the different characters.

Introduction

Write the words 'After ever happily' on the board or flip chart and explain to the children that this is the title of a poem they are about to read. Ask them to use the title to predict what the poem might be about, how it might be structured and whether it is a serious or humorous poem.

Distribute copies of the poem and, if possible, display it. Read it aloud with as much drama as you can, ideally using different voices for the characters and narrator.

Ask the children: what is unusual about the poem? (It is a fairy tale in reverse.) Were their predictions correct? Discuss how the title and the last line use humorous variations of well-known phrases to give an idea of what the poem is doing. Ask the children to spend a few minutes working in pairs to try to make the poem work in the usual way, that is by reading it backwards. Does it work?

Whole-class skills work

Explain that this poem has been written by the same writer as *The Silver Sword*. Invite the children's reactions to this – are they surprised? Why? Discuss the two types of writing and revise the features of the different genres Ian Serraillier has used. Refer back to other authors you have studied during the year and discuss whether they have displayed a range of writing styles or produced different stories or poems within the same genre.

Differentiated group activities

1–4: Ask all children to work in pairs to write their own backward fairy tale modelled on the poem. Suggest the following procedure:
■ Choose a well-known fairy tale.
■ Tell it in short sentences, starting a new line for each sentence. Do not worry about rhythm or rhyme (ie write in free verse).
■ Copy out the lines in reverse order.
■ Try to think of a humorous comment with which to finish the poem.
*The teacher works with Groups 1 and 4. You might suggest that the most able children try to write a fairy-tale poem with a circular plot (such as it ends where it began) and then to think of a way to set it out so that the reader could just keep on reading forever.

Conclusion

Ask selected pairs of children from Groups 1 and 4 to read out, or 'perform' if they are able, their backwards or circular fairy-tale poems.

Introduction

Ask selected pairs of children from Groups 2 and 3 to share their backwards or circular fairy tales written in the previous hour. Discuss how this 'narrative in reverse' structure might be use for ordinary prose stories. The discussion should lead towards the device of 'flashback'. This is a commonly-used plot technique in stories and films in which the development of the plot is suspended while a scene from the past is explored, or the beginning and end take place in the present, but the middle is a flashback to the past. Brainstorm a list of stories and/or films the children have read and seen in which this device is used.

Whole-class skills work

Revise the plot structures studied throughout the year, for example:

Beginnings: Description of character or place or action; dialogue.
Middle: Simple plot, building to a climax; sub-plot(s) within main plot.
Endings: Simple resolution; 'twist in the tale'; anti-climax; moral.

Explain the technique of flashback and examine the two recommended plot outlines offered on photocopiable page 195 (Flashback: Story Planners). Explain to the children that they should all plan a story with a flashback using one of the outlines on the sheet. Note that the second plan is harder than the first and should be recommended to children in Groups 1 and 2.

Differentiated group activities

1–4: Ask all children to begin to write their stories with flashbacks, encouraging them to get as far as they can in this session.
*The teacher works with Groups 2 and 3.

Conclusion

Ask selected children from Groups 2 and 3 to read out their plans and their stories so far. Invite positive comments from the rest of the class. Conclude the hour by asking the children what they found difficult about writing using the flashback device. What advantages and disadvantages does this device have for writers?

FURTHER IDEAS

■ An additional hour should be allowed for finishing and redrafting.
■ Find more examples of stories, films or television programmes which use the flashback technique and discuss how it is used.

AFTER EVER HAPPILY OR THE PRINCESS AND THE WOODCUTTER

And they both lived happily ever after...
The wedding was held in the palace. Laughter
Rang to the roof as a loosened rafter
Crashed down and squashed the chamberlain
    flat—
And how the wedding guests chuckled at
    that!
'You, with your horny indelicate hands,
Who drop your haitches and call them 'ands,
Who cannot afford to buy her a dress,
How dare you presume to pinch our
    princess—
Miserable woodcutter, uncombed,
    unwashed!'
Were the chamberlain's words (before he was
    squashed).
'Take her,' said the Queen, who had a soft
    spot
For woodcutters. 'He's strong and he's
    handsome. Why not?'
'What rot!' said the King, but he dare not
    object;
The Queen wore the trousers—that's as you'd
    expect.
Said the chamberlain, usually meek and
    inscrutable,

'A princess and a woodcutter? The match is
    unsuitable.'
Her dog barked its welcome again and again
As they splashed to the palace through
    puddles of rain.
And the princess sighed, 'Till the end of my
    life!'
'Darling,' said the woodcutter, 'will you be my
    wife?'
He knew all his days he could love no other,
So he nursed her to health with some help
    from his mother,
And lifted her, horribly hurt, from her tumble.
A woodcutter, watching, saw the horse
    stumble.
As she rode through the woods, a princess in
    her prime.
On a dapple grey horse...Now, to finish my
    rhyme,
I'll start it properly: Once upon a time—

This is a love story from the Middle Ages. The
Poet obviously knew his subject backwards.

Ian Serraillier

FLASHBACK: STORY PLANNERS

PLAN 1

PART OF MIDDLE: Describe the most exciting scene in the middle of the story.

BEGINNING & PART OF MIDDLE: Write a flashback explaining the events that built up to the exciting scene.

END: Explain what happened after the exciting scene and finish the story.

PLAN 2

END: Describe the scene at the end of a story.

BEGINNING & MIDDLE: Write the story from the beginning.

SUMMER CAMP EXPERIENCE

OBJECTIVES

UNIT	SPELLING/VOCABULARY	GRAMMAR/PUNCTUATION	COMPREHENSION/ COMPOSITION
WRITING SIMULATION 'Summer Camp Experience'.	Practise use of independent spelling strategies. Demonstrate use of extended vocabulary in own writing. Identify misspelled words in own writing.	Revise language conventions and grammatical features of a range of text types. Revise and use the impersonal voice and the passive voice.	Review a range of non-fiction text types and their characteristics. Use appropriate style and form to suit a specific purpose and audience. Secure control of impersonal writing.

ORGANIZATION (5 HOURS)

INTRODUCTION	WHOLE-CLASS SKILLS WORK	DIFFERENTIATED GROUP ACTIVITIES	CONCLUSION
HOUR 1 Examine a selection of activity holiday advertisements. Shared reading and discussion of 'Summer Camp Experience' advertisement on photocopiable page 200.	Examine use of persuasive language in 'Summer Camp Experience' advertisement. Revise language conventions of persuasive genre.	1: Write advert for a holiday activities club. 2 & 3: Write advert text for after-school club aimed at classmates. 4: Write simple advert promoting after-school club aimed at younger children.	Selected pupils show and/or read out their adverts. The class evaluates how effective these are.
HOUR 2 Shared reading and discussion of both 'Summer Camp Experience' and 'Summer Camp Experience: The Reality' on photocopiable pages 200 and 201.	Revise language conventions of recount genre.	1–4*: All pupils write an imaginary diary of a week spent at Heslington Hall, based on information on photocopiable page 201.	Selected examples of the diary accounts are read and compared.
HOUR 3 Examine documents written in formal language. Discuss use of impersonal style and passive voice.	Revise passive voice. Discuss examples of common phrases used in formal writing.	1–4*: All pupils write rules and regulations for holiday-makers at Heslington Hall, using impersonal writing style. *Group 4 can work in pairs.	Selected pupils read out their rules and regulations. The class discusses any difficulties in composing them.
HOUR 4 Display photocopiable pages 200 and 201. Use them to brainstorm points for a formal letter of complaint.	Revise conventions of formal letter-writing.	1–4*: All pupils compose a letter of complaint to the Manager of Heslington Hall, referring to their diary accounts from Hour 2 as evidence.	Selected examples of pupils' letters are read out and evaluated for their effectiveness.
HOUR 5 Review the information on photocopiable pages 200 and 201. Discuss what would happen if press discovered story.	Revise features of report genre.	1–4*: All pupils write newspaper report about Heslington Hall holidays, entitled 'The experience of a lifetime?'. They begin by role-playing a newspaper interview situation.	Selected examples of pupils' newspaper reports are read out and discussed. Summarize types of writing undertaken and chracteristic features of each.

RESOURCES

Photocopiable pages 200 (Summer Camp Experience at Heslington Hall) and 201 (Summer Camp Experience: The Reality), several 'activity' holiday advertisements (from newspapers) and brochures (for cutting out pictures, and so on), examples of documents using formal, 'impersonal' language, for example, consumer information leaflets, public notices, forms (including holiday booking forms), board or flip chart, OHP and acetate (optional), writing materials.

PREPARATION

Make enough copies of photocopiable pages 200 and 201 for one between two. In addition, prepare OHTs or A3 enlargements of both sheets. Collect several 'activity' holiday brochures or advertisements, asking the children's help.

HOUR 1

Introduction

Examine the selection of activity holiday advertisements and brochures (see 'Preparation'). Discuss the purpose of these, focusing on the persuasion aspect. Ask the children to identify the different methods that these texts use to entice the reader. Are there glossy pictures? Appealing descriptions? Lists of facilities available, and so on?

Now display the 'Summer Camp Experience' advertisement on photocopiable page 200. Discuss how similar it is in presentation and style to the other holiday advertisements. Ask the children: Does it sound exciting? Would you like to go? What aspects especially appeal to you?

Whole-class skills work

Ask the children to help you examine the use of persuasive language in the Heslington Hall advertisement as follows:
■ Make a list on the board or flip chart of all the words and phrases which try to persuade the reader (for example 'beautiful', 'easy access', 'comfortable', 'incredible').
■ Try to identify which part of speech the persuasive words belong to.
■ Explain how these words and phrases try to persuade the reader.

Now revise the general language conventions of persuasive texts, writing them on the board, for example as follows:
■ They usually consist of an opening statement followed by a series of different types of arguments (such as statistics, individual examples, opinions, facts, facts presented as opinion) and a conclusion.
■ They are usually written in the simple present tense.
■ They often use discursive connectives.

Can the children find examples of these features in the Heslington Hall advertisement? They should find that, though this is an advertisement, it still follows the above conventions. There is an opening statement about Heslington Hall followed by a series of points which are intended to persuade the reader to go on the holiday, such as these are a type of argument. The conclusion is the price information and information of requesting further details.

Differentiated group activities

1*: Write an advertisement for a summer holiday activities club for older children. Follow closely the conventions outlined in the skills session and include sections of persuasive description. The children should lay out the text in the appropriate format (a good IT opportunity), using pictures cut from the holiday brochures to make it as authentic and appealing as possible.

2 & 3: Write the text for an advertisement for an after-school club to persuade classmates to attend. Focus on using the conventions outlined in the skills section including some brief persuasive descriptions.

4*: Write a simple advertisement for younger children to attend an after-school club. Focus on using the language conventions outlined above. The children can use the Heslington Hall advertisement as a model.

Conclusion

Ask selected children to show and/or read out their advertisements. The rest of the class should comment on how effective these are at persuading the intended audience, and how well the conventions have been followed.

Introduction

Ask the children to look again at the 'Summer Camp Experience' advertisement. Are there any words and phrases that may be exaggerations, any phrases in small print, or any other text that may suggest the advertisement is misleading? ('The holiday experience of a lifetime' sounds like an exaggeration; the small print saying that activities are 'subject to instructor availability' could mean that not all the sports listed may be on offer; the address provided suggests that the Summer Camp Experience holidays are not based in the main part of the 'beautiful Georgian mansion'.)

Now display 'Summer Camp Experience: The Reality' on OHP. Ask the children: In what ways is the 'reality' different from the image promoted in the advertisement?

Whole-class skills work

Discuss recount texts. Can the children remember what their purpose is? (To retell for information or entertainment.) What type of texts does this genre include? (Descriptions; accounts of an event; biographies, diaries.) Ask the children if they can remember any of the language conventions of the recount genre, then sum up the main features:

- an opening paragraph which acts as an introduction and/or sets the scene
- use of chronological order for events
- use of past tense
- use of sequence (time) connectives – for example first..., next..., then..., and so on.

Write these on the board or flip chart to refer to in the group activities session below.

Differentiated group activities

Provide each pair of children with a copy of photocopiable page 201 (Summer Camp Experience: The Reality).

1–4*: All children work in their ability groups to write a diary of an imaginary week's holiday at Heslington Hall. Their accounts should be based around the information provided on the photocopiable page, especially the poster fragment. Ask them to express how they felt about the holiday and how they and the other children managed to make the best of it. Make sure that their diary accounts follow the appropriate conventions outlined in the skills session.

Conclusion

Ask selected children to read out their diary entries. Compare and contrast them, and identify the characteristic recount features in each. Discuss: Who managed to make the best of a bad situation? Who had the worst week?

Introduction

Show the children some examples of documents using 'formal' or 'official' language (see 'Preparation'). What do they notice about the writing style of these? (It's usually impersonal.) How is the 'impersonal' style achieved? (Through using the passive voice.)

Whole-class skills work

Explain to the children that the passive voice is a key feature of formal writing. Can they remember what 'passive voice' means? (A passive sentence is one where the subject is the person or thing acted on by the verb, rather than the one who performs the action.) Write the following sentence on the board or flip chart: *You can obtain forms for booking an activity from reception.* Now ask the children to help you turn the sentence into the passive voice. (*Forms for booking an activity may be obtained from reception.*)

In addition, provide them with some examples of common phrases that may feature in impersonal writing, for example 'it is expected that...', 'those wishing to...', 'it should be noted that...', and so on. Can the children suggest any more examples?

Differentiated group activities

1–4*: Ask all the children to work in their ability groups to write an information sheet outlining the rules and regulations for those children holidaying at Heslington Hall. This can include safety information (what to do in the event of a fire, personal safety and so on); security information (locking doors/windows, storing valuables); advice on safety and booking of activities; information on meal-times and location of facilities such as phones; rules on noise, behaviour, and so on. Emphasize that the style used must be impersonal, incorporating the passive voice as much as possible. Children in Group 4 can work in pairs to compose ten rules and regulations.

Conclusion

Ask children to read out their lists of rules and regulations. Invite the others to discuss any difficulties encountered in trying to compose the rules using an 'impersonal' style.

Introduction

Display photocopiable pages 200 and 201 again. Use them as a basis for brainstorming points to include in a formal letter of complaint about the 'Summer Camp Experience'. Jot down key points on the board or flip chart.

Whole-class skills work

Revise the conventions of writing a formal letter. Check that the children remember the details of layout, punctuation, inclusion of address, date, and so on. Explain that a business letter includes the recipient's address on the letter itself. This is so that letters filed for future reference (without envelopes) contain all the necessary information.

Emphasize that a letter of complaint should always be polite, and should set out the reasons for the complaint clearly. Finally, write out a letter format on the board or flip chart for children to refer during the group activities (see example illustrated).

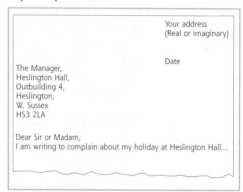

Differentiated group activities

1–4*: Ask all the children to write a letter of complaint to the Manager of Heslington Hall. Encourage them to refer to incidents in their diaries (from Hour 2) as evidence of bad experiences which they had on holiday.

Conclusion

Invite selected children to read out their letters. The rest of the class should evaluate which of the letters are likely to be the most effective and why.

Introduction

Review the information on photocopiable pages 200 and 201. Discuss what might happen if the local press got hold of a story regarding the huge number of complaints received by Heslington Hall. What kind of details would they focus on? How might they go about finding out more information?

Whole-class skills work

Revise the features of the report genre by asking what the class can remember about it. Jot their points down on the board. The end result should look something like this:
- A report usually consists of statements about a situation.
- It is usually written in the present tense.
- It may include sections of recount (using the past tense).
- A newspaper report is written to attract the attention of the reader; therefore, the style of language and choice of vocabulary are geared towards making the report sound more exciting and interesting.

Now tell the children that they are going to write a newspaper report in the group activities session, and ask them to keep the above features in mind during the exercise.

Differentiated group activities

1–4*: Ask all the children to work in their ability groups to write a newspaper report entitled 'THE HOLIDAY EXPERIENCE OF A LIFETIME?' Begin with a role-play exercise. Each group splits into two, one half as the manager and the disappointed children, the other half as the journalists taking notes during an interview. After a few minutes, swap the roles over. The children then write their reports, referring to the information on the two photocopiable pages, and using their notes to back up their reports.

Conclusion

Select some children to read out their newspaper reports. Discuss these in terms of how well they follow the writing brief. Conclude the unit by recapping on the different types of writing the children have undertaken and identifying briefly their characteristic features.

SUMMER CAMP EXPERIENCE AT HESLINGTON HALL

Heslington Hall is a beautiful Georgian Mansion deep in the West Sussex countryside, yet with easy access to South Coast resorts. Specially converted for use as a Summer Camp, Heslington Hall contains all the facilities your child needs for the holiday experience of a lifetime!

THE PACKAGE

★ Comfortable accommodation in small dormitories

★ An all-you-can-eat buffet every evening, prepared by our resident chef

★ The opportunity to visit local resorts and places of interest

★ Qualified sports coaches

★ All the activities you could dream of – see our comprehensive list

ACTIVITIES*

★ football

★ tennis

★ mountain bike riding

★ pony trekking

★ rock climbing

★ swimming

★ snorkling

★ sailing

★ wind surfing

★ orienteering

*subject to instructor availability

EVENING RELAXATIONS

★ discos

★ barn dancing

★ talent shows

★ local rock bands and folk groups

WANT TO KNOW MORE?

Then phone 0123 45678 for your free brochure or write to: HESLINGTON HALL, OUTBUILDING 4, Heslington, W. Sussex HS3 2LA

All this for an incredible **£99** per week per person! (Does not include travel to Heslington Hall, holiday insurance, optional excursions, lunches, drinks and personal expenses.)

SUMMER CAMP EXPERIENCE: THE REALITY

Heslington Hall certainly was an experience – but a bad one for most of the children who stayed there. Here are some photographs and a fragment of poster sent by one dissatisfied parent to the local newspaper in Heslington.

Comfortable accommodation in small dormitories?

Heslington Hall?

Mountain bikes?

Mike – the sports coach. He's nice, and he really was a tennis champion – but that was forty years ago!

ACTIVITIES FOR THE WEEK
- MONDAY – football
The football is in the cellar – organize this yourselves.
- TUESDAY – rock climbing
Cancelled.
- WEDNESDAY – mountain bike trail riding
We only have two bikes at the moment, so sign up early!
- THURSDAY – Day trip to Brighton – £20 (Includes Royal Pavilion Tour)
Trip will only run if we can get enough to fill a coach (30). Otherwise, walk into Heslington and take the service bus (fare is £2.40).
- FRIDAY – tennis
Free coaching from former champion, Mike Dorrington.
- FRIDAY NIGHT – disco
Ask to borrow the cassette player from reception.
- SATURDAY & SUNDAY – free time
Why not organize a talent show on Saturday night?

The holiday experience of a lifetime?

TALKING SLANG

OBJECTIVES

UNIT	SPELLING/VOCABULARY	GRAMMAR/PUNCTUATION	COMPREHENSION/ COMPOSITION
REFERENCE AND RESEARCH SKILLS Talking slang: a language investigation.	Understand the term 'slang'. Collect and define slang words and phrases, using a variety of information sources.	Conduct a language investigation through interviews and research.	Write a dictionary of slang. Locate information efficiently.

ORGANIZATION (1 HOUR)

	INTRODUCTION	WHOLE-CLASS SKILLS WORK	DIFFERENTIATED GROUP ACTIVITIES	CONCLUSION
HOUR 1	Discuss the meaning of term 'slang' and why people use it.	Research slang words for certain standard English words, using photocopiable page 204.	1–4*: All children work to complete the activity on the photocopiable sheet according to their ability.	Share outcomes of the group work and use to compile the beginnings of a class dictionary of slang.

RESOURCES

Photocopiable page 294 (Talking Slang), dictionaries of slang, thesauruses, board or flip chart, OHP and acetate (optional), writing materials.

PREPARATION

Make enough copies of photocopiable page 204 (Talking Slang) for one between two children. If possible, prepare it also as an OHT, or enlarge it to at least A3 size.

Introduction

Write the following sentence on the board or flip chart:

> The fuzz nicked the geezer who pinched the dosh from the bank.

Ask the children to explain what the sentence means. (*The police caught the person who stole the money from the bank.*) Do the children remember the term for the kind of language is being used? (Slang.) Discuss what slang is and why people use it. Emphasize the fact that slang is informal language (as opposed to the formal language of standard English). Slang is a deliberate use of non-standard English and marks the speaker as a member of a particular group. However, slang is not confined to certain groups of people – ie slang is used by all social groups. Slang, like other aspects of language, changes over time, and often words which were once slang are now part of standard usage.

Whole-class skills work

Write the words 'grotty', 'grub', and 'brill' on the board or flip chart. Ask the children if they can tell you what they mean (for example dirty, food, good). Distribute copies of photocopiable page 204 (Talking Slang) and, if possible, display it on OHP. Use the activity to model how the children might carry out a survey of slang words and expressions. Work through one of the webs using each of the methods suggested. Taking 'money' as an example, you might say: What slang words do I use myself that mean money? (Perhaps 'loot', 'dough'.) Then ask one or two of the children what words or phrases they use. (Perhaps 'quids', 'lolly'.) Then look the word up in a dictionary of slang and/or a thesaurus to see if there additional words given. (Perhaps, 'readies', 'bread'.) Write these in on the web.

Differentiated group work

All the children should work on completing the activity on the photocopiable page.
*The teacher supports groups as needed.
1: The children should work individually to complete the task, but have a partner who serves as the person they 'survey' about what slang words 'other people' use. They may wish to research more words, in which case they can use the back of the sheet to draw further webs.
2 & 3: As above, but work in pairs to complete the sheet, sharing the research and writing.
4: The children in Group 4 should work in small groups of three or four, so that they have a wider pool for their research.

Conclusion

Ask the children to share the outcomes of their group work. Did the children find that some standard English words had more slang alternatives than others? Why might this be the case? You might wish to make a master class version of the web activity using the OHT, or begin a class dictionary of slang to which the children can add words as they find them.

Because it is not possible to carry out an in-depth investigation or survey within the hour, suggest that the children may like to take their sheets home and survey members of their family and neighbours about the words they have been researching.

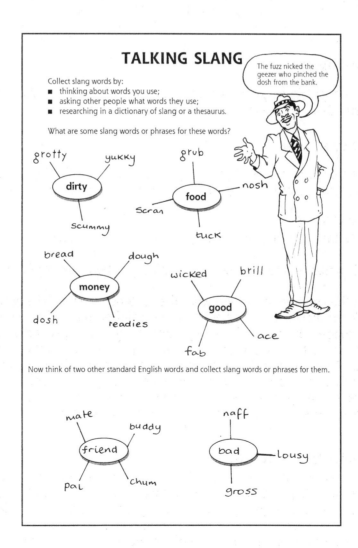

TALKING SLANG

The fuzz nicked the geezer who pinched the dosh from the bank.

Collect slang words by:
- thinking about words you use;
- asking other people what words they use;
- researching in a dictionary of slang or a thesaurus.

What are some slang words or phrases for these words?

grotty

dirty

grub

food

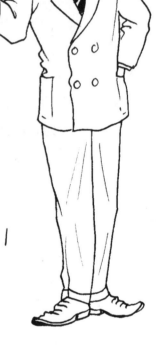

money

dosh

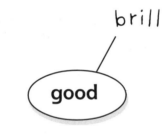

brill

good

Now think of two other standard English words and collect slang words or phrases for them.

EXPERIMENTING WITH LANGUAGE

OBJECTIVES

UNIT	SPELLING/VOCABULARY	GRAMMAR/PUNCTUATION	COMPREHENSION/ COMPOSITION
WORD PLAY Experimenting with language.	Experiment with language, creating new words.	Secure control of complex sentences. Understand how clauses can be manipulated to achieve different effects. Secure understanding of parts of speech.	Comment critically on overall impact of poem.

ORGANIZATION (1 HOUR)

	INTRODUCTION	WHOLE-CLASS SKILLS WORK	DIFFERENTIATED GROUP ACTIVITIES	CONCLUSION
HOUR 1	Share the poem 'Mean Song' on photocopiable page 207. Discuss how nonsense words have meaning.	Share the poem 'Jabberwocky' and discuss. Use grammatical awareness and context to 'decode' nonsense words.	1*: Rewrite 'Mean Song' with real words that are appropriate. 2: Compose a piece of writing using vocabulary from 'Jabberwocky'. 3: Use 'Mean Song' as model for own poem. 4: Make up a list of invented words on a chosen theme.	Selected pupils from each group share their work, followed by class evaluation and discussion.

RESOURCES

Photocopiable pages 207 ('Mean Song') and 208 ('Jabberwocky'), board or flip chart, OHP and acetate (optional), writing materials.

PREPARATION

Make enough copies of photocopiable pages 207 ('Mean Song') and 208 ('Jabberwocky') for one between two children. In addition, prepare them as OHTs or A3 enlargements. Practise reading the poems aloud before the lesson, giving particular attention to appropriate intonation and expression, especially with 'Jabberwocky'.

Introduction

Before giving children a copy or displaying it, read the poem 'Mean Song' aloud (with plenty of venomous expression!) to the class. What is their response to the poem? Do they like it? What is the poem about? Who is the poet talking to?

Distribute copies of the poem, or display it on OHP. Read it with the children joining in. Many of the words are made-up, nonsense words. Ask the children to identify them. Ask: If these are nonsense words, how do we know what the poem is all about? Focus attention on how we can tell what parts of speech these words might be from the way they look and from the surrounding grammar. For example, the s at the end of *snickles* and *podes* suggests they are either plural nouns or present-tense verbs. *That's what I wish you* confirms they are likely to be plural nouns. After reading *For fear that I might*, we anticipate a verb, so we read *Glom* as a verb. And so on. Discuss also the impact of the *sound* of the words. They sound harsh and mean to serve their purpose in the poem.

Whole-class skills work

Explain that you are going to read another poem that has invented words and that tells a story. Remind the children of 'Mean Song' and of how they figured out what that poem was about. Now read 'Jabberwocky' aloud (do not, at this point, give out copies or display it). Ensure that you read it with the appropriate dramatics.

Ask the children to tell you what the poem is about. If necessary, read it again. Now distribute copies of the poem or display it. Ask the children to identify the invented words and to suggest what they might mean. What effect do they have? Encourage children to relate the choice of words to the kind of atmosphere the poet was trying to create. Ask them to suggest why they think the first and last verses are the same.

Finally, ask the children if they recognize the name of the poet. Do they know anything else he has written (*Alice in Wonderland*, *Through the Looking Glass*, *The Hunting of the Snark*)?

Differentiated group activities

1*: Work in pairs to rewrite 'Mean Song', substituting real words for the nonsense words and ensuring that the new words fit contextually, grammatically and rhythmically. The more able children might also retain the rhyme scheme.
2: Using vocabulary from 'Jabberwocky' and other invented words, write about either the Jubjub Bird or the Bandersnatch.
3: Using 'Mean Song' as a model, write a similar poem with invented words, expressing another emotion.
4: Make up a list of invented words on a chosen theme, such as music or sport. Put the words in alphabetical order and give them definitions.

Conclusion

Ask selected children from each group to present their work to the rest of the class. Highlight their achievements and discuss possible ways of publishing or displaying the work. Finally, reiterate the organic nature of language and encourage children to take opportunities to play with words in their own writing.

MEAN SONG

Snickles and podes,
Ribble and grodes:
That's what I wish you.

A nox in the groot,
A root in the stoot
And a gock in the forbeshaw, too.

Keep out of sight
For fear that I might
Glom you a gravely snave.

Don't show your face
Around any place
Or you'll get one flack snack in the bave.

Eve Merriam

JABBERWOCKY

'Twas brillig, and the slithy toves
    Did gyre and gimble in the wabe;
All mimsy were the borogoves,
    And the mome raths outgrabe.

'Beware the Jabberwock, my son!
    The jaws that bite, the claws that catch!
Beware the Jubjub bird, and shun
    The frumious Bandersnatch!'

He took his vorpal sword in hand:
    Long time the manxome foe he sought –
So rested he by the Tumtum tree,
    And stood awhile in thought.

And as in uffish thought he stood,
    The Jabberwock, with eyes of flame,
Came whiffling through the tulgey wood,
    And burbled as it came!

One, two! One, two! And through and through
    The vorpal blade went snicker-snack!
He left it dead, and with its head
    He went galumphing back.

'And hast thou slain the Jabberwock?
    Come to my arms, my beamish boy!
O frabjous day! Callooh! Callay!'
    He chortled in his joy.

'Twas brillig, and the slithy toves
    Did gyre and gimble in the wabe;
All mimsy were the borogoves,
    And the mome raths outgrabe.

Lewis Carroll